Both Ways Are Best

A Journey Toward Finding Love

Pamela Dow

Both Ways Are Best

A Journey Toward Finding Love

Copyright © 2009, 2015 Pamela Dow

ISBN: 9780983923305

www.PamelaDow.com

1. Fiction. 2. Metaphysical. 3. Love. 4. Dow, Pamela.

Printed in the United States of America.

This one's for you, Thomas

About the Cover

I saw the water color on my friend's wall. "Ingalora, I love this! Is it for sale? I am looking for a cover for my first book, *Both Ways Are Best*."

I bought it, asked if she minded my using it for my book. She was thrilled. So am I.

Ingalora Dwyer is a wonderful artist who lives in San Miguel de Allende, Mexico. She has her own website. Thanks again, Ingalora, for making my first book even more special.

PEACE, Pamela

Also by Pamela Dow (in eBook and print):

Abduction

It began with an accidental kidnapping.

❦

Guide for the New Age

Bits of wisdom from A-Z, words like anger, wounded child, psychic attack, and more.

❦

The Power Series

Power Transfusion
Power Less
Power Shock

Both Ways Are Best

A Journey Toward Finding Love

Pamela Dow

PART ONE

Chapter 1

"Life is what happens while we're making other plans."

Penny — April 2007:

The call I'd been waiting for came early one bright Sunday morning in my home south of Nashville, Tennessee.

"Hi, Penny, this is Rob," was all I heard; if he said more I couldn't swear to it, as the familiar voice from the past set my mind in a spin, heart beating so loud I could hear it.

The conversation was over almost before I knew we were talking, yet I do remember making a plan to meet each other in June — two long months away — when I planned to take our grandchildren camping in Maine.

Who knows? Maybe it's a mistake to open old wounds, to re-visit our failures. All I want is to talk to you, to apologize for my part in the break-up of our marriage, to hold you in my arms once again. Honey, maybe you also want closure, I'm thinking.

Yes, it might be a mistake to see each other; after all, it's been over thirty-four years since the divorce. Yet, we both want to. I just know it.

Chapter 2

"Surfing: Either you do it like it's a big weight on you or you do it as part of the dance."

Baba Ram Dass

BETSY — Summer 1970:

As Cousin Penny breezed through the dining room she spied a photograph on the table. "Where did you get that picture of Melissa?" she asked anyone who was listening.

"That's me when I was five years old," I replied with an impish grin. Penny stopped dead in her tracks, stunned. It was good to see, as the little bitch is usually not at a loss for words. After a few seconds she softly asked, "Quite a family resemblance for someone who's adopted, don't you think?"

Yes, I had thought for many years that I looked a lot like some members of my adoptive family, especially Melissa, my Cousin Peter's daughter.

We were attending a family reunion at my Uncle Carleton and Aunt Winnie's home in Hampton Falls, New Hampshire. I had lost my father to lung problems many years before this; my mother died the previous year. There were often family gatherings that I was still invited to, even though I didn't feel especially close to my father's brother and his family. I never really felt accepted by any of them, so chose not to stay in touch. I was anxious to meet someone to fall in love with and start my own family. I had no intentions of following in the footsteps of my wild cousin Penny, who gave birth to a child out of wedlock years before when it was much more of a scandal than it would be now in 1970. No sir, this gal is not having any babies out of wedlock.

I was born in Portsmouth, New Hampshire on November 1, 1946 to a woman known only as a young girl from England, that fact being important to my adoptive mother, Catherine. For some reason she felt everything in England was better than "this nouveau riche country," the USA. Hayward and Catherine Hall were always honest with me, telling me even as a small child that I was adopted. It's just something I always knew. Yet, I never felt as though I fit in, which is a normal feeling for many of us, adopted or not. Catherine was a tall, formidable woman, one whose caustic tongue was often used to lash out at me. Many times I felt she hated me and had no idea what I had done to cause this reaction. My Daddy more than made up for the lack of affection from Mother, though. He was always there to protect me, and I felt his presence even when he was at his office, where he worked as an accountant and investor.

After both my parents died, leaving me a wealthy orphan in my early twenties, I found sheet music, love songs written by my parents when they were courting. Actually, my cousin Penny found the papers in Uncle Carleton's attic. She never told him she took them because she knew he was possessive, not just protective, of all things pertaining to family history. They obviously didn't belong to him, though. Penny and I were really surprised to see love songs written by a couple who certainly didn't act "in love" to us.

You know, I feel that many of us find, after the death of our parents, papers in their belongings that give us proof of who they were as people, sometimes showing how they, also, had once been in love. This discovery makes parents seem more human, more like adults whom we know and not parents whom we need. It's a milestone in our maturity, for sure. In fact, I believe some parents want us to find out about them. After all, doesn't everyone want to be "known," to be understood as to who they are? And sometimes the façade dies with the parent if we are not lucky enough to have letters or read between the lines of our memories.

My parents may have even wanted me to know about Ellie.

Chapter 3

"We are not human beings on a spiritual journey. We are spiritual beings on a human journey."

Stephen Covey

Penny — My future parents:

"Winnie, I have a splitting headache; I cannot go out tonight with Carleton Hall. Would you be a dear and go on the blind date for me? I hear he's quite handsome," Carol said.

My mother, Winifred Pearl McIntosh, was a second-year nursing student at Peter Bent Brigham Hospital and this was the first break she'd had from her studies since September. Thanksgiving would be the following week. It was an unusually chilly evening in Boston, almost too cold to go out. Yet, she had been raised in Aroostook County, Maine, a place that knew winter more intimately than Boston did. The year was 1931.

Wow! He is very handsome, Winnie was thinking as she descended the stairs into the lounge area of her dormitory. Ruth McCall and Robert Downing were going on a double date with Carleton and Winnie. Ruth made the introductions all around and, after a few minutes of pleasant small talk, the foursome was ready to leave for their dinner date at Schrafft's Restaurant in Cambridge. Carleton didn't appear to be disappointed that Winnie was a substitute date. There was clearly an immediate attraction between the two. At five-feet-four-inches tall, Winnie was five inches shorter than Carleton, with a slim figure, lustrous brown hair pulled back into a bun, popular in those days. Her blue eyes were those of a kind, gentle woman, which Carleton found sexy. Ruth just smiled, noting the chemistry between the two.

Carleton's green eyes penetrated Winnie's when he smiled. His muscular physique was something she took for granted, being raised on a farm where hard work was the norm, but she wasn't used to someone exercising just for the rewards of looking good and feeling healthy. The way he confidently held his body was something new for Winnie. Farm boys in Aroostook County were just farm boys.

Winnie, a serious student in Boston on a full scholarship, was self-conscious about her modest wardrobe, much of it handmade. She was the daughter of potato farmers, the oldest of five children, first to attend college. Four of the five siblings eventually graduated from college, one on a full scholarship to MIT. One of Winnie's goals was to marry into a wealthy family in order to get off the farm permanently. She was tired of working from dawn to dark. She wanted more leisure time.

One of Carleton's missions was to find a woman who would be a good farmer's wife. He wanted to raise chickens and live in the country. He knew he had the dedication necessary to be a farmer. One of Carleton's earliest memories was of wanting to grow food for his family, selling extras at a roadside stand. He wanted sheep, ducks, and cows. Perhaps he and Winnie should have talked about this.

My father, Carleton Elliot Hall, was born October 28, 1912 in Cambridge, Massachusetts to wealthy parents, Lillian Elizabeth Walker Hall and Fred Parcher Hall. He began to charm his way out of trouble (and into it at times) as soon as he could walk.

"Darling, Father and I are going to a meeting tonight. Auntie will stay late and look after you, okay dear?" his mother said one evening. They went out to business dinners almost every night of the week, leaving Carleton and Hayward with a nanny. He enjoyed their being gone, as Auntie indulged his every whim, always fixing his favorite supper of crushed saltines drowned in milk and sugar. Fred and Lillian were overprotective parents who kept him in the house while neighborhood kids went ice-skating in full view of his bedroom window. Carleton was a very spoiled, rebellious boy. Lillian, a large-boned woman six inches taller than her husband, was domineering and arrogant, a normal attitude for her economic class in the early 1900's of Boston society.

Fred was a banker and owner of many businesses, the first being a chocolate factory. Carleton complained years later that his father rarely took him to any business meetings, yet when he did he never acknowledged his son. Fred was a cold man, rather cruel at times, and Carleton once made reference to his father beating him when he was small.

Winnie was a very bright woman, a good student who got straight "A's," and couldn't spend as much time dating Carleton as he wanted. There was chemistry between them, but they spent the first eighteen months as friends. When Winnie graduated with High Honors the spring of 1933 Carleton was in the audience as one of her admirers. She was oblivious to her own beauty, lacking confidence, yet her blue eyes were filled with determination.

If asked to describe Carleton the term "playboy" would be on the list. He attended Boston University for three years, never taking studies seriously. Winnie was definitely the academically-smarter one of the two.

Winnie found a job as a public health nurse serving the poorest areas of Boston, mostly delivering babies. She quickly learned to buy a daily newspaper, as there were seldom clean rags or towels available with which to wrap the newborns. She shared an apartment with her good friends, Ruth and Carol, now also Registered Nurses. Life was good; she told her daughter many years later that this was one of the best times of her life.

Carleton did settle down and come to his senses; in the summer of 1934 he proposed marriage to Winnie. It was a love match, as shown in a letter she wrote to him during the summer of 1935 after she quit her Boston job. She lived with her parents on the farm in Maine, working in a local hospital while preparing for the wedding.

"Darling Carleton, I can't wait to be married to you September 1st. The plans for the wedding are coming along fine. My darling, I love what you do to me! I cannot conceal my passion for you. With Love, Your Winnie."

They couldn't afford a real honeymoon, yet were able to take a few days' honeymoon at the primitive cottage her family owned at nearby Portage Lake. There was no running water, but Carlton was thrilled to use the hand-pump and heat water on the ancient woodstove to wash his loved one's hair. The outhouse was a challenge, especially during the night when Winnie had to use it, as there was no electricity. No chamber pots under the sagging double bed or maids to empty them for this camping couple; they were madly in love and didn't care. It was a time filled with bliss and total happiness.

The passion and love they shared got an abrupt dose of reality in the form of an early pregnancy. Winnie conceived within a month of the wedding and Carleton tried to convince her to have an abortion, then a crude operation using a metal clothes hanger.

When a woman has a pregnancy she wants, yet the father of the child doesn't want it, his attitude often feels like a betrayal. Maybe it's the beginning of love turning to hate. This could be what happened to Winnie and Carleton, as she seemed to have more anger as time went on, not less.

Carleton was a spoiled, rich kid, foolish with money, counting on Father and Mother to solve his problems. He was barely twenty-three years old. He must have panicked about having the responsibility of a child.

Winnie thought he was smarter than she was, more important. Of course he liked her to believe that. Yet, she kept Carleton from forcing the abortion and was able to deliver their first child, Patricia, in July 1936. Winnie forced all her anger toward Carleton down into her body and soon began a lifelong battle with asthma.

By 1938 the threesome had moved to a farm in Westford, Massachusetts, near Lowell. Carleton's plan to be a serious chicken farmer was now being implemented. Yet, first he had to keep the roof from being blown off the barn by the Hurricane of 1938, one the history books show to be an unprecedented powerful storm, with steady 121 mph winds and gusts up to 186 mph. The storm was supposed to go out to sea after traveling from Florida north along the East coast; after all, New England "never" got hurricanes, especially inland. The storm surges, similar to a tsunami, hit Long Island, New York in the form of what looked like a fog bank, but was in reality a sixty-foot high wall of water, heading toward shore. More than six hundred people died in this storm, with over 9000 buildings destroyed.

Turkey Pond, still there in Concord, New Hampshire, was used to store pine trees that came to rest across the roads. Later the saw mills were again running and the government hired people at $2/day to help re-build from the storm. This was a welcome relief and help to the economy at the end of a difficult decade.

This farm is where two more daughters, my sister Peggy and I, were born. Meanwhile, Carleton realized he couldn't support his growing family on the small income from raising chickens. Winnie's health couldn't handle another New England winter, so Carleton spent the summer taking courses at Arizona State University in order to substitute-teach, planning to finish his degree later before teaching full-time. He returned to Massachusetts at the end of the summer session, selling the farm to a neighbor, and piled three kids and a very-pregnant wife into the faithful 1938 Dodge, which was pulling a small trailer. They headed to Phoenix, arriving in September of 1944.

The next part of their adventure had begun.

Chapter 4

"Our purpose in being here on Earth is to be happy."

The Dalai Lama

Penny, On Growing up:

I have vivid memories of Phoenix: fig trees in the front yard, apricots, pecans, and dates in the back yard of the small house where my family moved to in September 1944. My parents paid $2,000 for a house made of concrete blocks and stucco. The yard was enormous, large enough for us to have a trampoline, swing sets, and a horse. It was like being in the country, even though we had neighbors all around us. I have photos of the large horse, which was seventeen-hands high, but no clear memories of riding it except for the time my brother fell off the saddle while sitting in front of me, with my arms tightly wrapped around him. He was a squirmy two year old, who literally jumped out of my arms. I was about three at the time. I don't remember my parents being angry with me, so he must have been okay.

I learned to walk in the tiny travel trailer, which Dad pulled with Dottie the Dodge. I joked years later that I had walked across this country when I was fourteen-months old. My brother Peter was born in Phoenix two months after we arrived. Mom was thrilled to finally give birth to a son. My father was now fulfilling a lifelong dream of being a history teacher and physical education coach. He finished college, going to night school, while teaching during the day. I was very proud of my handsome and charming father. Mom held the family together with her well-kept home and handmade matching sundresses for the three girls. She was busy caring for four children age eight and younger. I believe this is where I first learned to keep a clean home and share the workload. One knows how to share when there are four kids in the family, especially when the mother often has asthma attacks, unable to handle all her responsibilities.

In those days there was no air-conditioning; swamp coolers were coming into vogue, but we couldn't use ours much because the dust was bad for my mother's lungs. I guess no one had filters in their cooling units then. A hose was hooked up and water ran through the unit with a fan blowing cooler, moist air into the house. Recently I received a catalog with a similar item for sale, unaware that the swamp cooler, or its latest "green version," was available. Of course, it is a smaller, portable unit. And not even two days before that arrived I had been thinking about the swamp coolers and wondering if they would make a comeback, as they seem to be a more cost-effective way of cooling a room. That often happens to me: thinking about something and there it is, as if I had manifested it into being.

Phoenix was really hot in those days; still is with temperatures occasionally reaching 120 degrees Fahrenheit in the summer. There are thousands of swimming pools and green lawns watered daily; the humidity has become more of a factor now in the dry desert landscape. The newly-transplanted Yankees brought their allergies with them when they insisted on having familiar plants and trees.

Dad missed New England; Mom loved the desert and thrived in Arizona. Yet, she had no choice when her husband bought, after four wonderful years in Arizona, another chicken farm, this time in Lee, New Hampshire. She had no choice, as he was the boss, which was the norm in 1949. All six members of the now-complete Carleton Hall family went back East, this time in "Sally," a 1949 LaSalle, a forerunner to the Cadillac. The same trailer returned to New Hampshire with us, the one that was my home when I learned how to walk. We all had trouble saying goodbye to a place thought of as being Paradise. All except Dad and me, that is. He was born with a suitcase in his hand, similar to the one I was born with. Trips and moving were seen as another adventure for us.

Carleton's father was contemptuous of his rebellious son's actions, especially when he chose to be a farmer rather than a successful businessman like Fred and his first-born son, Hayward. This was quite apparent when I found a letter written by Fred to his son Carleton about a gift of cream being on the edge of spoiling, belittling him and saying he'd better make good on it soon. That letter confirmed the nastiness I often sensed in my grandfather as I was growing up. Poor Dad.

My wings are flapping and I'm not even tired. I'm feeling powerful because my body is flying above my angry parents, just out of reach. They are planning to punish me for some minor infraction. I never do anything right. Criticism is a constant theme in my life.

Mommy accuses me of lying when I tell her I can see my Grampy (her father) and he's passed out on the couch in his den with an empty flask of whisky nearby. "Don't lie about my Daddy, he's not a drinker," my mother yells.

After that incident I learned to keep my visions a secret. I later realized it's not so hard to envision the future for others, yet I rarely could see my own. Of course, it's a good thing we don't know what's in store for us; otherwise, how many would have the courage to actually go there?

Chapter 5

"The man of perfect virtue, wishing to be established himself, seeks also to establish others; wishing to be enlarged himself, he seeks also to enlarge others."

Confucius

Penny:

Family holidays were always spent at Grandpa Fred and Grandma Lillian's beautiful three-story brick home on Fresh Pond Lane in Cambridge, Massachusetts. The home was built in 1910, but came up for sale after the businessman who built it lost everything in the 1929 stock market crash. Fred's father, John Calvin Hall, was also a self-made man and Fred learned at a young age when to buy and when to sell. The home was bought for very little money; more importantly, it was a well-crafted home, almost a mansion, with attention to detail and lots of nooks and crannies. The third-story attic was filled with every kind of hat, plus suitcases, some made of leather, others of tin; also shawls, parasols, tuxedoes, many kinds of walking canes, some with hand-carved ivory or wood handles. In the basement I used to sneak into the pantry and check out the cans and jars of kumquats, white asparagus, and other unusual foods, wondering what they tasted like. (When I did get to taste some of these items years later I was NOT impressed; after all, I was the child of organic farmers and had fresh everything to eat my whole life, not canned foods.) Some kids need toys. Not my brother Peter and me. Or my cousin Betsy. We had Fresh Pond Lane.

"Jenny, please serve the first course now," my grandmother, Lillian, ordered. I never could figure out how the maids knew to appear at the dining room until one day the secret was revealed when I saw Grandma stretch her right leg and press something on the floor. I peeked under the table and saw a tiny bump under the carpet. The buzzer that was built into the wood floor was under an Oriental carpet, well-hidden from a child's eyes. My cousin Betsy and I were disappointed to discover the truth; we preferred to believe in magic. Actually, Jenny was a magical maid, among the most gentle of women, escaped from Latvia, barely speaking English with a heavy accent. Jenny bought, with her hard-earned money, sugar Easter eggs with scenes of little chickens and bunnies inside and candied flowers outside, to give to the youngest grandchildren of Fred and Lillian.

The garden was also magical, with a rose trellis and bench, the backdrop for family photos of the 1930's and 1940's when many children were being born into this interesting family. The roses, irises, jonquils, tulips, and other flowers were tended to by a gardener, who appreciated the rambling English-style my grandmother wanted. To this day, I am a lover of a more natural look in a garden, not needing everything wrapped up in a neat package. That's my philosophy of life: no neat packages; let me be wild and discover my own style.

At one of these family gatherings, around 1950, Grandpa Fred brought out a strange camera that made pictures almost instantly. I remember commenting that the photos don't come out very clear; who would want them? Six years later, when he knew he was dying of lung cancer, my grandfather offered to sell his former chocolate factory in Lechmere Square, Cambridge to his friend who was leasing it for the camera business. Did he want $100,000 cash or more than that in stock in the new company, the man asked? Fred chose cash and sold the building to Ed Land. The company was Polaroid.

These family reunions were always interesting, even though I sometimes had to hide to escape reprimands from my stern grandfather Fred. Uncle Hayward was my favorite, although he was very quiet, almost sad. I would often seek him out to talk to. Catherine was not my favorite aunt.

"Mommy, why did Aunt Catherine and Uncle Hayward adopt Betsy? Am I adopted?" I asked when I was eight years old.

"No, of course not, Daddy and I are your real parents," my mother replied.

"Why did they adopt Betsy?" I persisted. My mother, a secretive woman, something I was aware of even at a young age, hesitated a moment before telling me that Aunt Catherine could not have children. "Mommy, if Aunt Catherine waited a long time for God to bring her Betsy why is she so mean to her?" I asked.

"My, you ask a lot of questions," and with that reply the subject was closed.

When I was cleaning out some of my father's things, after he died more than fifty years later, I was awestruck to see the same items I had played with in the attic at Fresh Pond Lane: the luxurious black wool tuxedo with a satin stripe down the side of each trouser leg, and matching coat with silver-gray brocade vest. All in perfect condition. The top hat was even there amongst Dad's clothes. I tried the entire outfit on; except for the brocade vest, which was a bit small, the tuxedo fit as though it had been made just for me. I swear I am going to wear it someday, even if it's just to a costume party.

My father collected things; was known as a packrat. After he died I found boxes filled with empty plastic yogurt containers, hundreds of them, and bottles once filled with herbal capsules. I'm talking many containers here, moved at great expense by professional movers from Phoenix to New Hampshire, where I got to unpack and dispose of much of it. Then, just to keep me on my toes, there were precious crystal plates at the bottom of boxes, packed underneath heavy chains, yet seldom even damaged. I also found clay marbles; thinking they were glass dulled by age, I washed them. Clay dissolves in water, something I managed to discover before ruining many of these antique marbles.

My father was a bit quirky. Must be the blood of an Englishman in him. It took me many years to appreciate being quirky; I'd often been accused of being weird while growing up. I'm like everyone else in that respect; wanting to be accepted by others as normal. Of course, it takes maturity to accept "being different." I remember as a teenager watching kids get into trouble, doing stupid things, hurtful things, and realized "being different" isn't all that bad.

Wow! That must have been in my early days as a teenager, as I soon "got with the program." I also learned how to do really stupid things.

Chapter 6

"O, for a life of sensations rather than thoughts!"

John Keats

Penny, Living at Solar Vista:

"Penny, you have to eat the blackstrap molasses and wheat germ before we can leave the table," Peggy whispered. She is older by three years and very bossy.

My father was a "health food nut" long before it became fashionable. We had to take our whole wheat sandwiches — bread made by Mom as she couldn't buy it in the grocery store — to school while the other kids brought food made with white bread that looked like cotton. When I tasted it years later I went yuck! It IS cotton.

I actually liked the nutty, hearty taste and texture of good whole wheat bread so I wasn't totally against Dad's health kick of goat's milk, using honey instead of sugar, brewer's yeast, and the un-strained carrot juice — well, THAT I was against and poured it down the bathroom sink whenever I could sneak away. We probably had the healthiest sink drains in the country. Yet, I had noticed the kids at school were often sick and I seldom was. Even as a kid I knew Dad had our best interests at heart most of the time. He knew a lot about the body, reading books by J. I. Rodale, Gaylord Hauser, Jack La Lanne, and other authors of "health food" books. We were sitting around the dining room table of our farmhouse in Lee, New Hampshire where we moved to in 1949 so that Dad could again be a chicken farmer. He was good at farming but could seldom make money doing it. I helped Dad make the cement walkway and spelled out S-O-L-A-R-V-I-S-T-A in bricks, which is still there today, named in honor of the view of the sun from our home. He always had a flair for the aesthetic, creative side of things, which I understood and shared.

But, wheat germ and molasses? Give me a break. I prayed to God: *Please help me find a way out of this.*

Peter and I loved the tree house our father built; we had to earn the right to play in it by exercising first. Dad made "traveling rings," connecting them to the tree that held the tree house. We had to climb up the ladder, grab onto the first ring, and travel hand-over-hand to the very end. Of course, there was another tree at the end. Poor Dad, he never got the athletic kids he wanted but Peter and I were the most interested in exercise. Peggy was nine years old and Patricia twelve. Peter was almost-five and I was six when we moved to "Solar Vista." Soon, we learned to sneak into the tree house when Dad was going to be busy for hours tending the new baby chicks or some such time-consuming chore. Eventually, we learned how to make a "tree house" on the ground from pine needles that fell from the many trees on our fifty acres. I'm still building houses today, usually of wood or bricks.

When lightning storms hit the area we lost electricity for hours and, after the storm subsided, we'd walk into the lower field to haul water; the artesian well couldn't work without electricity. Those springs gave us the best water I have ever tasted, along with tangy watercress growing next to the spring.

This is where I got head lice playing with chickens and had to endure the kerosene and steel comb my mother ran through my long, thick hair. It was absolute torture.

One winter day I got a gash on the head when Peggy knocked snow off the heavily-laden pine boughs with a sharp-cornered snow shovel. I was sitting on the ground, waiting for the "snow shower." She said it was an accident. But, it was evidence I needed to know this bossy sister really did hate me! I played it up big, laughing when she looked guilty.

One Fourth of July we were rousted out of our beds in the middle of the night — not just a fire drill, of which Dad had many — because party-goers had tossed firecrackers into the stand of huge pine trees that encircled our driveway, catching the grove on fire. We formed a bucket brigade and were making headway when the volunteer firemen and their water trucks arrived. Good thing, as it was getting too close to the house for comfort.

So, that summer afternoon when I am being coerced into eating blackstrap molasses, and all those things that are "good for you Penny," my three siblings are dreaming of going someplace — any place but there — and I am the only obstacle to their dreams coming true. I capitulated, bowed to peer- pressure, and ate the stuff. My sibs looked at me with relief and a new respect for I had held out for three hours. That Rebel archetype was always strong in me and served me well later in life, although it could just as easily get me into trouble as out of it.

My mother single-handedly started the hot lunch program at the Newmarket schools; they probably listened to her because she was a nurse. After that I was able to eat the hot lunch at school, as Mom made certain the food was nutritious. There was no blackstrap molasses or wheat germ on the menu. I do remember getting the "screamie meamies" from drinking milk at school. I would run around at night, sleepwalking and hysterical, not remembering anything about it the next day. They stopped giving me milk and the hysteria stopped.

Mom was a remarkable woman, something Dad didn't appreciate. I heard them arguing once when she demanded he stop treating her like one of his mother's maids. I suspect she shut him off in bed to make her point.

Sex education in Newmarket schools was begun by my mother; quite controversial at the time. Did you know Walt Disney made the first sex education films? Separate showings for boys and girls, of course. My sister saw one at the Stone School as a fourth grader.

Mom knew the western square dances, having lived in Arizona, and was popular as a caller. I remember full-skirted outfits with layers of crinolines, all puffed out. We were a controversial family because of the sex education both parents championed, but what they did next sealed their reputation. They cut down some trees and made the first hard-dirt tennis court in Lee, a lovely playing spot encircled by large pines. People came for miles to see it, slowing down, often stopping, to either admire it or shake their heads at our foolishness. I suspect many people judged us for being different.

This is the place where my sister Patricia, the first-born, was driving along Lee Hook Road with no license, being only fifteen years old, but gosh, Dad was with her so what's the problem? Someone called the police who came to talk to Dad, but they didn't seem too concerned. Maybe they also were raised on farms, where kids learn to drive very young. I was eight when Dad took me out driving but we never got caught.

To this day I drive thousands of miles each year, either being a tourist, driving to my second home in Mexico, or going on one of my Vision Quests. It is normal to put 30,000 miles or more on my cars each year. I still love to drive.

"Hey, what are you doing in there?" Patricia demanded to know one evening when she caught me on the floor behind the driver's seat, covered by a blanket. She and her boyfriend Alan, whom she married two years later, were going skinny-dipping and I wanted to see what being grownup was all about. I figured I'd get to see naked bodies doing something interesting. They were annoyed, but did take me back home, instead of killing me. I was eight and wanted to be part of the action I saw going on around me.

It was a good life down on the farm. I was bitten by the nature bug early in life. Someday, I told myself, I am going to live on a farm and never have to leave. Dreams are good; sometimes they even come true.

Chapter 7

"Security is mostly a superstition. It does not exist in nature. Life is either a daring adventure or it's nothing."

Helen Keller

Penny:

The winter of 1952-53 was very hard for my mother's health in general, especially her lungs, so my father sold "Solar Vista," the beloved farm. Our family of six piled into "Sally" the LaSalle, pulling that same trailer back to Arizona, the one we had brought to New Hampshire in 1949. We arrived in Phoenix just in time for school to start September 1953. Peggy and Patty attended North Phoenix High School, which was the "rich kids' school," having Barry Goldwater and other "bigwigs" living in the district. Peter and I were enrolled at Madison School #2, the latest in a series of Madison Schools, the newest elementary school in the northeast part of Phoenix, near 16th Street and Campbell Avenue. Dad was a teacher at the original Madison School, which was near Camelback Road. Phoenix had a population of less than 700,000 at the time; just a big cowboy town.

When I was twelve my friends and I were dropped off one night at "Sciot's Dance Hall" on Central Avenue to see Marty Robbins perform, along with other country/western singers. He was famous for "A White Sport Coat and a Pink Carnation." This was a fun and safe place for us to be then; we went to watch people dancing and hear the latest western music. The two-step was popular and my friends and I loved to practice it at home. Elvis was just starting to get famous, singing "Hound Dog" and "Don't Be Cruel"; the Everly Brothers and Fats Domino were some of our favorites. Sciot's Hall was torn down years later to make room for multi-million-dollar properties lining Central Avenue. Today no kids would be allowed to go to these places, and rightfully so. Yet, I feel that fear has taken over the United States and is becoming a self-fulfilling prophecy. Our addiction to it is actually attracting more fear and violence. The rest of the world (the parts not involved in wars, at least) is not filled with fear at all. It is nice to visit these places where people don't sue each other for tripping over the neighbor's dog or some activity that comes from lack of awareness.

If there ever was a place that could be called Paradise it was Phoenix in the 1950's, a vibrant desert town that hadn't changed much in the years since we first lived there, 1944-49. The desert is seared into my psyche; I owe it all to living in Phoenix at a special time when the city was magical.

In June of 1954, leaving Mom behind in Phoenix, Dad, Peggy, Peter, and I drove across country, pulling the same trailer, only this time it was to be our home for the summer while my father directed the playground summer program for the town of Newmarket, New Hampshire. It was free for the local kids to participate in activities like archery, paddle tennis, volleyball, horseshoes, and crafts. My father's favorite was Indian leg wrestling, probably because he was so good at it. For this game two people lie next to each other on a flat surface like the ground or a tumbling mat, heads at opposite ends, the inside legs hooked together; when the other person's body is flipped over the one who did the flipping wins. Got it?

I loved the playground, as did all the kids; it was a wonderful asset for the community. I loved the costume parades, making baskets and pottery, but most of all I loved the archery. It surprised me to be good at it since I am not normally athletic.

This was our last summer in Lee; as part of the sales agreement when Dad sold "Solar Vista" we could camp down by the chicken barn, using the outhouse Dad had built a few years before. The Lamprey River was our "bathtub" but I was terrified of the bloodsuckers in it. We kept lots of salt around to sprinkle on the parts of our bodies where the little suckers attached themselves to us. It usually worked and they would let go but it was gross. I remember one time scraping the damn thing off my ankle and it left a tiny hole where it had bitten me.

One day I played in the tree house, as the new owners had said I could, and accidentally (who would do it on purpose?) disturbed a wasps' nest. That's the day I learned that 15-20 stings from wasps can make a child pass out. I showed the stings to my sister after I woke up and felt okay to return to the trailer. We put baking soda on them and probably never did tell my parents, although they weren't overly-protective. I do know I never went back to the tree house. Years later I visited the new owners, the first black people, then called Negroes, to live in the area and saw that the tree house and chicken barn had been torn down. It was a lovely place for kids to grow up. Of course, all things change; the only constant in life is change.

I missed being on the farm but I did enjoy Arizona, with its endless blue skies and cacti blooming in the spring. The hot sun beckoned to me, as did the long, perfect days of sunshine all year-round. Yet, I would miss the pine trees in New Hampshire, in the winter heavily-laden with snow. I loved having deer come right into the yard; I even loved my traveling rings.

My experiences growing up, with Dad unable to decide which place is best to live, split my personality and today I divide my time living two extremely different lifestyles according to seasons: summer on a 75-acre haven in northern Maine, filled with all sorts of wildlife including bears, deer, bobcats, coyotes, eagles, wild turkey, and moose, then off to my other "wild" place to live my artistic life for the winter in San Miguel de Allende, Mexico, a life filled with music, fireworks, smells of all kinds, and lots of festivals. It's a wonder for all the senses as Maine is in another, more contemplative way. I find both of my lives quite healing. And I enjoy the adventure of living in two unique places, with good friends in both. Of course, my life did become perfect the day I stopped worrying about what I don't have and began to be thankful for all that I DO have.

Mom no longer had many serious asthma attacks once we moved back to Arizona, but she had to work hard to keep weight on her slender frame; reaching one hundred pounds was a milestone. That's one reason she stayed in Arizona the summer of 1954, to stay healthy. I suspect being away from the stress of living with Dad was better for her. The other reason she stayed was that she had a terrific job as a Registered Nurse at the Arizona State Hospital on 24th Street and Van Buren. She'd entertain us with stories of criminally-insane patients, the ward of her choice, the most famous patient being Winnie Ruth Judd, a woman with the same first name as my mother. Of course, this woman killed her lover, put his remains in a trunk, which she then shipped by train to Phoenix from California and, for some reason, ended up being declared insane. I guess the state had no sense of humor or failed, somehow, to understand the creative approach Winnie Ruth Judd used to get rid of a lover. That's how she, a California woman, ended up in Arizona State Hospital as one of my mother's patients. According to Mom she was a sweet lady who also made messes in her pants, then smeared crap all over the walls. Yes, a really sweet lady.

"How dare you betray me like that?" my father shouted one afternoon after my parents spent time alone in their bedroom. We had been back in Arizona a few weeks when this confrontation took place.

"Peggy, what's going on?" I asked, a bit nervous.

"Mom is divorcing Dad because she's got a boyfriend," my older and wiser sister answered. "Dad is going to try to get us to live with him; I'm warning you." I started crying and said I hated him and would never live with him. "The judge will ask us who we choose because we're old enough now to decide," she continued.

No way, I'm thinking, *I'll never go with him.*

Later that day Dad did take Peter and me aside and said we had to choose. Neither of us said a word, but we felt safer with Mom; my father's temper was scary. Besides, she could cook and he couldn't. As it was now, Peggy and I cooked dinner the nights my mother worked the 3-11 p.m. shift at the hospital. Since steak was only 39-cents a pound we ate it often, along with fresh veggies and always green salads.

Apparently this man Mom fell in love with was also an R. N. at the hospital. I don't know how he did it, but my father managed to get the guy fired. It was many years later that I realized he had also told her she'd never see her kids again if she left. He had the money for an attorney and she didn't. The social climate at the time was such that she probably would have lost her kids, as adultery was a no-no, even if we had told the judge we wanted to live with her. Women had few rights then.

Later, as an adult, I silently cheered for my mother, knowing she had found love in the arms of another man, as I knew how difficult my father could be. I was pretty much aware of his many affairs. By now I knew first-hand how easy it is to want revenge in the arms of another man when a woman finds her man is cheating on her.

I'll bet if someone interviewed women (and men) in long-term marriages they'd be surprised at how many couples stay together for the sake of their children. I admire my mother for doing that; I believe when we have kids we enter into a second contract. I realize she loved us more than I had thought while growing up. She was an amazing woman, my mother Winnie.

Chapter 8

"You must not lose faith in humanity. Humanity is an ocean; if a few drops of the ocean are dirty, the ocean does not become dirty."

Mahatma Gandhi

Penny:

I'd venture to guess that my adolescent years were no worse than those of others; few of us get through them unscathed. I suppose that's part of being enrolled in Earth School.

"Why are your hair and clothes damp? Have you been swimming in the canal, Penny?" my mother asked one day in 1956 when I was almost thirteen years old. We still lived in Phoenix near one of the many irrigation ditches that ran through the city as part of our water supply. I was returning from a neighbor's house where I'd gone to help clean, as the wife was recovering from an operation. The lady left to go shopping after paying me. As I was about to leave, the husband suggested I take a shower; I had gotten really sweaty washing floors and cleaning the oven, refrigerator, and bathroom. I reluctantly agreed. When I was in the shower I heard him trying to open the door, which I'd had the presence of mind to lock (yet wasn't smart enough to just go home to take a shower). My reluctance now turned to downright fear: I am thinking, *How can I escape from this unharmed*? Looking for a towel I realized he purposely had put the towels outside the safety of the bathroom, as he knew I had taken the linens to the laundry room when I cleaned. So, I put my wet body into my dirty clothes and cautiously opened the door. I can't remember exactly what happened next but I do know I got out of there safely, the molestation all in his mind, but fear of being harmed still in mine. It wasn't my imagination, though: he did plan to harm me.

Mom told Dad what I casually told her: Mr. Smith made me take a shower. My father stormed out of the house ready to kill the guy. Knowing my father I'd say he beat the shit out of the guy, and I did hear whispers later between my parents that confirmed my suspicions. If he had killed the guy it would be my fault, wouldn't it? After all, if I'd been smarter wouldn't I have gone home right after the wife left?

Two years later new neighbors moved in and I became friendly with the sixteen-year-old girl, Katie. She had just gotten her driver's license and a car, so we picked up other girls and went cruisin' Central Avenue on the weekends. That's when gas was less than 30-cents per gallon. We all flirted but it was innocent, none of us letting guys French-kiss or cop a feel. Litchfield Park was a nearby navy base, along with Luke and Williams Air Force bases, and these were great sources of guys from all over the country, which really appealed to me, being the traveler that I am. We'd sometimes call Luke or one of the other places and talk to whoever answered. I think at this point I must have been kissed at least once by someone, but don't remember who. I do know it would have been sweet and innocent kisses, as I was determined to "save myself for my husband." This non-existent, future husband of mine and I would have many kids, maybe a dozen, as I loved children and wanted nothing more than to be a good wife and mother. I would never look at another man, as "my guy" would be enough for me, and we would always be madly in love 'til death do us part.

One day Katie's twenty-year-old brother, Oliver came home for Christmas holidays bringing Mike, a fellow Marine, both stationed in San Diego. A blind date was arranged, Katie with Mike and me with her brother. We went to a movie but I can't remember the name of it. We then drove to the top of Squaw Peak Mountain.

"Ollie, when did you start drinking? Katie asked. She was shocked that her big brother who was brought up very religious was now offering us whiskey in Dixie cups. I declined; she did, also, but the guys drank some. Katie and Mike got out of the car to look at stars, which you could then see from up there, no houses being built until years later. There was a fabulous view because of really clean air in Phoenix then. The whole city was spread out below us. It was stunning and romantic, a popular "sparking spot." Ollie didn't wait long to make his move. Before I knew it he was kissing me and copping a feel and I was pushing him away, telling him to leave me alone, I am a virgin and plan to stay that way! He seemed like a different person than he had been at the beginning, before drinking whiskey. I started crying as he pulled my body under his, banging my head on the arm rest of the car. He unzipped his pants and pushed his eager penis inside me, just moving my panties aside, not taking them off. By then I was really crying and hitting him, begging him to just leave me alone.

Well, he did leave me alone but not until he had raped me. So much for the courteous boy next door, the upstanding military man who's protecting us from the enemy. With guys like him around we don't need enemies.

That experience shocked me to the core of my being, inoculating me with an anger I wouldn't face until almost twenty years later. Hell, I even forgot about being raped, just pushed it down into my body, although I did cry myself to sleep for weeks after that. I found out later the entire family heard me crying, but no one asked me what was wrong. Keeping secrets is a dangerous pattern of behavior, hurling us toward an inability to be intimate, thereby destroying relationships. It took me many years to learn what true intimacy is, and how to achieve it in my life. It is a lack of fear, an opening of the heart toward another person. It is worth discovering.

Katie didn't seem to know what her brother did and we lost track of each other when my family moved — once again — back to New Hampshire. Years later I found her on the Internet and visited her in New Mexico when I was on one of my *Vision Quests* to the Southwest. She was a bit hostile, which makes me think she knows what her brother did and wants me out of her life so she won't be reminded. We're no longer in touch.

Sex can be a powerful vehicle for intimacy and spirituality, but it can also be an abuse of power, a tool of violence. The rape planted a seed of promiscuity in me that I couldn't deal with for a couple decades. Rage took over my soul, making me feel power less and out of control. It helped complete the transition of innocent child to *Victim*. Many years later I found my way back to my *Magical Child*, realizing that being a *Victim* is a choice, as is happiness. After doing much work to forgive others, and myself, I found my true Self and began the journey to becoming whole. I now refuse to be a *Victim*. This is a journey that has been powerful and invaluable.

Chapter 9

"And what time do you ladies want to be knocked up?"

When checking into London's YWCA

Penny in Europe:

Europe was fun, I think. I drank my way through much of the continent the summer of 1960, abusing my newly-found freedom after graduating from high school a couple weeks before getting on the ship in Montreal, bound for Southampton, England. It was too early to be a hippie — and too late to be normal.

"Penny, have you seen my passport? Our handbags are similar; maybe I put it in yours. Can we look?" Sue, one of my cabin mates on the SS Iberia asked as we were pulling into the harbor. We searched both handbags, to no avail. Her passport had disappeared. I volunteered to go with her while she was "arrested." The immigration guys took us to their office and waited to hear from the United States that her passport is valid and can be duplicated today. I went out for lunch, leaving my "criminal" friend in the office, as she wasn't allowed out of their sight. The best I could find was a non-descript, tasteless ham sandwich on soggy white bread. The food situation was not to improve until a few weeks later, when we arrived in France.

Finally, about seven at night, we were taken to the train station, Sue's new passport in her hand, ready to buy tickets to London. "Oh no, Sue, you are not going to believe this! Your passport is here in my secret hiding place, so secret I forgot to look there before," I exclaimed when pulling out my money to buy the ticket. We had a good laugh and got on the train, tickets and passports well-guarded. When we arrived at the YWCA to sleep before continuing our travels the next day, the desk clerk surprised us by asking, "And what time do you ladies want to be knocked up?" Anyone raised in the United States in the 1950's and 60's pretty much knows "knocked up" means getting pregnant, but the English guy just wanted to knock on our door to awaken us so we wouldn't be late getting up. It was a day filled with adventure.

Sue flew to Switzerland to see family friends and I took a bus to tour England before going on to Scotland. The plan was to meet another group back in London a week later. The Lake Country was beautiful; also the place where a favorite poet, Lord Byron, lived and wrote. We went to the lake where he drowned in 1824. There was a plaque on the shore in commemoration of his life and career as an excellent writer.

Just a few weeks before this I had graduated from high school at age sixteen. And now my little side trip is taking me to Edinburgh, Scotland for a few days. It was a lot to handle for someone almost seventeen years old. I was much younger than I looked, partly because I had skipped two grades — school was really boring — before they put me back into second grade because I missed my friends on the other side of the one-room schoolhouse in Lee, New Hampshire. I was always expected to act older because of being taller and looking older than my age. Sometimes adults have unrealistic expectations, which can cause social immaturity in children. I know it caused many problems for me.

I spent my seventeenth birthday in cold, damp Edinburgh in a tiny room at the YWCA. My room cost the equivalent of $4, and was worth every penny. I was on a strict budget. All I could find for dinner on this so-called summer evening was bangers and mash — sausage and mashed potato — with soggy canned peas for a vegetable. I doubt that many awards are being given to restaurants in Great Britain even today, almost fifty years later.

I cried myself to sleep out of fear and loneliness, as I didn't know what to do next in life. Barely seventeen, on my own having to face "grownup land" when I returned in September was daunting at best.

I returned to London the same way I got to Scotland — by bus. And once again, I stayed at the YWCA. This time I expected the question from the desk clerk about being "knocked up" and got a good night's sleep, still a bit sad at turning seventeen by myself in Edinburgh. That was the last time I ever had fear while traveling alone. I faced my fears of loneliness that night in my closet-sized room in Scotland. The lack of fear to go through life alone served me well when I later needed it.

The next day Harold, our cute British tour guide, introduced us to the others. There was a married couple; not happily, it appeared to me. Tony and Joanne were sticklers for rules, easily annoyed by everything around them. We had the prerequisite lame-brain, Liz, who asked throughout the trip how much did that cost in real money? Most of us steered clear of her from the beginning, not wanting to give the impression of being "ugly Americans." One of the teens was Joy, who quickly became a good friend, one whose birthday is the same day yet one year before mine. She is a friend to this day, even though we go for years between actual physical visits. The group, totaling maybe twelve, got on our bus and began the tour of Europe by leaving for the ferry-boat to cross the English Channel.

Believe me, one can get really drunk and seasick while traversing that bumpy bit of water between England and France, and live to tell about it. When we are young we can survive almost anything. We landed in Le Havre, France the next morning, groggily happy to stop the seasickness, but still hung over. We proceeded to see Europe.

Europe was interesting; a bargain then, as souvenirs were actually affordable. It was a time when one could climb to the top of the Leaning Tower of Pisa, and we did. We toured the museums of Florence, Italy, seeing masterpieces that were later damaged or destroyed when a flood came through the city. Friends who have recently gone to Europe assure me I saw the place at its best. I don't think I want to go back; I'll just keep my fond memories of this trip.

I know people think of traveling with a tour group to be safer, but it has never been my favorite way of traveling. Structure, rules, and going by someone else's clock have never appealed to me, especially as a traveler, even at age seventeen.

One night a group of us partied in Heidelberg, Germany. Some local guys took us to a cemetery overlooking the city. It was beautiful, I think. After a few of those strong German beers things were not very clear. We're all sitting on a stone wall admiring the view, feet dangling over the edge of this wall when I looked down and realized the tops of the trees BELOW mean that, if we aren't careful, the ensuing fall is more than one hundred feet; not an injury-only kind of fall. I sobered up quickly. Isn't it funny what we remember growing up? Just recently I was talking about Europe with Joy, who was with me in Heidelberg, and she had also experienced that sobering moment, even though we didn't discuss it then. Too bad youth is wasted on the young. Yet, our angels are usually right here with us, especially welcome that night in Germany.

I love to travel. I travel to find myself; some trips are more of a Vision Quest than others. Around 1950 I asked my world-traveling father to tell me again about Dubrovnik, Budapest, Prague, Poland, and places my father visited in 1930 as a young man, bicycling all about Europe. He booked passage in steerage, sleeping with the cattle on the long voyage across the Atlantic Ocean from New York.

"Daddy, someday I am going to these places," I declared one day. He knew I'd be crushed at the news that all those places in his photographs were closed to tourists. Communism had taken over the countries. So, he told me as gently as he could. The eternal optimist in me retorted, "They won't always be Communist and when they're not I'm going there!"

I am very thankful for having a father who pushed us out into the world. I would never have been happy stuck down on the farm, even though that is where I am choosing to spend much of my semi-retirement. Thanks so much, Dad, for being the unconventional soul that you are, for giving me the love of travel.

Chapter 10

"A slave is someone who waits for another to free him."

Anonymous

Penny, Meeting Rob:

In July 1967 I was working long hours as a waitress at Fisherman's Pier Seafood Restaurant in Portsmouth, New Hampshire in order to support my three-year-old daughter, Heather and myself. Her birth was the result of a brief affair with an Englishman, Simon Stanhope, whom I'd met on board a P & O Orient Line cruise ship going from Long Beach to Australia via Hawaii, Japan, the Philippines, and Fiji, on a 60-day halfway-around-the-world voyage. After a tour of Australia we took another P & O ship, this time bound for England via Indonesia to Calcutta, then through the Red Sea to the Suez Canal. We stopped in Tangier and Lisbon, before arriving in Southampton, England.

Simon was about two inches taller than me, with a sexy, muscular body; a Rugby player, as it turned out. I later realized most Rugby players are huge fans of beer, looking for an excuse to work up a sweat so they can quench their thirst with more quart-size "pints" of beer. But, for now, I am smitten by his gorgeous blue eyes, dark, straight and thick hair that always needs combing, and lovely British accent. Of course, it didn't hurt my ego that he was totally taken with me.

Simon and I had to be careful not to be seen talking, as he was a bedroom steward in the first-class section of the ship and I was a passenger, with my own room away from my parents. He noticed me while waiting at the railing in Long Beach before departure and sought me out a few days later. He would have been fired and sent home from the nearest port had we been caught fraternizing. We spent time in the photographer's darkroom with his friends, drinking scotch — yuck! I tried it just one time and never again. We'd have a good time just joking around, all quite innocent.

"Hey, leave my fanny alone!" I said one night as Simon, his friend Harry, and my new friend Allison and I were all crammed into the tiny darkroom, trying to move at the same time, when my rear-end accidentally got touched. The guys, both being Englishmen, cracked up laughing, while we two American girls stood there, a little puzzled. Simon said, after the laughter subsided and he could actually speak, "Penny, your fanny is on the other side, not your backside." Allison and I had the good grace to blush.

Fortunately (or unfortunately, depending on who's doing the looking), my parents gave me a lot of freedom, so Simon and I met in my cabin frequently, just getting to know one another, kissing but nothing more than that, for the first 30 days. We got sexually involved only after the ship docked in Sydney, Australia. We went out one night to a few bars, returning to the ship and sneaking into my old cabin, which of course was vacant, as they were getting ready for the new passengers going on the return trip to Long Beach. My parents and I were waiting to meet up with the next ship, the "Canberra," for the second half of the voyage.

It took only one time of having sex with Simon to get pregnant with his child, something I began to realize a few weeks later when the trip was ending in London. I wrote to him and he was thrilled with the news, wanting the child and asking me to marry him. I didn't want to get married; I just wanted a child. It turned out to be a good idea not to marry Simon; when Heather and I visited his family in Birmingham, England eight months after her birth I was horrified to discover he was an alcoholic and liar. I broke it off with him after three weeks in England. Yet, I did keep in touch with his parents, sending photos and letters during all of Heather's childhood and teen years.

I look back at that time and am convinced that some of us women (or young girls, as I was then) need to cherish ourselves and make better decisions. I am also totally in awe of the journey that I have chosen and would not change a thing. Not even having a child out of wedlock. Not even meeting Rob, though later my heart was broken in many pieces, taking years to mend. I regret nothing.

"Brenda, stop the car! There's your sister Judy talking to some guys," I shouted to my friend as we were cruisin' the streets of Portsmouth one hot June night. Bless that lovely city, a wealth of dates for us local girls — with the Portsmouth Naval Shipyard in Kittery, Maine across the Piscataqua River Bridge from Portsmouth, New Hampshire. We also had the U.S. Marines and Air Force nearby at Pease Air Force Base. And, if that's not enough, I lived within walking distance of the U.S. Coast Guard station (now torn down) at Hampton Beach during my high school years. There's something about a uniform that makes red-blooded American men look really sexy. I say that, although we never slept with the guys we met; it was fun to flirt and hang out, just practicing our male-female bonding.

Judy introduced us to Larry, Mike, and Rob, the owner of the red 1946 Jeep they were all riding in. The convertible top was missing and the doors were welded shut, but it was paid for. I was immediately attracted to Rob's green eyes and light brown hair, along with his gentle manner. He was just the right height for me at 5 feet 9 inches, three inches taller than I. His slender body was muscular, with a really cute butt. He took my hand to help me climb over the side of the Jeep, asking me to sit up front with him. That night was the beginning of many nights when a few of us hung out in the little free time we had. Things soon changed when he began to follow me home to spend the night at my apartment in a lovely Victorian house owned by sweet eighty-five-year-old Mrs. Smith. Her roommate/caretaker was another story.

"Did you have company last night, dear?" Miss Harold slyly asked me one morning. I realized that the sounds I had heard from my closet, which shared a wall with her bedroom, were those of the nosy spinster listening to Rob and me make love. And make love we did, many times each night, both having such a strong attraction that we made a lot of noise. This was something neither of us had experienced before; it was phenomenal. Scratches-on-his-back kind of phenomenal. Bruises-on-our-pubic-bones kind of phenomenal. I was his first real lover, a fact that I should have paid more attention to because his need to find other experiences, to act like a horny teenager at age twenty-eight, was partly the basis for our break-up. But for now we were falling madly in love, not wanting to be separated even five minutes.

"Penny, will you marry me? I love you, and want to spend the rest of my life with you," Rob said one evening while we were sitting on the couch after putting three-year-old Heather to bed. I said yes. After less than three months of knowing each other we were planning our wedding to take place one month later, in a tiny stone chapel on the grounds of the governor's mansion in Hampton Falls, New Hampshire.

Sunday evening, one week before the wedding was to take place, Rob returned from a weekend visit to his parents, who lived more than an hour away.

"What do you think about postponing the wedding and getting married when I return from Antarctica?" he horrified me by asking.

"Rob, I thought you also wanted a baby; Heather is almost four now and you won't be returning for two years (hadn't even gone yet) so she will be at least seven before we can have a little sister or brother for her. I don't understand; is it that your parents don't like me because I had a baby without being married?" I urged him to reconsider with tears in my eyes. My willfulness overcame his passive nature and we got married one week later.

The minister married us, Robert Edwin Warner and Penelope Anne Hall, in front of family and friends inside the chapel next to the waterfall the second Saturday of October. The rushing water was our music; the sun and trees were our flowers. It was a lovely ceremony, a spiritual one; photos taken during the reception at my parents' historic home in Hampton Falls show us to be a happy couple.

Rob found a motel in Boston for less than $30. It wasn't great, but we felt lucky to get it because the weekend of October 8, 1967 was when the Red Sox were in the playoffs for the World Series. They almost made it, but not quite. These guys — Tony C., George Scott, and Carl Yastrzemski — were customers of mine at Hawaiian Gardens Restaurant in Seabrook, New Hampshire, where I now worked, as it was closer to my parents' home and less traveling from our Hampton Beach residence. I often had to pick up Heather late at night when Rob had to work late and my parents babysat for her.

Right in the middle of our first lovemaking session as a married couple, the phone rings. Rob is closer to the bedside phone so he answers it. I hear that his grandmother, at 10:30 on our wedding night, is calling to invite us to eat lunch the next day at the Ritz Carlton Hotel with the rest of the family. That is my first recollection, as a newly-married woman, of the power plays some people can make on younger, unsuspecting ones. She didn't improve with age. As a matter of fact, a few years later Rob and I took a trip across country and stopped at their home in Northern Michigan to visit this same grandmother. She was very nasty to me, but the problem I had was not with her behavior. I didn't have to live with her; she had to live with herself. Hopefully, she had a conscience. My problem was I felt betrayed by my husband for not standing up for me. I yelled at him after leaving their house that if my relatives had treated him that way — and of course they wouldn't because I don't have any nasty relatives — I would have said, "Grandma, please do not speak to my wife this way. I love her and cannot allow you to do so." I would be very calm, very firm. That is my first memory of thinking maybe I can't trust this man to be a good husband to me. It was the beginning for me of the love-that-turns-to-hate.

We were very happy for quite awhile; yet as I look at our wedding album, I am shocked that we got married barely four months after meeting each other! What could we possibly know about our new spouse in such a short time? I certainly didn't know he would betray me by not standing up to his grandmother. I also didn't know he would never talk to me or couldn't maintain any type of intimacy. His parents were right — maybe we should have allowed our heads to overrule our hearts. Of course, then we may have missed knowing and loving each other, the memory of which I cherish, in spite of all that happened later.

We didn't have much money — he made $85 each month from the Navy while I made as much each week waiting on tables six days and nights, about 72 hours a week. But, we were quite frugal. I could manage the food budget with lots of spaghetti and homemade foods. Shopping at the commissary at Pease Air Force Base really stretched our food dollars, helping me buy prime rib roast, which fed us for three days. At 39-cents per pound, it was often the same price as ground beef. Heather's clothes came from the thrift shops or my sewing machine. And gas for my Volkswagen was only 39-cents per gallon.

We settled into young married life in the same house at Hampton Beach where I had lived as a teenager and young adult, a house still owned by my parents, who rented it to us for a small amount of money. Six months after the wedding Rob got the duty he had requested in Antarctica. This was during the Vietnam War and Rob would have gone if they had sent him there, but he had long before volunteered for this duty. It was perfect for him, as he had wanted to be a Geologist since he was six years old.

Heather adored her new Daddy, and was eager to be with him evenings when I worked. Rob picked her up at my parents' house each evening on his way home from the Navy base. Things changed when he began training in Rhode Island. His jeep was broken down and he had to take our only car, my Volkswagen Bug, every Sunday evening, returning home Friday evenings. I had to change hours and work only Saturday nights that summer Rob was getting ready for Antarctica. They used Antarctica for research about astronauts landing in a hostile environment. In fact, when the first man on the moon landed in July 1969 Rob was one of the radiomen who patched through communications from the base commander to the astronauts, connecting the "last frontier on Earth to the first frontier in space."

Heather and I had a great summer, in spite of missing Rob during the week. I had a 1940's bicycle Dad had given me — bright red and lots of chrome — with fat, whitewall tires, crossbars for Heather to ride on. We also had a basket, which was handy for hauling groceries on the six-mile round trip from Hampton Beach to the town of Hampton. The A&P Supermarket was at the intersection of Lafayette and Winnacunnet Roads; they had torn down one of the most beautiful, old homes in Hampton to build this shopping center. I believe they call it progress.

The A&P is gone now; of course the old house is long-gone, never to return. This house, called the Tappan Homestead because that's the family who owned it, was a tall, big house similar to a New England Saltbox style, with natural shingles made of cedar. The homestead was quite a presence for many years, but probably wasn't old enough to have been there when one of my ancestors, Henry Hall, came north from Watertown,

Massachusetts in 1643 to become a "man of influence" in Hampton. The original group of founders consisted of seven families, along with a minister, who was required by law to be part of the beginning of every town in Puritanical New England. This group came from England, landed in Boston in 1637 and eventually WALKED north fifty miles to a town named Winnicunnet by the local Indians; the name was changed later to Hampton. Henry first went to Watertown to make his fortune in real estate speculation, taking advantage of a boom going on in the 1630's and 40's. He made a lot of money there and came to Hampton as a wealthy man with a new wife (having lost his first one in childbirth a few years earlier) and four small children.

Life in Hampton was not easy under the rule of the church; the Puritan founding fathers had many laws and used punishment as a way of controlling their followers. People actually were arrested for things like lying, fornicating before marriage, and not being in the courtroom as a spectator when your neighbor was being hauled before the court which was, of course, run by the church. Could that be why people historically have shown up for lynchings all over the world? Because it was an offense not to watch?

A man named Aquila Chase got arrested for picking peas in his garden on a Sunday. Who turned him in — a neighbor who was pissed off because he didn't get his share of Aquila's crop?

I don't know about their habits of "fornicating before marriage" but I do know there was a lot of sex — and a LOT of kids. "Go forth and multiply" seemed to be the motto of the Puritans. But, hush, don't enjoy it or tell anyone you want to enjoy it. That has to be where the United States got their preoccupation with sex.

Eventually some people who couldn't abide by the rules left the area. Aquila sold his farm to his brother and moved to Newbury, Massachusetts where there were more opportunities to earn a living. He was tired of being arrested. The church still ruled in Newbury, but he had lots of family members as allies there. Maybe things were better closer to the big city of Boston, now only thirty miles away.

Let's go back to three hundred years later in Hampton, New Hampshire.

Rob and I were surviving our own minor hardships and having our own great sex. We had survived six months of Rob's training in Rhode Island, his coming home only on weekends, so surely Heather and I could find enough to do while he was gone for one year. How hard can it be?

Hard as hell, is the answer. The thirteen long months he was gone was one of the worst times of my entire life. It hit me like a ton of bricks.

I cried for days after seeing him off on the plane to California, the first leg of the trip to Antarctica via New Zealand. We could communicate only by radio/phone patches saying something then "over" so the other could speak. This was before e-mail; the personal computer wasn't even invented. There was no room for spontaneous conversation, even if any intelligent speaking had been possible when I was awakened at three in the morning from a sound sleep to talk to my husband. Rob wrote an occasional letter to me. By now I was realizing he didn't know what to say to me in person, let alone in a letter. The contact was not often, and never emotional enough for me. It is easy to grow a distance between two people who are self-centered and immature, especially when one loves to write letters and the other finds it painful to express even the slightest hint of emotion.

In my selfishness and lack of understanding of who my husband was and how he operated, I allowed my anger toward him to grow, as I felt this old, childhood abandonment issue rearing its ugly head. I'm not proud of it, but I kept company with a married man named Rick Morrison, an executive with a big company that my brother-in-law worked for at their local division. We were introduced on one of his brief business trips to the Portsmouth area. He was happily-married, going through a rough time in his personal life, and I was madly in love with my husband, yet feeling very un-loved. We met for only a few times; it was just a sexual thing. I once cried in his arms out of loneliness for Rob. Rick understood me and was a beacon in the night during this agonizing time when the pain of missing Rob just wouldn't go away. I was fucked up, to say the least.

When Rob returned from Antarctica I felt his heart was no longer with me. That first night, in the motel where we stayed after I drove to Rhode Island to pick him up, I cried myself to sleep. He seemed like a stranger to me, all pale and unhealthy looking, so withdrawn, unable to talk to me. I hoped it would get better as he got work and we settled down like the "newlyweds" we were. To make matters worse, we had been trying before he left to have a child and continued after he returned, but were having no success. He had adopted Heather, claiming he loved her as his own, but I had doubts about his sincerity. My *Mother* archetype was strong, and I wanted a little sister or brother for Heather. I have learned some of my greatest lessons through being a mother. I was also willful, so it became an obsession. One doctor said Rob had low sperm count, another said it was low but may just be a problem with the two of us together. As Rob told me what the second doctor said I got a flash of insight: in his passive-aggressive anger his body was denying me the two things I wanted from him — love and a baby. Maybe our fields of energy know more than our heads and hearts do.

Rob immediately found work in construction, supervising the demolition of very old, historic homes in Portsmouth in order to make way for a major thoroughfare. He brought home wooden doors, beautifully-crafted and not readily available today, along with glass and porcelain doorknobs and unusual windows. We gave away some items and kept others in anticipation of building our own little hippie home on the 150 acres we bought in Maine. We both worked hard toward our goals. We had all these dreams of making a good life, a simple life, homesteading and growing our own food. I learned to make head cheese, lard, and sausage when we slaughtered a pig; became a gourmet cook who made bread three times each week, sometimes even sauerkraut, which I couldn't perfect. Once I made Duck L'Orange from Julia Child's cookbook and spent three hours doing what should take one hour; then the thing got eaten in ten minutes.

One of the ways to live a "simple" life is to get down and dirty, climbing fifteen feet or more in the air on a heavy-duty extension ladder to rip off and replace four-inch, original wooden clapboards on a New England Saltbox built in 1722. While Heather was in school and Rob was working in construction, often away from home during the week, renovating our "new" home (for which we paid $10,500 cash) was exactly how I spent my time and energy. Of course, we had gardens on our small plot next to the train tracks in Newmarket, New Hampshire so I canned a lot of tomatoes and made pickles. And froze green beans, peas, and wild blueberries Heather and I picked.

"How could you do that?" Rob yelled, as he came home from work and walked into the house, seeing my latest project in the living room right next to the kitchen where I was cooking dinner. He picked up a plucked ear of corn that was waiting to go into the boiling water and threw it at me — to emphasize his words, I guess. My feelings were hurt; after all, it wasn't a load-bearing wall. Even I knew better than to tear one of those down! We had talked about re-doing the living room, tearing out the old, horsehair plaster and lathes to put up sheetrock, as this was one wall where the plaster couldn't be repaired.

I must have made some comment like, "Well, the house is still standing, what's the problem?" He stomped off, having no sense of humor. I stood there, puzzled at his anger. If I'd known my husband better I'd have seen how frustrated he was by his job; after all, he just wanted to be a Geologist, not a Project Manager for a construction company. I'd have offered to put him through college if he could have articulated this disappointment in his life.

This was during the last three years of our marriage, although neither of us knew it at the time. We were busy making three apartments out of this huge, sixteen room house, where we un-boxed the original, hand-hewn wooden beams (and saw the builder's chalk-written name, Josiah Somebody). Beams were thought to be too crude during the Victorian era and therefore covered with smooth wood boards and painted. We got two apartments rented out right away, leaving the renovations of our six-room apartment until the end.

We both had big dreams. We just wanted to live the simple life, which is what hippie-ness was all about, anyway. He fulfilled these dreams with another woman in the next part of his life.

"What are you doing?" I asked my husband, who was lying on the bed with a girl, both naked. "What does it look like I'm doing?" he answered defiantly.

This was to be our last New Year's Eve party together, although neither of us knew it that night when we walked into Joe's cabin in the woods for what promised to be a fun night. I guess some people had fun, but I wasn't one of them. Joe's Vietnamese Potbelly pig "Oinky" was already drunk; weighing two hundred pounds she could drink a lot of beer. Many friends, old and new, greeted us as we entered the kitchen and handed the bartender our bottle of wine for sharing. One of the new "friends" to greet us that night was a fifteen-year-old girl with a woman's body that was looking for action. I never did get her name. After touring the house that Joe had been building for three years and now had a few levels, very cleverly designed, I went downstairs to find food and music. Someone was playing his guitar and singing.

"Where's my husband?" I asked no one in particular as I walked into the kitchen to get a glass of wine.

"Oh, he's outside looking at Billy's new truck," someone answered nervously.

"Billy was here when we arrived and there was no new truck outside then. I'm going to look for Rob," I said.

"Oh no, don't do that, he'll be right back," the guy said.

"Now I know I'm looking for him," I said, as I marched toward the stairs. I don't know to this day if anyone followed me or if what I saw I saw alone, but I do know I knew what I was going to see. It was NOT my husband's finest hour.

We left early that night, I think. I was in shock, not just because my twenty-eight-year-old husband had screwed a fifteen-year-old child, but also because I now knew what I had suspected for a few years: my husband not only didn't love me, he hated me. I felt humiliated; it also brought up memories of my being raped at age fifteen. In my grief over knowing the end of the love story with Rob was now here, I blamed myself: maybe if I'd been prettier, better in bed, had a better body, was more lovable, more whatever, maybe then he would have loved me. I realized later that he didn't love me because he didn't love himself. Yet, I obviously wasn't able to love myself then, either.

We never discussed that night, even after the father of the fifteen-year old called and threatened to press rape charges against Rob. I do believe my husband was sorry for doing what he did and told the father so, as the man called later to talk to me and told me they had been having problems with their wayward daughter. He and his wife had decided not to press charges; he then told me I was the one he felt sorry for. I look back and realize I was like an indulgent "mother" with my husband; any other woman would have screamed and yelled about that night, but I was an enabler with him, as I turned out to be later in life with my children. I feel his behavior kept getting worse because then I would kick him out and he wouldn't have to make a decision to leave — it would all be my fault, not his.

You'll never guess what I did to solve this problem. I suggested we try to have an "Open Marriage," based on this new book by a couple of marriage counselors who, by the way, also got divorced later. They wrote that we could learn to not be possessive of each other if we took other lovers. Maybe we could get our relationship back on track.

Young and stupid are two words that come to mind.

A lot has been written about the 1950's and 60's. I haven't felt the need to read about that time, as I lived it. What I remember is hypocrisy, a glossing over of the American family ideals, encouraged by TV shows like "Ozzie and Harriet" and "Leave it to Beaver."

My mother tried her best to be a version of "the Beave's" Mom, June Cleaver, the lady of the house in high heels and dress, while effortlessly making a fancy meal three times every day. Mom did a good job but underneath it all she was seething with anger.

Well, shit, who wouldn't seethe? The men? I look back at this era and feel that some of the men may have wanted an equal partner. What a burden on a man to be the primary breadwinner. And, because of a woman's sense of powerlessness she is, underneath the surface, resenting the hell out of her husband. Or her kids. Or maybe she doesn't really know who or what makes her angry. She may not even be aware of her own anger.

And now you've got career opportunities available for both men and women in the 1960's that just weren't available in the previous decades.

Remember "Rosie, the Riveter"? She was a real woman who worked for the war effort, World War II, in Detroit. Her photo became part of a media blitz to encourage women to work in steel mills, lumber and freight yards, as taxi drivers, even operating heavy construction machinery. The slogan was "Do the job he left behind."

Wow! I can really earn as much as men can by doing the same job? Not really. Women not only did the same job for less money, but were forced to leave work as soon as the men returned, even if they had been widowed, with no other means of support.

The women of my mother's generation got a taste of learning new skills and making more money than they could as domestic workers or secretaries, but still not as much as the guys doing the same job, a fact which became the catalyst for the "Women's Lib" movement in the 1960's.

When my mother was in her 60's I asked her what she really wanted to be when she was growing up, in her heart of hearts, thinking she might say a doctor, as she was a Registered Nurse and loved it. The answer came quickly: "Oh, Penny, I'd have given anything to be a pilot, I so loved to fly; all my brothers were pilots. But most women had little opportunity in the 1920's and 30's to fly planes," she lamented.

Amelia Earhart's plane was lost somewhere over the Pacific Ocean in 1937. What a huge loss, as she was a great example, like "Rosie," telling girls and women, "We can do this!" She was barely forty years old when she became part of history.

I guess the thing I remember most about the 1960's is that it was a time of turbulence, of great change; a real loss of innocence for our nation with the murders of John F. Kennedy, Dr. Martin Luther King Jr., and Robert Kennedy. That may be when fear began creeping into the fabric of our otherwise idyllic lives.

❦

"You know what I'd love to change about you?" Rob asked. We were heading toward the end of our marriage by then. I had decided, after a few months of having an "Open Marriage," that it was crap and I wanted out of it, but didn't say anything to Rob, just stopped doing it and watched in horror as his behavior seemed to become more reckless. I no longer trusted him or his ability to be a soft place for me to land. This experiment of ours did not work, except maybe to show me there's a better way of loving one another, a way without other lovers forming a wedge that tears apart a couple like a mall splits the chunk of wood that heats our home.

"I'd like you to go through a door and close it gently behind you," Rob continued. There are moments in our lives when we make a spiritual connection with a loved one that goes beyond intimacy.

I hesitated for only a moment before looking at him and quietly saying I also wanted that for myself. And then, unable to sustain the deep, momentary connection between us, I continued, "But what makes you think I will want you when I get there?"

Today I'd be much kinder, more gentle with my husband if that conversation were to take place. Of course, it wouldn't happen today, for many reasons and not just that I now close doors gently behind me. Or that he's married to someone else, a woman who wouldn't allow us to have any conversation at all, even if it's what he wanted.

"Mom, when did you first learn of Dad's cheating?" I inquired one day as she drove us to the grocery store while Dad watched Heather. After I had stopped having other lovers I noticed Rob wasn't coming home on time at night or sometimes spent the weekend with his parents if he had a job out of town near them, rather than come home for the weekend.

"I didn't realize you kids knew about that," Mom finally replied, as if thinking about it was painful. I knew how she felt, as even the idea of Rob's cheating on me hurt like hell. "Your father began his affairs when Peggy was a baby," Mom continued. I was shocked to hear that he strayed so soon. Surely, it must take couples more than a few years to learn not to love each other; yet I remembered that Rob stopped loving me after only two years of marriage.

"Mom, Rob has a girlfriend; I don't ask because I'm afraid of the answer. I don't want to lose him," I said, starting to cry, "but I guess I already have." Mom reached over to pat my hand as she knew what I was feeling. I was touched by her show of concern as she's usually quite reserved, even cold. Mom drew her hand away and the moment was broken by her making some innocuous comment about groceries on our list.

I had a bad dream one night: "Penny, I need to talk to you about something," Rob said in a tone that frightened me. *How bad could it be,* I'm thinking. *We've already hurt each other a lot.*

One good thing about dreams is that they are not "real," although often turn out to have some truth in them. This dream was no exception, yet subconsciously played a role just a few months later in the direction our marriage took. I had forgotten the dream but the seed had been planted.

"I have a girlfriend and she's pregnant; I'm leaving to be with her," Rob continued in the dream.

Of course I was shocked, as my good news that day was going to be, "Guess what, honey? We're having a baby!" We had wanted a baby for a long time, but this was unexpected. In my dream I'd gone to the doctor that day to find out if I was anemic, as I was tired all the time. I thought missing one period and being "late" for a second one was from stress, as we had been going through a rough time.

When I awoke from the dream I dismissed it, only to discover the significance of it many years later.

That summer I turned thirty; on my birthday I vowed that things would be different between Rob and me by my thirty-first birthday or I would be out of there. I made the mistake of telling Rob that. He heard *I'm out of here,* while I was saying I want things to change for the better.

It took me many years to understand that Rob shut me out right from the beginning, not because he was a bad person; he just didn't know how to be a husband. I had married a man with the emotions of a teenager yet neither of us realized it. Maybe it was his passive-aggressive nature at work, refusing to take responsibility for his own actions, allowing me to push him into marriage then blaming me for his lack of interest in maintaining the relationship. Yet, I hid myself from him, also. I never told him about being raped at age fifteen; that trauma added much anger toward men. I didn't try to share myself with Rob, probably because I had no clue who I really was. You have to become an "I" before you can become a "WE."

At the beginning of our marriage I had asked why he wouldn't argue with me, or even discuss things with me. You know what he said? If we argue it means we are getting divorced. Well, guess what, honey? We never had an argument but we did get divorced.

Chapter 11

"You cannot change other people. You love them the way they are or you don't."

Don Miguel Ruiz

Betsy — My adoptive parents:

My mother, Catherine Eleanor Paulsen, was born in Massachusetts to George and Rose Paulsen, originally from England. He owned a shoe store in the village of Lincoln, where Rose worked for him, adding feminine touches and designing eye-catching storefront displays in order to market the products better. His business flourished, partly because of her easy manner with the customers. They were attracted to each other and would have been sweethearts except for one barrier: George wanted to leave England for better financial opportunities and Rose couldn't bear to leave her family.

In 1896, at age twenty-nine, George immigrated to the United States, coming to Boston on the Cunard Line's "Cephalonia," a transport ship which pre-dated the luxury liners that Cunard owned years later. His brother Arthur had already settled in Medford, Massachusetts and wrote to George of the wonderful country with its vast wealth and chances to be successful. George and Rose parted as friends, yet wrote letters to each other for more than ten years, neither of them marrying.

"My Dear Rose," George wrote in the summer of 1907. "It is in my heart to ask for your hand in marriage. I am well-established here in the Boston area; as you know, I own a lovely shop where I sell the latest fashion in quality shoes. A friend has suggested I add millinery items, along with other accessories for women, to make this shop the very best it can be. Now my dear, I don't want you to misunderstand my motives for asking this question, as I am very clear of the place you hold in my heart. Is there a place for me in your heart? Will you marry me? We can build this shoe store into something we'll be proud of, the kind we often dreamed of owning back in England. You would like it here very much; I have good friends who will welcome you with arms wide open. Another surprise I have for you is that I have commissioned a man to build a lovely home in Medford. Will you share it with me? Will you share my life? My love has always been strong for you. Yours, George."

My grandmother, Rose Wheeler, came to Boston from Liverpool on the Cunard Line's "Saxonia," arriving in October. The usually-reserved Rose was bubbling over, excited to see George and have this adventure with him. She stayed with Arthur's family until they got married Christmas Eve, 1907. Their daughter, Catherine, an only child born to this couple late in life, arrived January 9, 1910. She was raised in the upper-middle class world of Medford society, yet preferred England with all its pomp and circumstance. She got very excited each time she and her mother took a ship to England to spend a month with relatives.

George returned only once to see his elderly parents before dying of a heart attack in 1920 at the age of fifty-three. Rose lived to the ripe old age of sixty-eight before dying of unknown causes in Medford in 1936.

❦

My father, Hayward Fred Hall, was born in Boston on August 1, 1906 to Fred Parcher Hall and Lillian Elizabeth Walker Hall. Fred was a successful businessman/investor who celebrated his first son's birth by giving his wife a beautiful ruby ring, set in white gold surrounded by diamonds. It was passed down to my Cousin Penny fifty years later.

My father lived a rigid, yet highly-privileged, upper-class Boston life as the spoiled, over-protected only child of Fred and Lillian until October 28, 1912 when his brother Carleton arrived on the scene. By all outward appearances Hayward was thrilled with his new brother, but inside he was thinking *good, now they have a baby to smother and will leave me alone*.

That didn't happen. Letters found many years later, over one-hundred of them between Hayward and his parents starting in 1924 and ending in 1962, allude to their son's health. There was weekly correspondence, mostly Hayward asking for money when he was a student at the University of Vermont. Later they wrote letters when he was a lodger in Boston working as an apprentice at a major accounting firm, and more after he was married and I had arrived.

"I hope you're wearing the new scarf I sent you; you know how cold New England winters are. I hope you're eating right, dear. I hope you're feeling well, dear," or similar words of caution, were often written by his mother, admonishing him about his health. In spite of that, my father was sickly much of his life, dying in his fifties of complications from emphysema.

Hayward was in his late twenties when a mutual friend, Alice, introduced him to Catherine on a blind date. He was successful in his career as an accountant; now the pressure was on him to marry and produce the first grandchild for Lillian and Fred (although Carleton, the baby brother, did beat him to it).

"Hayward, may I present to you my friend, Catherine. She's a student at the Conservatory, your mother's alma mater," spoke Alice as the two shyly shook hands and murmured the necessary niceties. The tall, red-haired man replied, "It's very nice to meet you, Catherine."

It was a cold, crispy October night in Boston, with a promise of winter coming soon. Catherine's chestnut-brown hair and green eyes were complemented by her choice of dresses: a gray satin evening gown with a matching silver fox coat. Her long gray gloves and silver pumps completed the outfit. Catherine's pearl necklace and earrings were family heirlooms given to her by an aunt in England. Catherine's tall, patrician figure helped make this formal outfit look elegant and not overdone.

The new couple-to-be kept stealing glances at each other while the discussion about restaurants, the weather, and life at the Boston Conservatory of Music went on until Hayward said that Bishop, the chauffeur, was waiting to take them to the Algonquin Club. His parents were members of this social club known for excellent food and impeccable service. Throughout the evening Hayward and Catherine continued to peek at each other; he thought she was a possible candidate for a wife. Catherine knew he was a good catch.

By the end of their second date, to the opera, Hayward realized he and Catherine had a lot in common: they both loved all things pertaining to music, including playing the piano together. Their social standing in the community was as important to Catherine as it was to Hayward. Hayward felt she would be a good wife, an asset, as he climbed up the ladder of success. She wanted to be married to a man who matched her ambitious nature. Material "things" were of great importance to Catherine. Her schoolwork did, however, take precedence over dating which limited their social life to weekends for the next two years. Even then she often had to study for exams and write papers for school, having to cancel a date last-minute to catch up.

They dated for more than a year before Catherine was invited to the new home of Hayward's parents, who had recently moved to Fresh Pond Lane in Cambridge. The event was one of Lillian and Fred's frequent Sunday afternoon parties. They also dated for more than a year before he kissed her. He did have other women he visited to satisfy his physical needs, though; this was an accepted part of upper-class Boston society in the late 1920's.

"Catherine, dear, would you do me the honor of being my wife? We have a lot in common, you must admit," Hayward said one evening during the Christmas holidays of 1931. "Do you love me, Hayward?" she asked. "You've never said so." "Yes, of course I do," he replied.

It was time for Catherine to be married; she was twenty-one and ready to settle down and raise a family. This could work with Hayward. And she did love him, although one thing they had in common was the inability to express the love they felt for each other, both being quite rigid and formal.

A guest book found after my grandmother, Lillian, died shows there was an engagement party for the couple Valentine's Day weekend, 1932. Catherine's mother, Rose, a widow for many years, signed this book. Lillian's diary describes the party as a joyous affair filled with music, laughter, and good food. Mrs. Bryce, the weekend maid, set up a lovely buffet for which she made poached salmon with dill sauce, along with tomato aspic; baked ham, sliced thin and served with her special mustard sauce, was also on the menu. These were accompanied by many salads: Waldorf, tossed green salad, gelatin fruit salad, New England potato salad, along with freshly-ground coffee for which Lillian supervised the preparations. Keswick Pudding, a recipe brought over from England, was made in honor of Catherine and her mother. Lillian and Fred often served a dessert of sliced bananas and oranges with clotted cream or eggnog sauce, which was yummy, but this new dessert was a special hit with all the partygoers.

Card tables were set up in the living room with the logs in the fireplace burning brightly and name tags placed by each plate. Small frilly paper baskets with tiny handles made of twisted paper held the mints and nuts set by each place setting. After dinner the card tables were put away, table cloths taken to the laundry chute to drop into the basket below in the basement washing area, and everyone gathered around the Baby Grand, singing songs accompanied by Hayward and Catherine on the piano. This is the party where they sang the first love song they wrote together.

The August wedding of my parents took place at her mother's home in Medford; the backyard was spectacular, a typical, overflowing English garden — perfect for a wedding — with many roses, peonies, hollyhocks, and other colorful flowers and trees. The ivory satin gown, made especially for Catherine by an English designer who had recently settled in Boston, had a discreet neckline and round cap with veil. Hayward wore the required formal tuxedo. The newlyweds enjoyed their back yard celebration, yet clouds were gathering which forced the reception to end a little early. The downpour came as Catherine was changing into her dark blue traveling suit made of silk shantung suitable for the train ride to Quebec City, where they were to spend a brief honeymoon.

Clouds also moved into their relationship within a few years after the wedding. Catherine showed her unhappiness by using her sharp tongue all too frequently, while Hayward retreated further into himself, creating a chasm neither wanted to bridge even if they'd known how to do so.

Chapter 12

"You are all born here to go to Earth School."

Caroline Myss

Ellen Rose Hill — everyone called her Ellie — was a natural beauty, being given the gift of a flawless, creamy complexion, perfect curvy body and glistening, dark curly hair she usually kept long. Those big brown eyes looked right through a person with gentleness rather than a challenge. She had a beauty that women admired, while men were stunned at the first sight of her. When you talked to her she treated you as though there was no one else in the world. Most importantly, Ellie was genuinely nice, very kind; a sweet soul.

She and Parker Hill grew up together in Farmington, a small factory town in New Hampshire. He was a local boy, his family having been there for too many generations to count. She was the second child of immigrants from Quebec, Canada. Her parents, George and Ellen Lavoie, came to the United States as a young married couple in the early 1900's to seek employment in local shoe factories, as there were many. An expensive shoe in those days cost about $2.00/pair, but were still being made in the United States; those sold on the East coast were made in New Hampshire beside rivers where waste could be discharged. Ellie had no opportunities to be educated beyond elementary school, as her wages were needed to help the family survive; she had been making shoes for six years when she married Parker at age eighteen.

Parker found a tiny apartment in nearby Rochester, where he and Ellie worked in a factory; she sewed tongues on shoes while Parker operated the large cutting machines, a higher-paying job. Their new home was filled with furniture and household goods donated by both families. Life seemed fine for the newlyweds until December 8, 1941 when they heard about Pearl Harbor being bombed by the Japanese. Parker enlisted in the United States Navy, one of thousands of young men who went off to war the winter of 1941-42. A barely-pregnant Ellie kissed her husband goodbye, trying unsuccessfully to fight back the tears. That cold, somber, gray January day was the last time she saw her husband; he did not live to know about his son's birth the following August. Ellie named him Kevin.

After Parker's death, and the birth of her child being imminent, Ellie moved in with her parents so they could help her. Since Ellen also had to earn money she was able to care for her grandson only occasionally, so Ellie found work where she could usually take Kevin with her, cleaning homes and caring for the children of other families. Being a bright, hard-working woman, Ellie was limited only by her lack of education and training.

The summer of 1945 arrived, along with an opportunity for Ellie to work at Camp Cambridge on Lake Winnapesaukee near Alton, New Hampshire. She was excited to be able to spend the summer working and living in a beautiful place, but also to have three-year-old Kevin with her, as the duties were mostly cooking meals and light cleaning.

Lake Winnipesaukee, spelled Winnapesaukee many years later, was called "Beautiful Water of the High Place" by the local Indians, part of the Algonquin tribe. Lake Winnipesaukee, with its 274 islands and 72 square miles of water, along with 183 miles of shoreline, was indeed a high place of beauty. The Indians saw it as a sacred place that gave them salmon, bass, and lake trout, along with wild blueberries, blackberries, gooseberries, and plenty of wild game. In the winter there were pickerel and perch to be found under the ice, even two hundred years later in the 1870's when Camp Cambridge was built.

Nearby Alton was founded by a group of Roxbury citizens; that Massachusetts connection continued with the group of friends from Cambridge who bought land in 1871 and built four buildings a few miles north of Alton: the main house, dormitory, kitchen, and boat house. Camp Cambridge was built as a Social Club, a place to entertain business and family friends, and had a long glassed-in porch overlooking the lake, with a view of the tiny island directly in front of them. It was a year-round club, where visitors coming by train were dropped off at the water tower next to the compound. They came to ice-fish and hunt for game in the winter, and to go boating, swimming, and picnicking in the summer.

The nearby ice-house provided much-needed employment for locals in the winter.

It was in this beautiful natural setting on Lake Winnapesaukee that Hayward and Ellie first laid eyes on each other.

Chapter 13

"You can't make-believe you're calm when you're not."

Baba Ram Dass

Ellie and Kevin arrived at Lake Winnapesaukee by train early one June afternoon; bright, hot weather greeted them. The area was alive with noisy bugs talking to one another. The scent of pine trees and cool breezes coming off the lake were soothing after the long train ride.

There to greet them, also, was Hayward, the elder son of one of the owners of Camp Cambridge. "Hello, Mrs. Hill, I'm Hayward Hall, here to help with your luggage. Is this all you have?" he asked, as he picked up the small suitcase she and Kevin shared.

Ellie's smile made her eyes twinkle even more than usual as she said, "Please call me Ellie, and yes, we do travel light. This is my son, Kevin, whom I'm certain will show his best manners throughout the summer." Kevin hid behind his mother's skirt while Hayward quietly said hello.

Ellie's routine quickly became established: up early to fix breakfast for guests, sometimes as many as seven or eight. Then light cleaning of the rooms, including emptying out the "thunder jugs" that were under each bed. Every morning Ellie walked along the shoreline a discreet distance from the buildings in order to dump them as far from the swimming area as possible. Often Hayward would watch her walk, enjoying the natural movements of her sensuous body. Sometimes a child came to visit and Kevin had someone to play with, but the Social Club was mostly for adults, business acquaintances. Everything in the upper-class world of Boston came down to business, even vacations at the lake.

"Good morning, where are you going this fine day?" Hayward asked, as he spied Ellie walking along the shoreline, carrying some pots.

"Oh, good morning, Mr. Hall," she replied.

"My name is Hayward. Mr. Hall is a bit formal, don't you think? Please call me Hayward."

"Yes, well, uh, Hayward, I am going to wash out the thunder jugs," she said, embarrassed. "Thunder jugs" was the local expression for what they called chamber pots in Boston, used no matter where one lives for a call of nature in the middle of the night. Even country folks were hesitant to walk to the outhouse during pitch black nights. Since Hayward was used to having maids do all the domestic work he wasn't inclined to offer help, no matter how strong his attraction for Ellie.

"Ellie, the launch leaves in fifteen minutes for Alton. We could use your help in buying food."

"Yes sir, uh, Hayward, it is my job to buy the food. I will be there in fifteen minutes. Sir, may Kevin come with us? He's very well-behaved," Ellie said.

"That is entirely possible. I will wait for you both at the dock," he said, watching her as she hurried toward an area good for emptying the jugs. Hayward was beginning to feel a little protective toward Ellie, a new feeling for this privileged upper-class Bostonian who had grown up getting whatever he wanted, and having to bear few consequences when he made mistakes in his personal life. Father and Mother took care of things.

Hayward began visiting Camp Cambridge nearly every weekend, often arriving late Friday morning. He had taken a sudden interest in going to Alton on the camp's steamboat launch. Hayward brought foods from the big city: kumquats, canned gooseberries, water chestnuts, and other exotic items showed up in the pantry at the camp. Maybe Hayward's desire to go to town was partly because Ellie needed help carrying the two bags of groceries.

One weekend Hayward brought his wife Catherine to Camp Cambridge. She normally disliked roughing it so Hayward was surprised that she asked to come along for a visit. Even though they tried to hide it, it was obvious to many that their relationship was strained, a fact betrayed by body language and tone of voice. Catherine couldn't speak in a kind voice and Hayward was unable to give much response to her comments. Ellie noticed the tension between Hayward and his wife. It was different from the friendship he was developing with Ellie.

One evening Ellie and Hayward ran into each other. They stood there in the fading light, talking yet not saying much, both of them a little self-conscious.

"Oh, look at the moon peeking through the haze," Ellie said, pointing. Hayward drew in a breath as he realized how lovely and intoxicating she looked in the pale moonlight. Ellie, a beautiful yet modest woman, was used to men's stares but not comfortable with them. *Hayward's different*, she thought, looking at his thinning, red hair in the moonlight and his lean, yet masculine body. He was an accountant who spent most weekdays in his office, which gave him a pale softness in the winter; in the summer he was more active. He was now tanned and healthy looking. The attraction between them had been growing right along with their friendship since the first day they met. He reached for her face, taking it gently in his hands, kissing her with a passion that took her breath away. "We mustn't do this," she gasped, as she broke away. *Yet*, she thought, *we both want to.*

Chapter 14

"Desiring to heal is not the same as having the will to heal. Some people who want to heal may not have the will to make the life changes required in order for them to heal."

Caroline Myss

"Ellie, I can't stop thinking about you. I dream we're together as a family; I feel us making love. I dream Kevin is my son and we have another child together. I can't eat; I'm hopelessly in love with you. I wake in the middle of the night when the dreams are so real that I ache," Hayward said one cool evening in early September. Ellie had taken a break from packing Kevin's clothes, some of which no longer fit him. He had grown a lot during the summer and become as brown as the hot sun could make him. Kevin, the beautiful curly-headed child with a sweet disposition, was peacefully asleep in their dormitory room. Hayward had waited for Ellie at water's edge far from the camp, as arranged ahead of time.

"Did you mean it when you said you could find a way to come and see me this winter?" Ellie asked in a voice beginning to crack with emotion, her eyes filling with tears.

"Yes, my love," he replied, while holding her close, not wanting to let her go.

She and Kevin left the next morning on the train to return home; during the few hours between Camp Cambridge and Farmington a plan was forming in her mind. She had saved money all summer and wanted her own apartment. Parker's service pension gave her a small nest egg; she knew where she wanted to settle into a new life with Kevin: Portsmouth, New Hampshire. This was a brave thing for a war widow to do but there were many others in her situation; maybe she'd be able to find a roommate, another widow, to share expenses.

"I miss you with all my heart and soul; I ache to be with you," Hayward wrote in the fall of 1945. Ellie and Kevin were settled in their tiny apartment on Market Street, a stone's throw from the Portsmouth Harbor, where seagulls performed for Kevin, always asking for more bread crumbs. The sea air, with its frequent fog, combined with the sound of the moaning fog horn, surrounded Ellie like a protective bubble. She longed to be with Hayward, yet was always aware that he belonged to another woman.

Ellie found a job in a dress shop and occasionally treated herself to a simple frock, one she knew Hayward would love to see her wear when they finally did spend some time together. They wrote to each other on a weekly basis; she saved some of his, which showed up in her personal papers after she died. Yet, as a married man, he was not able to save hers.

"Mommy, will we see Uncle Hayward again?" Kevin asked one day when she picked him up from the lady who babysat for Kevin while Ellie worked. "I hope so, my dear, I hope so," she replied.

One day Ellie received the letter she had been waiting for: Hayward was able to visit her for the weekend! A week before Christmas he took the train to Portsmouth rather than Camp Cambridge to go ice-fishing, as he sometimes did. He booked a room at the Rockingham Hotel, but went directly to her apartment without un-packing his things.

"Ellie, I'm in love with you; I didn't mean for it to happen but it has. I don't know what we can do about it except enjoy this weekend. I have nothing to offer you, can make no promises; I know only that I love you very much. I've never felt this way before," Hayward said that evening as they sat in the kitchen, each sipping a hot cup of tea. Kevin was in the other room playing with the ball Hayward brought him.

"No throwing it, okay, Kevin?" Ellie called out before answering Hayward.

"Okay, Mommy, I'll be good," Kevin replied.

"Yes, Hayward, I can be happy with what we have, even though I know you cannot make me any promises," she softly replied after a moment's hesitation.

That evening Kevin developed a bad cold and cough and was put to bed early. Ellie hoped the small amount of cough syrup she had just given him would help her son sleep. Within minutes Kevin was out like a light.

Conversation, which usually flowed freely between Hayward and Ellie, was a little tense. They both knew what was going to happen; a new intimacy in their relationship was beginning. The night was blustery cold outside, wind howling, mirroring the passion and excitement building in the hearts and bodies of the expectant lovers. He gently unbuttoned the front of her new dress, the bluish-gray one with gathered sleeves and tiny pink bows in the fabric. She touched his hand, encouraging him to continue. She caressed the back of his hand as he softly reached under her bra, fondling her breasts, toying with her nipples, showing a patience that comes with maturity and experience. He unhooked the back of the bra and her full breasts popped out, offering themselves to his hand and mouth. They both sighed with great pleasure. His lips found that small, sensuous curve of her neck, sending shivers up and down her spine. He smiled into her eyes as he reached for her mouth to kiss.

"Mommy, I hurt," Kevin cried from the other room as he began a round of heavy coughing. Ellie quickly kissed Hayward and buttoned her dress while going to help her son. Hayward spent the next two hours helping Ellie with a "croup tent," finding a blanket to make one, and boiling water to set up a pan of steam. He felt very protective of both of them and could see he was also beginning to fall in love with Ellie's little boy.

"It's late, you have neighbors; I must go back to the hotel. I know Kevin will be better in the morning. I love you very much, my darling," Hayward murmured to Ellie.

"Me too, I love you, too, Hayward," she replied, as they kissed.

Sunday arrived and Hayward went to her apartment after a restless night at the hotel. Kevin was well on the road to recovery, but because of his illness they spent all day inside the apartment made cozy by a gas heater inside the living room wall. Their only other source of heat was the gas stove in the kitchen, which Ellie often used in the winter for both cooking and heating. As Christmas was coming the following week they exchanged gifts: Hayward gave Ellie a gold locket with the initials "H" and "E" engraved outside and a tiny snippet of his reddish hair inside. She showed him the tie tack she bought for him with the letter "E" in the center, but of course he couldn't take it with him so she kept it to be worn by Hayward when he visited her and Kevin.

Ellie seldom took off the locket until years later. Hayward never wore the tie tack. These items were found by her son after she died.

At 1 p.m., after a lunch of crabmeat sandwiches and cucumbers, Hayward said goodbye to Ellie, both fighting off tears. "I must leave for the train. I cannot miss it," he lamented as he put on his overcoat and rubber overshoes. "Goodbye, Kevin, be good for your mother," he said as he hugged the boy.

After a few quick kisses they parted and Hayward took a taxi to the train station to return to Boston. A few hours later he arrived to find his 1942 Buick where he had parked it at the station. He reluctantly drove home to Catherine.

Chapter 15

"The curious thing about healing is that, depending on who you talk to, you can come to believe either that nothing is easier or that nothing is more complicated."

Anatomy of the Spirit by Caroline Myss

One bitter cold day in February, 1946 Hayward called Ellie at the dress shop. "Honey, I can get away for the weekend. We can be together for two whole days," he exclaimed!

"I can hardly wait to see you, darling," Ellie replied, filled with much anticipation.

Weekly letters were still being exchanged between them, often crossing in the mail. They both cherished these letters, reading them over and over again, but of course Hayward had to throw out his after a couple days. His secretary surely would have recognized the handwriting on each letter, yet never let on that she knew he was having an affair. The men in upper-class Boston often had mistresses, but it was all done discreetly.

"The train ride was longer than normal; the snow train had to go in front of us, and I thought we'd never get here," Hayward greeted Ellie as she opened the door of her apartment. They went inside and embraced warmly. "Oh, honey, I missed you so," Hayward began before being interrupted by Kevin, hugging Hayward's legs and shouting,

"Pick me up, Uncle Hayward!" Hayward tossed Kevin in the air while the three-year old roared with laughter. "More, more," he begged. After a few moments of rough-housing Kevin scooted off to play with the gift Hayward brought, a plastic chicken that lays eggs. Kevin cherished the toy and passed it on to his own kids many years later.

That evening, after Kevin was bathed, Hayward read him his favorite book of Robert Louis Stevenson's poetry, each poem illustrated with a scene that popped up as Kevin eagerly opened the page: the girl who swings high, showing her petticoats and buttoned shoes, the boy who laughs as he throws the ball to his dog.

After Kevin was asleep the couple kissed as they sat together on the sofa. The words were unspoken, yet each knew tonight the love they had felt growing over the past eight months would be consummated.

Hayward gently ran his hand up her thigh as he kissed her lips, making contact with her inner being which was warm and moist with desire. She slowly stood up as he took off her silky underpants, the ones he had bought for her at Filene's in Boston; the panties matched the pink silken fabric of her bra. He kissed the tiny mound of her tummy, moving to her thighs, along the way filling her with a longing that made her moan. They took turns gently exploring the other's body, with passion increasing each time they kissed and touched each other. As they moved their bodies together they looked into each other's eyes, knowing they had found something very special. There was an explosion of pleasure, with satisfaction unlike anything they had felt before, which made them cry out in ecstasy. Their bodies shuddered as they both began to come back to Earth. They glowed in the aftermath of their passion.

This is the night their child was conceived.

❧

"Darling, I have news for you; good news and bad news," Ellie wrote one cold New Hampshire day in April 1946.

She and Hayward had been writing their weekly letters for more than seven months, and their love and understanding of one another were increasing with each correspondence. Yet both were wary, as this was a forbidden affair between a forty-year-old married man and a twenty-three-year-old war widow. It could go "nowhere" and this saddened them both.

Ellie's cozy apartment was the scene of many, yet never enough, family moments with Hayward and almost-four-year-old Kevin. These scenes warmed her heart and broke it at the same time.

"Hayward, I have something to tell you and I must just come out with it:

I am expecting a child in the fall. I am excited because it is our child, made from our love, yet frightened because I don't know what will happen to Kevin and me. I want to tell the world about us, yet cannot. Please call me at the dress shop when you receive this," Ellie wrote.

Hayward, of course, reacted with shock. He had spent a few wonderful nights with Ellie not trying to become a father, while the first ten years of his marriage were spent dealing with infertility, along with an eroding relationship with Catherine. Maybe it was the lack of a child that made Catherine increasingly unhappy, yet they never discussed their problems. Catherine got her own bedroom when they bought the house in Wellesley Hills, out in the country, in anticipation of adopting a child.

The demand to adopt was increasing while a large number of men away at war helped keep down the supply of available babies. Also, it was easy to pose as a war widow, which allowed some women to keep their children.

Only Catherine knew her reasons for being unhappy with Hayward, yet he was miserable living with her cold, shrill tongue and angry demeanor. The happiness he had with Ellie was exquisite, especially when comparing it to his marriage.

"Darling, I will be there Friday evening and we will talk about this. Please wait up for me, as I will take the late train. We can find a solution, I promise," Hayward almost shouted over the phone, which had a bad connection.

❧

"Oh, where have you been? I've been worried, darling," Ellie said, as she greeted a drenched Hayward at her door late Friday night.

"The train was delayed because of the rain storm, trees down all over the place, cars stalled and no taxis in sight. I walked here from the train station," Hayward said, clearly out of breath.

"I'll draw a hot bath and fix a bowl of chicken soup for you," Ellie offered, as she hung up his overcoat to dry and helped him take off his galoshes. She quickly got the bath started and put out the robe he kept there.

After the soothing bath and a bowl of soup Hayward felt like a new man. "I want you to know I won't desert you, that we are in this together. I promise you that, darling," he said as he gently put his hand on her tummy. "To think we have a baby inside here is really exciting, but scary. We need to think about options. Can you keep this child and raise it alone? I would help with money, of course."

"Hayward, I have been a widow for almost four years; there could be no passing this off as Parker's child. The baby needs a better life than I can give it: two parents, a nice home, the education I never got. Poverty is not romantic, darling," Ellie stated.

"I know abortion is out, as you may be too far along anyway, even if you wanted to do that," Hayward said.

"Abortion is not an option," Ellie said, "but putting it up for adoption is."

They agreed to work on this as partners, to come up with a solution best for all concerned. As they walked to the bedroom he thought of how much he loved this woman, how wonderful it would be to stay forever with her, Kevin, and the new baby.

Hayward was almost afraid to make love with Ellie as he didn't want to hurt the baby; but they couldn't keep their hands off each other. Their lovemaking was more gentle than usual.

Hayward returned to Wellesley Hills with a plan hatching in his mind: he and Catherine could adopt this baby that was part of him. But first, he must tell his father. He would discuss this plan with Ellie when he figured out the details. His hope was that Catherine would never find out where this baby came from.

"Father, I have a problem and I need your help," Hayward said the following morning when Fred was not distracted by business at the bank or the chocolate factory. Fred was a Vice President at Boston Safe Deposit & Trust Company, which he preferred doing rather than running the factory, which he later turned over to a manager. Hayward caught his father in a favorite den, which was filled with books, paintings, and tobacco pipes, all the things Fred needed for leisure time.

"What is it, son?" Fred asked. Hayward knew better than to beat around the bush with his father whose time was precious: "Father, I've been having an affair and she is pregnant with my child, due in November," Hayward hurriedly answered.

Fred didn't bat an eyelash, as this was not the first time one of his sons had come to him with this problem. The second-born, Carleton, seemed to have a goal of bedding every attractive woman who came within touching distance. He tried to be discreet, having these lovers only when he spent time out of town, away from his lovely wife and four children.

"What do you propose to do about this? Pay her off?" Fred asked.

"Father, I love this woman and she is having my child. I know there will be no divorce from Cath…" he started to say.

"Damned right there will be no divorce if you want to stay in this family!" Fred yelled.

Hayward continued, swallowing hard. "I know there will be no divorce. I'm thinking Catherine and I could take this child and raise it as our own."

"Would Catherine consent to this? Does she know about the affair?" Fred asked.

Hayward had no intentions of telling Catherine about the affair; the more he thought about it the more determined he was to pass this off as a normal adoption. Hayward lied to his father and said she did, knowing his parents would never speak of it.

Catherine need never find out the truth.

❦

"Darling, I am coming up this weekend so we can talk about our problem. I will be there Saturday noon and stay at the Rockingham Hotel. I'm sorry this has to be a quick trip but we need to talk. I think that I have found a solution. I love you," Hayward wrote.

May had arrived, although the weather was still brisk, when Hayward took the train for the last time to Ellie's apartment on Market Street. The early afternoon sun made everything bright, including Hayward's hopeful attitude that all would be well soon.

Kevin was excited to see his "Uncle Hayward" and let him know it with a hug of the tall man's knees. "Kevin, you're getting so big I can hardly lift you now," Hayward said, as he picked him up. He brought Kevin a gift of a light blue metal dump truck and matching shovel; this summer his mother could take him to the beach to play in the sand. Ellie would have to quit working soon, as she was beginning to show her pregnancy.

As Kevin ran off to play Hayward spoke to Ellie, tightly hugging her as if he couldn't bear to let her go: "I have a solution; let's sit and discuss it."

The emotions between them were intense: some relief, some tears, a lot of love and laughter, more tears. Later a sense of calm came over both; they knew it would be okay. Hayward explained how he and his parents would pay for all of it — the apartment, the hospital stay and doctor's visits, along with extra money to help Ellie and Kevin live comfortably. He and Catherine would adopt the baby. Ellie agreed to this, as she knew the baby would be safe with its father.

Now that they had a solution they relaxed and enjoyed his brief stay. After Kevin was asleep they had a tender, poignant lovemaking session, knowing this might be the last time they ever made love together.

But, it wasn't.

Chapter 16

"No one can make you feel inferior without your consent."

Eleanor Roosevelt

Catherine was excited to hear from the adoption agency that a baby was to be born in a few months and it would be theirs. Boy or girl didn't matter, as long as it was healthy. Fred had arranged this adoption through the same agency that placed Catherine and Hayward on the waiting list five years before. Fred and Lillian's lawyer was the go-between, just as he had been in charge of sending monthly payments to Ellie. It was done discreetly; no one need ever know the truth.

Elizabeth Kate Hall — known as Betsy from the beginning — was born on a cold November morning in the Portsmouth Hospital. She was a beauty, easily the prettiest in the entire nursery: dark, curly hair and big brown eyes. Ellie had a normal labor and delivery, but was all alone — no mother, no Hayward, not one single friend to visit her. Her neighbor cared for Kevin the week that Ellie was in the hospital recuperating from the birth.

Her heart would take much longer to heal from giving up the only daughter she would ever have.

Ellie told no one in her family about the pregnancy. Even though major highways would later make the trip between Farmington and Portsmouth no more than one hour long, in 1946 it was a trip few working-class people could afford to make. She also never told Kevin of the birth, yet years later he realized that period in his young life had a piece missing, as though he subconsciously knew he had a sister. For years he remembered his "Uncle Hayward" was no longer coming around, yet knew better than to ask his mother.

In spite of taking pills to dry up her milk, every time Ellie heard a baby cry her breasts would tingle, aching to be drained of milk by her baby, the child she held only briefly while nursing her after the placenta had been delivered. She un-wrapped the swaddling cloth the little beauty had been wrapped in, checking all of her baby's toes and fingers to make certain she was perfect. Betsy, who had no official name yet, stopped nursing when Ellie burst into tears. She looked at her mother as if she knew of Ellie's pain at letting her go to live with another family. Ellie held her daughter tightly while tears flowed down her cheeks, tears that would take years to dry up, long after her milk had ceased to flow.

Ellie took solace in the fact that Hayward would be raising their daughter; the child would become the joy of her father's life.

It was good that Ellie did not know her daughter would become the focus of Catherine's anger.

Chapter 17

"When an illness is part of your spiritual journey no medical intervention can heal you until your spirit has begun to make the changes that the illness was designed to inspire."

Why People Don't Heal and How They Can by Caroline Myss

Catherine and Hayward had arrived at a more peaceful co-existence because of the shared excitement about the new baby's pending arrival. The nursery contained everything one could possibly buy for an infant, including a canopy bed, rocking chair, changing table, and dozens of expensive stuffed animals. It was the perfect nursery for a child born into an upper-class Boston family in the 1940's. The new parents-to-be were ready for the phone call informing them of the birth of their child — at last they were to have their very own baby after more than ten years of heartbreak over Catherine's inability to produce a child.

Betsy was brought home to her lovely new room filled with yellow and green bedding and accessories. She had been placed in a foster home for a few weeks while waiting for the adoption papers to be ready; the final adoption would take place six months later, long after Betsy had bonded with her new parents. Catherine and Hayward were eager to claim her as their own.

"Hayward, look at how the sun is shining in here to welcome our daughter. I am so happy," Catherine said the day before Betsy was to come home with them.

Hayward replied, as he put his arm around his wife's waist, "I am also, Catherine. I have no doubt we will be good parents."

For the first time in many years Hayward was content with Catherine. His thoughts of Ellie were filled with tenderness, a bit of sadness and longing, but most of all, gratitude for the gift he and Catherine had been given.

The sun that was shining down on the new family in their 1930's English Tudor brick home that wintry day in early December kept the atmosphere warm and cozy inside for many years.

All was well. Until Catherine discovered the truth of Betsy's parentage.

She never got over it.

Chapter 18

"We cannot love ourselves unless we love others, and we cannot love others unless we love ourselves."

Thomas Merton, Catholic mystic

One early fall day in 1950 Catherine had a gall bladder attack and was hospitalized, requiring surgery. Hayward was in charge of Betsy, who was now almost four years old. When he realized Catherine would be in the hospital for awhile, he called Ellie, who now had an apartment in Dover, closer to her parents. The new place carried no painful memories for Ellie.

Hayward and Ellie had kept in touch; their letters during the past four years were still being exchanged, yet not as frequently as when he was "courting" her. Hayward often sent photographs of Betsy as she grew into what he thought was the "spitting image" of her real mother, Ellie.

"Darling, I have a surprise for you," Hayward said, when he phoned Ellie that morning. "I'm driving up there to see you and Kevin, and bringing Betsy. Would you like that?"

Ellie had yet to see her daughter in person since she was a newborn; she was a bit nervous. "Hayward, I would love to see you both. I just hope I can handle it," Ellie replied, with anxiety in her voice.

Friday morning Hayward drove his new Buick, which Betsy named "Boopsie," to Dover, New Hampshire and took a room for himself and his daughter at Jensen's Guest House. It was close to Ellie's apartment on Sixth Street. He was excited knowing he'd see Ellie; also wondering if Kevin would recognize him. They had agreed not to see each other after Betsy was born; it would only prolong the goodbyes. But he needed to see her one last time. She wanted it, too.

The love between them felt stronger, more enduring than before Betsy was born, as though a child born to them was glue that bonded them. They were strongly attracted to one another physically; time had done nothing to diminish their feelings.

"Look at your little girl!" Ellie exclaimed when she saw Betsy. "What a beauty!"

"Yes, she looks just like her mother," Hayward replied before he could stop himself. Betsy heard the official story of her adoption when Hayward made up bedtime stories, always starting with, "One day a beautiful, little girl named Betsy was born…"

"Uncle Hayward, I remember you," Kevin said, as he hugged Hayward's now-not-so-long legs.

"Kevin, you're so grown up now. You are so tall; how old are you now, eight?" Hayward asked as he bent down to return the hug.

The kids ran off to play with the wooden puzzle of the United States map; the pieces were colorful and each state had a red knob which you could use to put it into the puzzle. Kevin and Betsy played well together, Kevin relishing the role of older friend.

That evening, with both kids asleep in Kevin's room that was furnished with bunk beds, Ellie and Hayward went to her room. He kissed her gently, treating her like the treasure she was to him. Their kisses quickly became quite passionate filled with pent-up desires. Hayward looked into Ellie's eyes and they breathed into each other as he penetrated her. The softness of her inside being made them both moan; he was very sensitive to her receiving him, making Hayward even more desirous of her. Love-making between them now had a sense of urgency as though they had to make up for lost time. Somewhat like a long-married couple re-discovering their desire for each other, familiar and intimate, yet new and exciting. Their bodies moved together as two combined to make one. His eyes bore into hers as the orgasmic explosion rocked their souls.

"I love you and always will; you know that, darling," Hayward moaned. Ellie began to cry, sorry for what they had lost, yet thankful for what they shared.

"I feel the same way, Hayward; no matter what the future holds I will forever have you in my heart," Ellie said, between sobs. The long, gentle, passionate kiss between them was the goodbye they had postponed when Betsy was born. They were both sadly aware they may never see each other again.

The next day Hayward and Betsy left to return home to Massachusetts, planning to visit Catherine in the hospital. The charge nurse kept an eye on Betsy downstairs near the lobby, but Catherine could wave to Betsy from her window as they left. As father and daughter continued the journey to their home in Wellesley Hills, Hayward said, "Honey, you know not to mention this trip to Mother, don't you?"

"Yes, Daddy, I can keep a secret," she quietly replied, with a note of conspiracy in her four-year-old voice.

Betsy never spoke of the trip. Although Hayward and Ellie never again made love together they did see each other years later.

Chapter 19

"Your playing small doesn't serve the world. There is nothing enlightened about shrinking so that other people won't feel insecure around you."

Marianne Williamson

"What's this letter inside your pocket? I took your suit to the cleaners and found this. Unfortunately for you, I read it," Catherine said, her voice seething with anger. "Who's Ellie? Is she Betsy's mother? Did you have an affair or is this some scheme you and your parents cooked up? You actually took MY daughter to see THAT woman? Answer me, Hayward!"

Hayward wouldn't answer her; he quickly left the house, which is the way he normally handled conflict with Catherine. But he was caught and knew it. He wondered if he was secretly hoping she'd find Ellie's letter so it would all be out in the open, as he was usually careful about destroying all paper evidence of Ellie's existence.

He almost expected Catherine to allow her anger at him to turn into resentment toward Betsy for being Ellie's daughter. Unfortunately, he was correct in thinking this. Over the next decade Betsy had only her father to turn to for comfort when Catherine's rage was turned on her. It poisoned the atmosphere in their home to the extent that his brother noticed the tension and questioned Hayward about it. Hayward played dumb, unable to give a reason for the estrangement between him and his wife.

It took Catherine's stroke years later, which paralyzed her right side, leaving her face permanently distorted, to bring teenaged Betsy and her mother to an understanding. Betsy began to see her mother as an adult who was frustrated with life's offerings, rather than just an angry woman who seemed to disapprove of Betsy's every move.

It was a beginning, at least.

Chapter 20

In 1961 the entire family was visiting Grandma Lillian at Sparhawk Hall Hotel overlooking the ocean at Ogunquit, Maine. This turn-of-the-century resort had been the scene of Hall family dinners for almost three decades. Patricia and Penny usually celebrated their birthday here with a delicious dinner and cake in the large dining room because their grandparents vacationed there the month of July. Now there was only Grandma Lillian, as Fred died five years before. The party was for Penny and Patricia. They were born the same day, seven years apart; Patricia was 25, Penny, 18.

Hayward, Catherine, and Betsy were there, along with Carleton, Winnie, and their other grown children, Peggy and Peter. Things were different this year: Hayward was suffering from emphysema and had to use an atomizer to breathe. He no longer could dance; years of smoking, now age and illness, were creeping up on him. He was only fifty-five years old, yet this disease did not take Hayward totally by surprise; his father had died from lung cancer.

Since male dancing partners were often in short supply at Sparhawk the bellhops were required to work Friday and Saturday nights in the ballroom, being charming and dancing to a live band with the women guests who were alone. These bellhops were usually students who worked there summers (as the place was open only during the summer), living in cramped, hot dormitories while earning tuition money for college in the fall. One of these students was Kevin Hill, who was entering the University of New Hampshire on a full scholarship in September.

"Sir, do I know you from some place? You look familiar," Kevin asked Hayward when he returned Betsy to her seat after a slow dance. Little did he know he had just danced with his own sister. Hayward muttered a denial, yet realized he was looking at Kevin, the little boy he grew to love as a three-year old, now all grown up. He sucked in his breath, but not just because his lungs needed oxygen.

Hayward later looked over toward Kevin, who was staring at him. Hayward looked away. Unbeknownst to him, Kevin's parents and younger brother were also in Ogunquit staying at a smaller, less expensive hotel nearby, on a short visit to see their son halfway through the summer season before he left home for college.

Sunday morning was gorgeous, a perfect summer day, with the fog just burning off as Hayward took a walk along Marginal Way, picking wild blueberries, cautiously making his way on the narrow path. After the party the night before his brother Carleton and family drove back to their home in Hampton Beach, just an hour south. Hayward's illness made him too tired to drive in the evening so he, Catherine, and Betsy shared a room at Sparhawk Hall. This was his last visit to a place he loved very much. He knew he was dying.

"You always did like blueberries," a familiar voice said. It startled him. Ellie was also walking along Marginal Way and, in his concentration on picking the now-ripe berries, he had not seen her coming. *Oh my God! She's more beautiful than ever*, he's thinking.

"Hello, Ellie, it's good to see you; you're as lovely as ever. Yes, I must have my annual taste of these blueberries; maybe it's the sea air that makes them so good. We're here for a family birthday party, but we'll be leaving soon," Hayward replied, having to take a puff on his atomizer. "Why are you here?" he managed to ask.

There was a charge of almost-visible electricity between them, with much left unspoken, as they stood there looking at each other while she told Hayward about Kevin going off to college soon, about her second son, now eight-years old, and her husband who was very good to her. They lived in Rochester, New Hampshire and owned a successful country store, where they sold everything from big sour pickles in a barrel to yard goods for women to make dresses for themselves and their daughters. She and her husband worked long hours with the assistance of a clerk, who was now minding the store so Ellie's family could have this short time together.

"How's Betsy doing?" Ellie's question interrupted Hayward's thoughts of the past, of how it could have been different if he had the courage years before to rebel against family tradition, to forego the family money if he disgraced them by divorcing Catherine and having the affair and pregnancy out in the open. Ellie's happy life could have included him.

"Betsy's doing well; she's almost fifteen, as you know, and is a straight "A" student. She wants to study botany in college. She's a beauty, looks just like her mother." Hayward hesitated a moment to catch his breath, then softly said, "Thank you, Ellie. Thank you for my daughter; she's been the light of my life."

Hayward was getting tired and needed to conserve his energy for the drive home, as Catherine did not drive. Reluctantly, he said goodbye. Before Hayward turned away to go back to the hotel he looked at Ellie with much love in his eyes and gently touched her face while saying, "Please remember me; I'll remember you."

With tears in her eyes she put her hand on his and replied, "Forever, my love, forever."

Ellie turned away, hesitating, not wanting this moment to end, and slowly walked back the way she came. A few minutes along the path she encountered a young girl with dark, curly hair and a quick smile popping perfect, black-ripe blueberries into her mouth. They were nodding to one another when Ellie realized who she was: her daughter, the baby who hungrily nursed at her breast while looking into her mother's eyes as though she knew Ellie's pain, the baby who was taken from a sobbing Ellie and put into a foster home while waiting for the adoption papers to be ready for her real father to adopt her. The photos from Hayward had stopped years before, along with the letters, but she'd know this child of hers anywhere. Ellie held her breath for a moment before walking on by.

This was the last time she would see either Hayward or Betsy. Hayward passed away the following winter, having little energy, often gasping for breath, before being released from his pain.

Betsy didn't know she had just seen her mother for the third time. Letters found later in Ellie's home would comfort Betsy during her search for the truth. The truth was that her father and mother loved her. And they loved each other.

Chapter 21

"We don't see things as they are; we see things as we are."

Anais Nin

Penny — My brother, Peter and Edie:

"Get out of here; this isn't your house," Peter snarled as he shoved Edie off the steps. As she landed on the ground she felt a sharp pain in her ribcage and just sat there, stunned and gasping for air, having just enough breath needed to sob.

How did it come to this? she's asking herself as Peter goes inside to call the police.

My brother Peter married a Chilean woman after getting out of the Peace Corps; the marriage lasted long enough to produce a daughter, Lisa. When Maria left Peter and returned home to Santiago she reluctantly left her daughter with him, feeling he could take better care of her than she could. Peter and ten-year-old Lisa were living together in Concord, New Hampshire when Edie came into their lives.

The first time I saw Edie was when I visited Peter, unannounced, one November evening in 1979. I had never met or heard Edie's name mentioned, so she was a complete surprise to me, although I didn't keep close tabs on him. Edie, looking very much at home, was cooking something on top of the stove.

Okay, I'm thinking, *what do we have here*? I quickly found out "we" had a love triangle going as Edie was waiting with her son to be picked up by her husband on his way home from work, maybe three hours later. She and her almost-three-year-old son Christopher had ridden home with Peter after his Montessori School closed for the afternoon. Edie was an assistant there and Christopher was a student.

Edie, the older of two kids, was born in 1950 to George and Evanthea

Stanopoulus in Erie, Pennsylvania, a community where many Greek immigrants lived. Her parents and grandparents owned and operated restaurants, serving Greek food, of course.

Edie stood just short of five feet tall, full-figured yet slender, with long, straight black hair and brown eyes. She was sorta pretty, I thought. I would come to appreciate her intelligence and good character only much later; right now, in my judgment of her, all I saw was a married woman going after my baby brother. Later I began to understand how important timing is for relationships: sometimes we need to, in order to survive, get out of a marriage that doesn't serve us well. Maybe the term "forever" means until the end of the reason for being together.

After Edie divorced Andrew, moving in with Peter, eventually marrying him, she began to come into her own as a woman. It took me years to realize she is a healer, has a gift she's tried hard to conceal, and is able to help others with clearly seeing the principles of human behavior and relationships. Eventually, in leaving my brother she taught him how love really is: non-judgmental, patient, sometimes confrontational, ultimately focused on the positive aspect of each situation. Much later, they became very good friends, with no inclination toward romance, yet certainly great intimacy and honest communication.

"Dear, it's okay, she has a good heart; it will be fine," I heard Edie's mother say as I walked away from one of many confrontations in life, this time with Edie. I don't remember what it was about, but I can guarantee my being judgmental, rude, and obnoxious had something to do with it. Edie's calm patience, firm boundaries, and graciousness were clearly ruling the day, as they usually did. She rarely "lost it." And I rarely found it in those days, being stressed to the max by a destructive, yet ultimately, great learning experience, a marriage filled with incompatibility between David and me, along with a three-year-old son so wild that neither of us knew how to handle him. I have found that one can know intellectually that something is radically wrong yet not know how to change it.

"Penny, Edie and I have split up and will be getting a divorce. She found a boyfriend," Peter said one day in March of 1995 after fifteen years of marriage.

His version of the events that led up to their divorce differed greatly from what she observed and lived.

"I get so tired of people focusing on the so-called breaking of the marriage vows when one spouse finds a lover," Edie stated a few years later in Guanajuato, Mexico, where she and I had gone on a short trip the winter of 1998. She had spent the previous four days telling me her side of the divorce, as I was one of those in the family who partly believed my brother's version, not having much contact with Edie for a few years. I had called her, asking if she'd go with me to Mexico, hoping to reconcile our friendship. "It's so typical of a man to respond with 'she found a boyfriend' instead of how he broke the vows first. What about the vow to love, honor, and cherish?" she continued. "I never felt loved, honored, OR cherished during the entire marriage. It was 'my way or the highway' from him at all times, pretty much how your father treated your mother."

It was during this vacation that Edie showed me, by example, how to say "yes" to life, a trait I will always treasure. When strangers were friendly, offering to show us the way to some place or tell us who has the best woodworking shop or the best restaurant, Edie always said "yes" and thanked them and we would be open to going there. Before then I had been saying, no thanks, I don't want to bother you. Wow! A good way to shut out people, wouldn't you say? I think it boils down to developing our intuition and trusting it so we aren't tempted to follow some murderer into an alley.

Later, as I evolved, I realized that Edie is a woman who knows her power and uses it wisely. To those of us who have yet to find our own power — and when we do find it we often give it away to others — the confidence I saw in Edie that first day I met her may appear to be arrogance. I've found that, as I become more centered and aware of my surroundings, there are some who are threatened by my happiness and seem to delight in trying to knock me off my perch of power, to weaken me in order to strengthen themselves. Of course, they no longer succeed, as I pay no attention to them once I've ascertained what their game is. I suspect Edie has always been challenged by others trying to pull her down, jealousy being a nasty, yet human, trait.

"What attracted you to Peter in the first place?" I asked Edie on that

Mexican trip.

"Peter hooked me the day I watched Christopher fall asleep on his shoulders and he just went about his business of running the school with a tiny, curly-headed blonde toddler relaxing against him. It was comforting as I had never seen him have that kind of relationship with his own father. We were totally focused on the kid-family thing the first ten years of our marriage. When the kids grew up and Peter decided to sell the school and become a Rolfer, our individual needs began to surface. And they turned out to be so radically different as to be incompatible," Edie answered.

"Peter promised we'd leave New Hampshire and go to Nova Scotia after he finished Rolfing training. That's why we'd spent two summers and a lot of money building the house on our 135 acre farm near Bridgewater. I thought we had agreed to a plan of living there full-time but Peter changed his mind, saying he needs to be where he's known so he can build up his Rolfing practice. I understand that, even though I dislike living in New Hampshire, so agreed to the new plan. I asked can't we at least sell this old house with tiny rooms and dark corners and find a more spacious, light-filled space to live? He said no, this is good enough. I had spent two years paying all the bills so he could train to Rolf people. He's really good at it so I wanted to support it, even though it meant he was gone to Colorado for three months, home one month, then back to Colorado for another three months. This went on for two years. At the end of holding my part of the bargain he reneged on his promises," Edie said.

"You know, Edie," I said, "I'd have felt really betrayed, like what I want doesn't matter. David's the same; I can hardly wait to leave him in a couple years. I feel so powerless when he's around." I continued, "But I guess I need to find my own power, regardless of being with David or alone."

"Yes, we all need to do that. Now I can follow my own flow, have my own studio space and bathroom," Edie continued. "I think that all we need to do is respect our different ways and not try to become the other person. But, Peter's lack of respect for me is what did us in."

"Edie, I've heard Peter's version of what happened that night the cops came; I want to hear yours," I said.

"I'm sure mine is different from his," she replied with a laugh. "I can laugh about it now but at the time it was pretty upsetting. Peter was finally certified, finished with training, and he called to say he'd be home in a few days. It was then that I realized I didn't want him home, I wanted out. When he came home all we did was argue for months. Finally, I moved into the apartment I'd been making for a tenant at the river house; I knew I could quickly get another space in the house ready to rent as I wanted my own income besides the real estate commissions I was earning selling houses. I had met Mark, a true craftsman, who was building the apartment and could finish the second one. In fact, Mark and I were attracted to one another and later became lovers, eventually roommates after awhile."

"I didn't know about Mark; is he the guy Peter told me was your boyfriend?" I asked.

"He wasn't my boyfriend when I moved out; I didn't move to be with another man, I moved out to be with myself. I thought I could just walk away with my best parts, leaving the old stuff behind. I found out we leave the old stuff once we've learned what we need to know from these 'challenges' and not until then."

"Peter and I were going back and forth, sleeping together, trying to work it out living separately until one night he tells me no more sex, he's now with Sharon, whoever Sharon was, just like that! Bet Peter didn't mention that part to you, did he?" Edie remarked.

"No, there's a lot he hasn't said, but I can see he also twists things. What happened next?" I asked.

"Peter was with Sharon; I began the affair with Mark, then realized there's no going back for Peter and me so came to the house to get the rest of my things. Emotions escalated when he wouldn't let me in and I pushed past him, which pissed him off so he grabbed me and pulled me out of the house — all the time I'm yelling, why doesn't he get out, it's my house, too. This happened three times. Finally, he managed to toss me into the mud, holding me down on my back in the rain with his knee in my stomach, before getting up and running to lock the door. I had no purse, no shoes, as I always take my shoes off when I go into a house. I was in pain, although the ribs weren't broken, just bruised," Edie sighed, shaking her head.

"That's good; what happened next?" I'm eagerly asking.

"Next, after catching my breath, I got a shovel from the porch and broke the glass in the old door, unlocking it and going inside. I sat down on a stool in the kitchen, listening to Peter on the phone with the police: 'Yes, I did. No, she didn't' and after he hangs up I ask if they're going to arrest me and he says no, they plan to arrest him!"

"No way. Why?" I asked, more than a bit surprised.

"Because it's my house, too, and I have a right to be there, and he assaulted me. And that I have the right to break a window in my own house if I choose to do so, believe it or not," she continued. "When the cops came I asked them not to arrest him, but they said it was out of my hands. Peter got a Restraining Order, which said I couldn't even talk to him or use our bank account for thirty days, which isn't good because I pay all the bills, including the mortgage. I called a lawyer friend and he said I need Peter to get the R. O. lifted because, yes, it does mean I cannot pay the bills. So, he did. He can't write checks, you know," Edie explained.

"What? Why not?" I asked.

"He must have gotten his aversion to money management from your Dad; he can't handle checkbooks at all," Edie said. We both laughed.

"You know, Peter never told me this; his version was a bit self-serving," I said.

"Yes, I've heard his version," Edie replied.

"How did you go from assault charges and broken glass to being best friends today?" I asked.

"Six weeks later he came to my office and said he was told by a lawyer and other smart friends: 'Oh Boy! She's got you now; she'll get everything you own because of the assault.' So, he said to me he was forced to assess who I really am, and he came to the conclusion that I am not seeking vengeance, just a fair deal. We dearly love each other, and now are really close and can talk in a way we never could when married. We just cannot live together,"Edie said, with a hint of sadness in her voice.

It's funny how we can love each other, yet learn to hate each other later. We're the same two people. Or are we really the same? Shouldn't it be possible to once again learn to love one another? I surely hope so. Maybe it has to do with judging others. Being non-judgmental means accepting a person "where he is at the moment," not shutting him out because he isn't perfect or as "evolved" as we are. We truly are all ONE; this I know deep inside. Of course, many make horrible choices, often evil ones, but we cannot judge others, only discern who they are without being invested in the outcome.

After all, when we judge others we could be wrong.

Chapter 22

"Remember that sometimes not getting what you want is a wonderful stroke of luck."

The Dalai Lama

Penny, Without Rob:

Finding that I was over-qualified for many jobs and under-qualified for those I knew I could do, I decided to finish my college education. I had spent one year at Phoenix College almost right out of high school, following my instincts of studying mostly languages and literature. The fact that I had few credits in any other area is what enabled me, many years later, to take the CLEP exam for $25 and earn twenty-two credits toward graduating from the University of New Hampshire.

"I drove my car to the desert, expecting to see wildlife that I could photograph," I wrote during a Creative Writing course that first year. "I have some beautiful images of coyotes, roadrunners, and other wild life I've experienced in my many years of taking pictures, which I manipulate and superimpose onto modern city images, creating opposites in one piece of art. The affect is stunning, and others must agree as my work sells very well in the nearby city of Phoenix. Maybe the stress of concrete-living makes the urban dweller crave the relief of living a more natural life.

'I don't care if you don't have the money; you owe me $10,000 and we aren't leaving here until I get it,' I heard an angry male's voice yelling, which was very frightening. I guess I was so intent on making everything perfect for my shot that I never heard a car or people hiking until this argument began.

I quietly hid in the relative safety of a nearby rock crevasse.

'Mike, please be reasonable; you know those guys stole the last shipment and ran off to no-one-knows-where,' the second male voice said, pleading for leniency. 'I'm asking for more time,' he continued.

I heard a brief scuffle, like two men fighting, then a thud and a man's voice filled with pain as he was either dying or losing consciousness.

I was terrified. What will happen to me if I'm spotted? The only sound I heard during what seemed like an hour but was probably only minutes was the very loud beating of my heart. I was sure they could hear it and would catch me hiding.

Did they see my car in the parking area? How can I safely get away from here?

'Cut!' I heard a male voice yell. 'That's a wrap. Good job, guys.'"

After Rob and I split up I entered into one of the most exciting growth periods of my life. This writing course was one of my favorites, as I was re-discovering the fun I had as a child writing poems and short stories. I discovered many parts of me that I had denied during my marriage to Rob. I now could paint my bedroom walls any color I wanted, rather than having an all-white house as Rob had insisted. Penny was discovering Penny. And liking much of what she saw, determined to change what she didn't like.

What I wanted to change was my anger toward men and life in general. Where did all this crap come from?

I don't believe in living in the past; I don't even trust modern psychology to go to the heart of the matter. It tends to encourage intellectual change, which isn't really change. One has only to look at the many therapy sessions it takes, remembering past transgressions by our parents, to know there is a better, more powerful road to growth and change.

I paid for four $90/hour sessions with a psychologist named Michael Banks before being finished with using traditional psychology as a way for me to grow. He sat there, telling me all his marital problems for one hour — a session I was paying for while making $75 each week as an office clerk. Finally, I said to myself, *enough is enough, Penny*. I left and never returned. I knew there was a better way; I just hadn't discovered it yet.

What I did get from these sessions was how passive I was, how I had to stand up for myself and get what I need. Gotta learn who I am first, I guess, before knowing what I need. I should have refused to pay him for wasting my time and money being HIS therapist. Yet, the lessons were powerful; in the long run it was worth the time and money spent. It's like watching my older sister Patricia, a lost soul if ever I saw one. I knew, even as a child, *this is how NOT to be, Penny.*

Rob and I separated in January 1974; by May we had sold the house and Heather and I had moved in with Jill and her five-year-old daughter, Michaela. Jill was renting a rambling, old house in Durham, New Hampshire and needed a roommate to share expenses. Heather, age ten, shared a bedroom with Michaela, but the age difference wasn't a problem, as they got along fine. Jill and I ate the same way — natural, organic foods when possible, and lots of salads and fresh veggies — so we decided I would cook and clean up Monday, Wednesday, and Friday nights, while Jill got Tuesday, Thursday, and Saturday duty. Sunday was a free-for-all kind of day, cooking only when a child needed to eat.

It worked like a charm. Jill and I cooperated in keeping the house clean, as did the girls. Rob came to pick up Heather a few times in the two years we lived there. One such visit, right after the divorce was final, on the exact same date as our wedding seven years before, I took Heather's suitcase to the truck and saw his girlfriend, a very pregnant Sandy, in the front seat, glaring at me. I chuckled, knowing that I am finally seeing how angry I've been for most of my thirty-one years on this Earth, and she's really young to be this bitchy. Poor Rob, he didn't learn his lessons and now has another angry woman, or nineteen-year-old girl, in her case. Good luck, Rob; I bet she gives you a good run for the money.

The first course I took as a full-time college student at the University of New Hampshire was an eight-week session in summer school, beginning June 1974. Just to get my feet wet. I can't remember the exact title of the course, but it was "Group Dynamics" or something like that. The premise was to see how peer pressure changes individual behavior. The first exercise was to go outside on the lawn near a sidewalk where others will be walking by and go up to a perfect stranger and ask if I can hug and kiss that person. Without thinking, I jumped up from our little circle of nineteen or twenty and asked a good-looking man, maybe twenty-five years old, the question assigned to us. He shrugged "okay." I did as I was told.

The group's cheering me on, but surprisingly, I am the ONLY one who will do this! I credit my having "hippie power" and maturity, as the other students were probably younger than twenty years old.

That was easy. So was the second experiment a couple weeks later: Each one of us had to envision being in our house as it's burning down and rescuing the one thing we can't live without. I was surprised to hear some declare they can't live without their favorite painting or family photos, as I wasn't thinking any material thing is more important than my own life.

"Damn, I'd save my life! I can't imagine anything else being as important," I wisely offered. I was the only one there thinking like a hippie.

There might have been other basic experiments, ones I don't remember, but the final one was a big one for me.

"Okay, students," Professor Wilson began, as he clapped his hands to get our attention. "Let's divide into two groups — ten people over here, the rest need to gather there," he said, pointing to the other side of the room.

The idea was this: one group had ten minutes to make a list of questions to ask the members of the other group. I was in the group being questioned. It started out fine, the inquiries and answers rather innocuous. I raised my hand to answer some, but was ignored while others in my group got to answer. Everyone got to give answers, except me. About fifteen minutes into this experiment I'm starting to get pissed off. Issues such as being an intelligent person who was never listened to now or in my childhood, surfaced. Issues due to my lack of power, leading to extreme anger, surfaced. I stood up and told the group I don't know what's going on, but you guys are really pissing me off. The professor took over, saying this was an experiment to show group dynamics issues when one person is being ignored. And lucky me, I am chosen by the questioners because they saw me as the one who could best handle being ignored. Of course, I could "handle it;" after all, I'd been married! Right in front of the entire group I told the teacher that I feel this little experiment of his is cruel. He can see I am almost in tears by now. He apologized, saying he is not going to do this experiment again.

I got an "A" in the course. But, more importantly, I was willing to look at my reactions to this experience. And make changes. It wasn't long after this course that I realized I now wanted to look at my hatred toward men, and eventually was able to forgive the guy who raped me at age fifteen. Forgiveness was in order in many areas of my life — beginning with men.

I owe a lot to my brother Peter for showing me the way of meditation, a practice I started soon after this psychology course ended. I could plainly see that psychology didn't have the answers — hell, they didn't even know many of the questions!

Once I began the process of calming my mind through meditation the debris gathered during my childhood started to fall away. I was now on the path to finding my strength, my inner power, which is the only power we truly have.

"We can't give you these right now; you don't have the right paper work," the bank teller said the first time I tried to get food stamps issued by the government. Her voice was filled with resentment, as if she had to give me the $80 out of her own pocket. I had accepted help from welfare the last nine months of school because I was working thirty hours every week, raising Heather, and taking a full load year-round so I could graduate in less than three years. I was studying a lot rather than partying.

Because of practicing meditation I knew I no longer needed to react to the anger of others, but this was the "light bulb moment" when I realized I really CAN stand here, calmly not reacting, waiting until she gets over her frustration. Without my saying a word, just energetically sending her patience filled with love, she found the paper which was there all along.

Then she apologized to me for being impatient! This non-reaction of mine was beginning to become a habit — even if I'd had to "fake it 'til I make it" for a few weeks previous to this experience. This is the day I proved to myself that non-reaction works. Being neutral, with no anger or judgment, does work in dealing with others. And it only gets stronger inside me as the teachers and lessons come with even more subtle ways of tempting me to react, which would give them power. After all, if I react they get energy from me, don't they? And energy is power.

Great lessons were coming to me. So was great music. I got my priorities straight: one morning, after Heather went to school, I left the dishes in the sink in order to line up, along with half the student body, to buy my $7 ticket for the "Rolling Thunder Revue." I chuckled as I watched many of the students lighting up joints and smoking right in front of dozens of police.

Yes, Joan Baez, Bob Dylan, and Emmy Lou Harris graced us with their presence for the most memorable concert of my life. Dylan came out in total white-face, made up almost like a clown. Joanie and Emmy Lou sang like musical angels. It was worth it to blow one-third of my week's grocery money to see and hear them perform for us. Money well-spent.

The last year I studied at UNH I got an opportunity to go to England for three weeks during the January 1976 break between semesters. My parents paid my air fare and my friend Cathy took Heather to her house as her three daughters were good friends with mine. In exchange for my gorgeous, antique, oak chest of drawers with claw feet Cathy fed and cared for Heather just like her own. I figured it was a good deal for both of us.

In England we went to classes to learn how the Social Workers deal with aging issues there. When I got my degree in Social Work my specialty was going to be Gerontology, the study of old people. We visited four nursing homes, all in the same neighborhoods the elderly clients came from. The atmosphere in each of these facilities was more like home, much less institutionalized than in the USA.

I looked up Simon by calling his parents, who contacted him; I was surprised when he called my hotel. He had to meet me secretly so his wife wouldn't find out. We met in the hotel bar and hugged one another. "How are you, Penny? I've missed you," Simon said, with emotion in his voice.

"It's good to see you, Simon. Let me show you the latest photos of Heather," I said matter-of-factly, having met with him only out of curiosity. After all, he is the biological father of my only child. Even though he wanted to go to my room I wasn't interested in being the "other woman." It was obvious his marriage was in trouble but I had no need to get involved. We said goodbye on a friendly, yet cool-on-my-part, note.

It would be twenty-five years before we'd see each other again.

❦

In December 1976 I earned my B. A. in Social Work — with a GPA of 3.78, no less — after going to school full-time, year-round, summers and all, while working hard to support Heather and me. Rob was paying $100/month child support which enabled us to eat. We were living quite frugally, eating lots of pasta. I couldn't get my degree in Business Administration as previously planned because I tried Accounting 101 twice and the details of the subject drove me right up the wall. One of my most difficult classes was Economics, where the professor gave us what looked to me like many bowls of spaghetti with puzzles we had to solve. Graphs were not my strongest suit. Lordy, that man was good-looking, but such a taskmaster who made the subject far more complicated than it had to be.

"You used to be married to Rob Warner, didn't you?" a young woman asked me one day after class got out. I think her name was Donna, but I recognized her only by sight; it was a fairly large class.

"Yes, I am Penny Warner," I answered. Then she proceeded to tell me far more than I ever wanted to know about Rob and his new wife.

"I used to live in a house with Sandy and two other girls; I was the only one who wasn't having an abortion that spring. She had met Rob while hitchhiking months before and he told her he was married and not getting divorced. She came home that night and told us she had met the man she was going to marry and she figured she could get him away from his wife. When Sandy told Rob she was pregnant he said it couldn't be his and she needed to get an abortion," she continued.

"Was it Rob's?" I asked.

"I don't think so; it was pretty much a party house and I was appalled at the lack of morals and left at the end of the semester, but she swore it was his baby, which I really doubted, she was such a liar," Donna replied. "He was just the weekend boyfriend — she had many others — even when she got pregnant the second time. She did, however, go for the abortion during the first pregnancy, couldn't do it and got off the table, leaving the clinic. When she told Rob she wanted to keep it he told her he would leave, that he had no intention of marrying her, he was already married," she continued.

"That's news to me," I said, "as I had already filed for divorce and he knew it. He had told the counselor he wanted the divorce and there was no chance of reconciliation, which didn't surprise me; I was planning the divorce the minute he left."

And I'm thinking back to the night before he left, knowing he was leaving because we had discussed it. I was worried that I might be pregnant, asking him what he would do if I were? And he replied that he would leave. When I asked, "What if it's yours?" knowing I'd had no other lovers for almost a year, he said he'd leave anyway. I told him to leave the next morning. I was done with him. I knew for sure that if he had told me to get an abortion I'd have told him to fuck off, I'll see you in court, buddy.

Sandy did have the abortion, but quickly got pregnant again and he married her when our divorce was final. It's obvious she had a plan to hook him right from the first meeting, no matter what it took.

Who says we don't have "someone" watching out for us at all times? Obviously, he was meant to have babies with her and not me. And, for the first time since marrying him, I felt very lucky that I had not given birth to a child of Rob's, as I couldn't have counted on him to stick around. He had adopted my daughter, saying he felt like she was his own child, yet was never the "hands-on" Dad I hoped he'd be.

"Hello, I am here to pick up Heather," I announced as Rob answered the door one day months after his re-marriage. He had sporadically kept in touch, but I wasn't keen on her going to their place because she always returned home sick from allergies and it took all week for her to recover from the visit. Rob said he'd get Heather and her suitcase so I waited at the door; seconds later Sandy appeared and said, "Heather really loves ice cream and macaroni and cheese. You should see how she gobbles them down," she said, using an evil tone filled with glee.

I looked at her, trying not to strangle her; after all, she was pregnant and fat and such a young, short girl I wouldn't have felt right punching out her lights, so I calmly said, "Heather's allergic to all dairy products and gets really sick from eating them."

"Oh, I didn't know that," she retorted. *Yeah, right, bitch.*

His new wife was sneakily cruel to Heather; one can only guess what she did when I wasn't there or Rob wasn't paying attention, which was most of the time. I was glad that she seldom went to their house after the baby was born. Rob did pay child support on a regular basis, however.

In his weakness he allowed the wife, who was jealous and threatened by our existence, to drive a wedge between him and our daughter, causing Heather many emotional problems. I believe it was partly his lack of love and attention that put her in a vulnerable position to be sexually abused, a tragedy I knew nothing about until many years later. Poor child, my heart goes out to her, and I totally understand what she went through during that time.

Our deviousness will always catch up with us. Be careful what you want, as you just might get it.

Rob had jumped right from the frying pan into the fire, something I would do a few years later.

Chapter 23

"If you don't go when you wanna go, when you do go you may find that you have gone."

Penny, with David:

I "jumped" after seven years of being single (or on my way to being single, as the divorce took close to a year). The guy I chose was David Michaels, an engineer with a heart of stone. Of course, he didn't show that when he courted me, vigorously going after what he wanted. What he wanted was a wife so he could look good to others; any wife, I guess, as long as she was good in bed, could cook and clean well. What he turned out to be was a bully, a control freak, a man filled with fear and negative energy. He had a huge poverty of spirit, which I finally recognized many years later, and that idea of poverty showed itself in a number of things, mainly money matters. He could have a million dollars in the bank and still feel poor.

How perfect that I chose to find myself in him, through him. I discovered the bully within me, the fearful, unhappy woman, who had what could be called a nervous breakdown just a few years after marrying him. Talk about jumping right into the fire. My ego issues — and there were many like abandonment, need to control others, verbal abusiveness, and fear of doing damage to another child, even though I wanted to "do it right" — soon came to the forefront. Yet, by clearly looking at them, I could see they were going away by being brought to the light. I changed by facing the truth about myself. Eventually, after many years of being married, I got strong enough to say to these ego issues, "Hey, ego, it's time to take a back seat." Only then was I able to find my *Higher Self*, a *Self* I had been running toward and away from my whole life.

"Peter," I said, between sobs. "Mom really hates me; I got a letter from her and she doesn't like me, probably never has."

"Well, you have been feeling this for years," he replied, "and at least now you know your intuition was telling you right all along. What you need to understand is that you chose these parents before coming here," he continued.

"Oh shit, that's a scary thought," I said.

"Penny, you chose all the lessons, maybe not all the circumstances of how they happened, but you did choose to learn certain Truths about your soul so you could evolve during this lifetime. You don't want to go back and do it all over, do you?" he asked.

"No, of course not, why would I?" I almost shouted over the phone to my baby brother, who was always the leader for me in spiritual issues.

"Then do it right this time. Understand that you won't grow until you forgive Dad and Mom for being bad parents. Tell me, do you think they made these mistakes out of being evil or did they just do the best they could, even if it wasn't looking good to you at the time?" Peter continued.

"No, they're not evil," I quietly replied, realizing maybe it was time to take responsibility for my own life, rather than saying my parents were the "problem."

In spite of David's contention that we were "always broke" I managed to eke out the money for vacations. I'd pack up my car with a tent, sleeping bags, and lots of food in the cooler, taking Benjamin to state parks. Sometimes we'd go back east to visit family for a few weeks, often without David. Just about the only peaceful time I had was without David. I was nervous most of the time; I felt as though the warrior got his deer, shot her right in the head, and there he was, lying on the couch, basking in the feeling that he had "bagged the quarry." I was the quarry.

In 1992 we expanded our horizons and bought a house in Nova Scotia, one right next to the ocean, built in 1820 by a sea captain. Capt. Wenzell's heirs were upset at having to sell but they needed the money; our buying it meant we were the first people outside of the family to own it. We were the first foreign owners since it was built. We respected that fact. And we really appreciated having it.

The house began as one of those tall, center-spire houses, similar to the Cape Cod style. These are common in Nova Scotia and look as though the French built them but the province was founded by the Scottish, the conservative ones who chose to leave Massachusetts and take land given to them by the King of England. They settled Nova Scotia, loyal to the Crown, while we Rebels stayed in Massachusetts and fought the American Revolutionary War, winning independence before becoming the United States of America. Houses like Captain Wenzell's had a local name, "The Lunenburg Bump," because of the separate entryway in the center-front of each house, which distinguished it from a regular Cape.

Anyway, two brothers inherited the house in 1900, along with fourteen acres. Only problem is they hated each other. So, one says to the other, how about we cut the house in half (not literally) and add "wings" (my term, as this is how it looks) and you live in one half, out of my sight, while I leave you alone and live on the other side?

So, they did. And so we bought it, ninety-two years later, as a place to retire because David wanted to build a wooden boat which he could keep at our dock on the Lower Le Have River, right across from the inlet where the Atlantic Ocean comes in.

Wow! Talk about windy! I've never been to a place with such a force of wind, so much that one needs to put solid wall fencing all around the gardens to keep plants from drying out. They also had to be high and strong enough to keep the bears and deer from eating everything.

The hill behind the house was a joy to climb, as the views were to "die for." The faraway islands seemed to be poking up out of the ocean and the architecture of the nearby houses really old and historical. We could see everyone else's gardens, with vegetables and wildflowers, while watching the activity on the river. There were wild blueberries at the top of the hill, which we picked when we were there in July.

The property was a problem for us right from the beginning, a money drain, like a pit you just keep throwing dollar bills into. The rents from both apartments were supposed to be paying for the house and its upkeep. Soon after we bought it, the insurance game changed, now charging double the rates for foreigners, just because they could. And the government got their hands into our pockets with every move we made. A few years after buying it a neighbor turned us into the health department, saying our sewer was going into the river. Yes, it was, but so was everyone else's along the river. We, being the foreigners, had to come up with an expensive pumping sewage system, while no one else had to make changes, probably because they were homeowners and not landlords charging rent for two apartments.

I came to believe the place had a curse on it, just like my marriage with David. By 2001, when we separated, David and I were supporting the place, continually making repairs needed just to keep tenants in it. (I didn't know until later that if it had been a single family house, left un-rented, just for our occasional use, the investment would have been a far better one; we might even have made money selling it.)

Ironically, after the divorce, when I bought out my share of the property from David, the problems disappeared. I sold it anyway, as it wasn't part of my retirement plan.

If a person focuses on the lack of something, that "lack" keeps growing bigger. David never understood that to focus on abundance would make abundance come into our lives.

I was barely holding my own, feeling totally powerless in this marriage. Penny was disappearing right before her very eyes. But, maybe I had to deeply feel the pain of no personal power in order to ask, how the hell did I get myself in this pickle?

The next question was just as important: How do I get OUT of this pickle? How I got out of this "pickle" was to read every self-help book that spoke to me, go to every seminar I could afford to go to (which weren't many), and be committed to making the best of my time while fulfilling my duties as a wife and mother the best I could, without continuing to compromise to the point of self-annihilation.

The first books I found were *Anatomy of the Spirit* by Caroline Myss and Gary Zukav's *Seat of the Soul*. They both spoke to me so deeply I had no choice but to change. Of course, I also had the necessary tools: commitment to growing spiritually and time to breathe.

This was a period when I no longer cared that we had no money and refused to work outside the home for more than twenty hours each week, mainly because I got no help or cooperation at home from either male, Benjamin taking his cues on how to treat me by watching his father. By now, he was a freshman in high school, the first time he'd ever attended public school. (I home-schooled him until age ten when we found a Montessori School he attended until age fifteen.) The changes in my kind, gentle son were shocking to me; he began to speak to me with disrespect for the first time in his life. Of course, he was a teenager by now. I figured out why teenagers can be difficult: so that we can let them go with relief, rather than sadness. No empty nest syndrome for me, ever.

Metaphysical books kept popping out at me, literally falling off the shelves of the bookstores, where I would go to read (sometime for hours at a time) without buying them. The bookstore people knew I'd buy from them when I had the money to spare. Lots of people were using the comfy couches and oversized chairs to spend the day reading; we even sometimes fell asleep in them.

One of the books asked a hard question: How does your energy affect others? Does it empower them or dis-empower them? After giving my answer to this question I began to look seriously at my own power — how do I get it, what should I do with it once I have it? I began to realize that David and I were blatantly incompatible because he operates differently from me — his whole thing was getting power by taking it from others, especially those of us whom he thought of as weak. Being a water sign, a *Cancer* (Moon Child), my whole thing was to find my own power within, knowing this is the only place true power resides, and quit giving it away to others. Of course, this is a process, one not usually "finished" overnight; one with many levels of awareness and strength.

I now became very aware of the HUGE responsibility of using my power wisely.

I then realized forgiveness is also a big one. We talk about forgiving others, but what about forgiving ourselves? Who are we to judge ourselves? Hell, the world around us is so quick to judge us, why shouldn't we be kind to ourselves? Maybe then we can have the habit of kindness so strong inside that we are able to be kind to others — without even having to think about it. I read that the Dalai Lama said: "Be kind whenever possible. Kindness is always possible."

I was a work-in-progress, desperately needing to learn all these lessons that kept popping up, sometimes hitting me in the head.

It was during this time that David began traveling a lot for his job. This was a good thing. I loved being alone! He seldom called home, even when gone for three or four days, and I was thrilled to be away from him. We had long-ceased to have sex together — although there was probably a lot of solo sex going on, just to relieve the tension of living with each other. I was renovating our house; one of the rooms I was fixing was my own bedroom.

I had begun my first major renovation job with the oldest house I'd ever lived in, the sixteen-room New England Saltbox built in 1722. Rob and I had worked on it together in Newmarket thirty years before. Now, it was rather appropriate that I do the last renovation as a married woman, living with another husband.

This house was a Cape Cod style with expanded upstairs, yet only five years old, one of the newest houses I'd ever lived in. What a job! The previous owners' five dogs had the run of the house, peeing and pooping wherever the mood struck, which was often and all over the place. This was the most difficult project of my entire, substantial career as a renovator of houses. The heating/air conditioning guy came to clean the furnace and AC units, and ended up steam-cleaning the entire galvanized-metal duct-work , filling garbage bags with debris from these ducts, including, guess what? Dog poop, of course. Lots of it. Worst job I ever did, tearing up and throwing out the pads underneath, urine-soaked carpets and all, then scrubbing, spraying the particle board sub-floors with pet-neutralizing solution before painting them with Kilz's "Cover Stain." Then, and only then, were we ready for new carpet to be installed.

I chuckled at the thought that the last house I'd ever be renovating as a woman married to David Michaels was one that needed such a difficult, major cleanup before I could move on. Kind of a metaphor for one's life.

It's not that every moment with David was horrid — we did have a beautiful, healthy baby boy together about three years after our simple wedding at a friend's house. I can laugh now but at the time I was horrified that his idea of a honeymoon was to go to a matinee and see some stupid animated film. This was the second time I had gotten married but had yet to receive an engagement ring, both husbands being "too poor" to afford one. I realized many years later that the Goddess would never allow herself to get involved with a man who doesn't cherish her and their relationship, and a beautiful ring, yet not necessarily expensive, is a good way to show that commitment.

There were some wonderful times. I choose to remember them, rather than the feeling of suffocating, that I was going to die at any moment. Actually, looking back I can see that what was "dying" was the ego garbage, something that had to leave before I could get to the good stuff.

I planned to leave David from the time our little boy was around six years old. It's not that I had a plan; I just knew that if things didn't get better by the time Ben turned eighteen, I was out of there. I kept waiting for things to change until I realized those "things" were my husband; he wasn't going to change and I couldn't change him. I could only change myself. This "light bulb moment" began the process of my life being perfect, as I now, finally, was beginning to be thankful for what I have and stopped worrying about what I don't have. Yet, for a long time I did hate him; he was a worthy adversary.

The break-up with David came after twenty-one years — there's that seven-year cycle thing again, something I was beginning to write down, doing timelines, as I searched my life for meaning, for a pattern. I became acutely aware that it all has a rhythm, something I find comforting and predictable. And very true in my lifetime, for sure. I began to see the ebb and flow of events, coming to an awareness of what I was to learn, then getting a respite before the next seven-year cycle began.

I did leave David once Ben turned eighteen. But I wanted to leave with kindness, with an appreciation for what he had given me, even if it had been adversity that taught me my lessons. My husbands and children turned out to be my best teachers; and for that I am thankful.

Did my husband deserve this kindness? Probably not, as he was a subtly-cruel man. But let's face it, whatever we wish for others we are also wishing for ourselves. In the long run I came to love David for giving me my son, and for being the person who pushed me so hard I was forced to look at myself, asking why was I attracted to him in the first place? What soul-level thing was going on? We were so incompatible that I am certain he wasn't getting what he needed from me, especially once I began to fight back.

Those of us who are interested in having deep relationships — and not everyone is — want to be accepted and loved by a partner, someone who "gets" us. I got David okay; I just felt I was sleeping with the enemy and no longer wanted what I got. Yet, would I be who I am today if he had not been in my life? Probably not.

David went on to marry a woman who was the boss in their marriage, which amused me because he had been so bossy, and now had reversed roles. Maybe he is happy for once. He still tried to dis-empower me after the divorce. Of course, that just proves the saying, "People treat us the way we train them to treat us."

I half-jokingly tell people I have a PhD from Power Play University, as the experience of living with David taught me to clearly see ALL power plays coming my way, including those in the political world, relationship world, all around me. As I got stronger I found more of my own power with each encounter with him; even when he cheated me out of money I handled it well. It's a matter of taking responsibility for who I am and how I operate.

I chose to see myself as a *Victim* until I realized that happiness is also a choice. I now choose to be happy. It truly is a CHOICE.

Chapter 24

"There are no great deeds — just small ones done with great love."

Mother Theresa

Penny, the reunion:

It dawned on me as I got older that I'd be losing my parents soon. I decided to become a tourist and stay at a campground when I made my yearly visit to New Hampshire, rather than at the homes of relatives. I brought a tent and set it up in a campground in Northwood. Now that I had my own "kitchen," which consisted of a propane camp stove and ice chest, I wanted to have a family reunion.

I love reunions! What is it about getting together with those in our present time who have been with us in the past? Comfort, continuity? A sense of belonging? Hopefully, some of my favorite older relatives, like my mother and her younger sister, my Aunt Bea, would be there.

The day of the reunion was cool and hazy, threatening rain all day, something New Hampshire does well. The covered party areas of the campground were all reserved so it had to be an outside party, rain or not.

After preparing some foods — like my famous potato salad and Boston Baked beans — at my brother's house I bought organic salad fixins' at Shaw's Supermarket, along with gallons of spring water. I didn't forget the watermelon; it's a staple at all summer gatherings. Forget about buying it for the kids — I'm the one who spits the seeds as far as I can, just to watch them fly.

Aunt Bea and her daughter Pearl brought their famous foods, also: green gelatin and marshmallow dessert and three-bean salad. If my Aunt Thelma's mother, Grammy Bessie, were alive she'd be bringing her soft molasses cookies, definitely an item that brings smiles to all of us lucky enough to have eaten our share of her goodies.

Memories of my mother's family farm in Aroostook County, Maine came flooding back: Grammy's salt and pepper shaker collection that inspired me to start my own when she died, leaving maybe 100 pairs for her "children." Since I was only a grandchild I didn't get any so I started buying my own. I also remember Grampy eating a huge raw onion with every meal, which seemed strange to me until I was much older and realized that the smell covered whiskey on his breath.

I saw the reality of my mother's harsh upbringing on a potato farm when reading her stories about winters where they had no money and little to eat except for what they had in the freezer: venison, chickens, and moose and bear meats. They also had canned produce from the garden: corn, green beans, tomatoes, and pickles. The cows gave fresh milk and cream, from which they made butter, the best I have ever tasted. They sometimes had wheat berries they hadn't sold for cash and could make their own bread. Maybe it all sounds good unless one is forced to live this life of poverty. The potatoes, of course, were king and had their own "castle" called a potato house, a building often bigger than the farmhouse. Mom was frail as a child and not allowed to work much in the fields; she became the "inside daughter" while her sister Beatrice was the outside farm hand, helping their father.

Grammy, my mother's mother, was cruel to her daughter by verbally abusing her; her father did the discipline with wooden paddles, and my mother's frail health probably didn't save her from at least an occasional whipping. Was Grammy's cruelty toward her daughter ever justified? No, of course not, but one can see where it might come from by looking at the harsh way they lived. Her son, my Uncle Earl, told us after we became adults that Grammy was fun until she "got religion."

Imagine my sadness when, after Mom's death, I read a memoir of her childhood: "The hardest thing for me growing up was when my mother said to the photographer taking my high school graduation pictures, 'Do what you can; there's not much to work with!' I've never gotten over that," Mom wrote. In the same journal I read this about her father: "It was said that our father was an alcoholic. My reaction was an internal kicking and screaming fury — but in all honesty I understand why they thought it was so. If others had only known all the internal injuries and consequential diseases he had, they would have forgiven his solace in the bottle," my mother wrote, defending her beloved father.

Yet another case of why none of us has a right to judge others: after all, we could be wrong.

I'm sorry you had a hard life, Mom. I always thought you were beautiful and smart, a good Mom.

At five in the afternoon of our reunion at the campground I asked the Universe to PLEASE hold off the rain until the party was over. Do it for Mom.

We had a delicious, almost-magical supper. There were fewer than ten of us because Mom got tired in large crowds. By 8 p.m. it was dark and Mom was ready to leave. Mosquitoes were trying to crash the party, which didn't help the atmosphere. It was time to go so we said our goodbyes. Mom said to me, "This was the best night of my life; thank you, Penny."

Oh, Mom, you are welcome. You always were so easy to please.

Five minutes after everyone left the rains came. Who says no one is listening?

My mother passed away the following summer but I got to see her twice before she died.

Chapter 25

"Learning to manage your personal power means that you have to become aware of how you work your energy and whom you give it to."

Invisible Acts of Power by Caroline Myss

Penny:

My sister Peggy and I had a nice visit with my parents when we flew to Phoenix in February, seven months after the reunion at the campground. When we said goodbye Mom hugged me longer and tighter than ever before. We had tears in our eyes because we both knew this was our last hug.

I knew Mom was failing during the following summer. I was planning to visit her, so it wasn't a complete shock to get the call from Peter saying that Mom was in the hospital, dying. I kept my vehicles in top shape; it took me little more than an hour to pack my van and take off for the two-day trip from Kentucky to New Hampshire, arriving Sunday evening at the hospital.

My mother hated my father, even on her deathbed. As I stood by her side, holding her frail hand and gently stroking her dry forehead, she relaxed and found the strength to answer "yup" to my question: "It's hard for you to have so many people around you, isn't it, Mom?" When my father walked into the room and spoke, her entire energy field filled with hatred. Her hand tightened while her whole being seemed to tense up. It was interesting, yet not surprising, for me to see. She had not forgiven him for his treatment of her or his many infidelities. I will never know if she did in the few days before she died.

Mom operated differently from me; she was like an iceberg where she hid most of what she was. Yet all that I am is out in the open, sometimes too much so. Men are often attracted to that very feminine, often flaky, aspect of my personality. Yet, I'd never had a sexual relationship with a man who had my best interests at heart. Maybe I needed the false security of the linear thinker to offset the capriciousness of my intuitive way of thinking. I jump to grab the answer, rather than start at "A," solving that before going on to "B," and then to "C," having solved "B."

The linear thinkers are the bureaucrats, the mathematicians, the ones who run the ego world. They comprise 75% of the world's population, while we creative thinkers — the ones who fly by the seat of our pants — are in the minority. Yet, we are able to see the whole picture, understanding relationships and why people do what they do. The intuitive thinker is stifled by the rules of the linear person and the linear one doesn't at all understand the more creative one without a lot of opening up of his or her heart to the other.

I certainly have learned my much-needed lessons from these men: how to value myself, which comes down to having personal integrity. I also learned how to value these men for the gifts they have given me, and not just my babies.

I don't know if my mother came to any realizations as she lay dying. But I do know that from her I learned to stand up for myself, even if the way she taught me was to silently say "Don't do this; there is a better way."

Thanks, Mom; I love you and honor you for being my mother in this lifetime.

Chapter 26

"I can do nothing for you but work on myself. You can do nothing for me but work on yourself."

Baba Ram Dass

Betsy:

"I'm dying, Betsy; I guess you know that," Mother said one blustery March morning. She had been admitted to New England Baptist Hospital with pneumonia two days before this conversation took place. I didn't want to talk about it; dying is something you have to do but no need to share it with anyone, especially a twenty-three year-old daughter.

Catherine's face, a little misshapen by a stroke a few years before, had clear tape on it in places to hold her facial muscles tight, to look more normal. The tape helped her ability to speak but she had never fully recovered from the mild stroke, and her speech was slightly slurred.

Of course, I didn't want my mother to die, but we weren't all that close. I was still grieving over Daddy, who had died a few years earlier. She didn't seem to miss him, but I did. He was the only person who has ever really loved me.

"Oh, don't be silly, Mother, you're not dying. They have penicillin for this now," I insisted.

I couldn't wait to cut my visit short, as Mother and I rarely had much to say to each other, even when she was well. How does one forget the verbal abuse, the barely-hidden contempt that I'd gotten from her my whole life?

I did feel a moment of sympathy for Mother, however, after witnessing an argument between my parents, which left me feeling a bit insecure. About ten years before this I'd gone to bed early because I didn't feel well. When I decided to ask Mother to make me a cup of tea I tiptoed halfway down the stairs before hearing my parents talking in the living room. Mother was partially visible, standing near the chair with her back to me, but Daddy was out of sight.

"You're NOT sending this photo to that woman! She has no right to see what our daughter looks like. Betsy's ours, not hers," Mother yelled.

"Catherine, calm down; Betsy will hear you. I'm not even thinking about sending this to Ellie; I don't know where she is," Daddy said. I didn't know it then, but Daddy had kept up with Ellie, sending photos over the years, along with bits of news about me, while apparently not hearing from her in return. Of course, I was wondering who Ellie was.

"I'm the one you're supposed to love; I'm your wife," Mother continued. "Why don't you love me?" my tormented mother, as she fell into the chair, crying softly into her hands. Daddy left the room, saying he was going to the kitchen to make coffee. I lost my appetite for tea and quietly returned to my room, a little frightened.

I had never before witnessed an emotional scene between my parents, who were usually polite to one another, although there was always tension in my home. There wasn't a lot of talking like other married couples. Who knows? Maybe it would have been easier for her if I'd been a more loving daughter. I learned early not to question things, not to mention anything personal, or to share my feelings. It was like that with Mother. Daddy and I were a different story when we were alone. Not a day goes by that I don't miss him. But, even on his deathbed he didn't mention my real mother. And I didn't ask. As close as we were I was smart enough to know there were things we just didn't discuss.

After my father's death, I went into his den where he kept his special suits and extra clothes. The smell of him was permeating the closet and room. Sometimes I felt him right there with me. Maybe he was, in spirit. I found a letter he'd written to me and placed in a suit coat pocket. How could he possibly know Mother wasn't going to throw out all his clothes? Maybe she would have if she hadn't been sick so much.

"My dear Betsy," the letter began... "If you are reading this it means I am no longer here with you and Mother. Please take good care of her. She needs you to be strong. She loves you very much but has a hard time showing it. Be patient with her. I love you, Betsy. Your Daddy."

I sat down on the closet floor, amidst all the hanging clothes, and wept because of pain from losing my father, of feeling so un-loved all the years I was growing up. I was a financially-privileged child, yet deprived emotionally. It had been difficult for me since Daddy died. I had given up after-school activities in order to help Mother take care of the house with the help of Rowena, our maid who had been with the family since before I was born. I didn't mind not staying after school, though; I had no friends. I was shy, lonely, fat, and depressed.

Mother died a few weeks later, after rallying then taking a turn-for-the-worse, before succumbing to the complications of pneumonia.

Apparently, the pneumonia was worse than I thought.

Chapter 27

"People treat us the way we train them to treat us."

Betsy:

It was a lonely time after Mother died. I couldn't figure out what to do next. I needed to grieve over my mother and deal with my anger and resentment toward her. My only friend was the maid who helped me with cleaning, so I didn't even have much to do in order to work off this sense of loss.

"Betsy, you are the sole heir to a small fortune and we want to make certain you understand how much you can tap into, and how to do so. We want to answer any questions you may have," Mr. Chapman said; he was the executor of my mother's will. He was also the administrator of the trust fund that my grandfather had set up at his bank, Boston Safe Deposit & Trust Company.

It was settled that I would attend Boston University in the fall, as Mother and I had originally planned before she needed me to stay home with her when she got sick. I was to study Botany.

My college courses were fun, but not easy for me as I was distracted by many parties with too much alcohol available. I was a top student in high school, but this party-mentality at college didn't do much to help my academic status. College was a lot more work than high school. I floundered a bit, flunking a few courses, not taking it seriously. One day I decided to quit school in the middle of the spring semester, looking for a way to fit into this new world that I was thrown into, the world of grown-ups. Hooray! The diet I'd been on worked and I began to lose weight, taking an interest in what I ate and how I looked. For the first time I felt almost pretty.

I was ready to have an affair, and went to London the first week in March, in time for the rainy season. I was in search of a man to love. Maybe he'd brighten up my day and make the sun come out.

Chapter 28

"Be the change you want to see in the world."

Gandhi

Betsy:

"But, Vera, I'm not sure I want to be fixed up with your brother; I can find my own dates," I protested as Vera raced around our small flat, tidying up because Patrick was making his way up to the third floor by lift, rather than using the stairs.

"Betsy, trust me, you'll have a fun time with Patrick. Get on that new red plaid skirt with matching red sweater you just bought — the red looks lovely with your dark eyes and pale, creamy skin. You are so pretty, do you have any idea how you look?" Vera insisted as I reluctantly went to my room to change clothes. It had been a long week and I was looking forward to a hot bath and staying in my nightgown and robe all evening. I had found a good job as an office clerk the very first week I arrived in London, along with a two-bedroom flat, complete with Vera as a roommate.

I heard the doorbell ring. Vera greeted him, speaking loudly to warn me he was there. Patrick let out a soft whistle as I came into the sitting room. I was thinking, *I hope he's not a wolf;* I've had zero experience with men, never even been kissed. He was four years older, with at least some experience, I was sure.

"Vera wasn't lying, you do have beautiful eyes. Hi, I'm Patrick and pleased to meet you," he said, as he extended his hand for me to shake. Nice solid handshake, strong hands. "It's good to have a proper introduction, don't you think?" he continued.

"I'm starving, Sis; what's for dinner?" Patrick asked, as he walked to the tiny kitchen, opening the refrigerator door. I said nothing; the cat got my tongue. But, I did notice his tall, skinny body, which was kind of sexy; maybe anyone would have turned me on at that point. His brown hair was thick and straight, and his brown eyes focused on me as he talked. Even with my lack of experience with men I knew Patrick was a bit flirtatious, and interested.

"Betsy, we can make our own pizza; look at all the stuff in the fridge," Vera said, as Patrick set things on the counter next to the sink. "When did you buy these items?" I started to answer "last evening," but the brother-sister team had already started the pizza dough. So much for a quiet evening in my robe.

The pizza was yummy, music excellent, and I felt I had friends for the first time in my life. We enjoyed each other's company, in spite of my initial reluctance. Patrick and I had a great first date — my very first ever. I was falling for Patrick Eric McConnell.

Patrick and I went out every weekend — to dinner, to the cinema, to pubs to drink: "shandy" for me, which is a drink of lemonade and ale together, and dark lager for him. We played darts and got pretty good at it, too. He came to visit me at the flat practically every night. I found out later he wasn't working as steadily as he had implied, and that our dates were often funded by Vera.

We dated for six months before he kissed me, which was disturbing as I was experiencing many passionate thoughts and feelings of my own and couldn't wait to find out about sex. Didn't he find me attractive? Many others thought I was and a few guys at work asked me out. I declined because I wanted to be with Patrick. I was in love.

Finally, Patrick asked me to marry him. "Yes, let's do it soon," I answered. We went to the English equivalent of city hall and got married one afternoon with only a few mates of his attending. Vera came too, of course. He didn't seem close to any of his family, which I thought odd, but didn't question why they weren't there at our wedding. Imagine my disappointment when, on our wedding night, all Patrick wanted to do was talk a little, kiss even less, and pet a little. It took us two weeks to consummate the marriage. Both of us were virgins, something he never told me even though I was upfront about my status as one. I told myself things would get better with time, once we had more experience with sexual intercourse and marriage.

We moved to the United States within three months of the wedding; it took that long to get his visa. With the proceeds of the sale of the Wellesley Hills house — now legally my home since the estate of my mother was settled, but not a place we wanted to live — Patrick and I bought a home west of there, near Springfield, a good-sized city with more job possibilities for him. He found a job driving a truck, but was home nights and weekends. We became a happily-married couple who was settling into life together, making all the necessary adjustments one makes to live with another. And soon we found out I was pregnant, which delighted us both.

Plants have always been of special interest to me, and I planned someday to return to college to get my degree in Botany. I tried my hand at raising orchids because I like them; I love the air of mystery about them. Maybe I wanted to dazzle people with my beauty just like they do. One has to admit they are gorgeous; I suspect I went through a cocky stage where I also wanted to be gorgeous. God knows I have always been finicky, just like orchids; and a little vain.

"Honey, where do you want me to put this shelf I made for you — near the window?" Patrick asked one weekend shortly after we moved into our new home. I had bought "grow lights" and was doing more reading about orchids, being almost ready to try my luck at growing them. The budding sexuality in me was fascinated by the orchid bulbs, which looked like testicles to me, already a subject of interest, as Patrick's mates called him DB for "Donkey Balls." Some people throughout the world use the ground-up bulbs as an aphrodisiac, but I couldn't see doing that; we didn't need any help with being "randy," as they say in England. We spent a lot of time in bed, although sex decreased the closer I got to delivering the baby.

The last month of my pregnancy I chose to take naps rather than tend to the flowers as much as they needed. It was often hard to know when to water, how much light to give them; then there was the question of fertilizer. My time was precious — had to get the nursery ready, buy Christmas gifts and do all the extra things necessary for wintertime living, like snow removal, furnace maintenance, etc. Patrick was gone a lot driving the truck, coming home later at night because of the road conditions. The flowers took a back seat to all the other activities in my life. I woke up one morning in a cold room because the furnace went out during the night. The flowers had died. That was the end of my orchid-growing experiment.

Questions about my birth mother began to surface: *Did she want to give me up, did she ever see me, was she happy now, would she love me if she saw me?* All this confusion was swirling inside.

"Honey, look at our perfect son! Oh, thank God he looks just like you, and not me; what a head of curly hair he has!" Patrick exclaimed, interrupting my thoughts. "Those big brown eyes of his are looking so serious and curious! Oh, honey, thank you so much, I could watch him all day," my more-than-happy husband said. "Let's check his fingers and toes," he went on, as he un-wrapped the swaddling blanket.

All the while I am thinking as I look at Matthew, named after Patrick's twin brother who died at birth, *I hope I can be a good mother. What if he won't breastfeed? Maybe he won't like me.*

"Betsy, let's give him the middle name Hayward, after your father," Patrick said, as I put Matthew to my breast. The baby latched onto my nipples like a pro. I guess I was wasting time worrying about breastfeeding. No problem, I'll just find other things to fret about; that's my nature.

As a small child I had dreams that my mother died and left me alone with Daddy. He found my birth mother and we all lived happily ever after, together as a family. I'd never shared these feelings with anyone, not even Patrick.

"Betsy, you shut me out. You never tell me about yourself or how you feel. Don't you like me? You act as though you don't. Even in bed," Patrick said in frustration one day. We had celebrated our first anniversary but already the "bloom was off the rose," so to speak. Patrick was beginning to suspect I'd never had a real orgasm, yet I couldn't talk to him about it or tell him what I wanted, as I didn't have any clue what I needed or even who I was. I just wanted to be loved, but probably didn't know how to receive love even when it came to me.

"Patrick, everything's fine. I really don't know why you keep harping at me; you nag like an old woman," I said.

"I give up," he yelled, as he stomped out of the house. Patrick often ran away when things got heated; I fumed and shut down while he fled the scene. Neither of us discussed our frustrations, but they were keeping us both on edge. To make matters worse, after the birth of our son I hated sex with him. We could have benefited from reading a "Virgin's Lovemaking Manual." Too bad it didn't exist. Looking back, I wish we had read some books about sex, yet that still wouldn't have solved the problem I had with his lack of good hygiene. He told me that in England people don't take daily showers like we do in the United States. I was hurt that he didn't take into consideration how I felt about cleanliness, so I was sexually turned off. I did, however, feign passion and interest in sex with him. I faked orgasms; seemed easier that way.

We spent only one Christmas with my Uncle Carleton and his family after my parents died. I wasn't close to them; was actually a bit envious of the four siblings having so much fun together when we were kids, getting dirty, yelling and getting along with each other. I envied them for that. But there were advantages to being an only child: more presents on my birthday and at Christmas, and a lot more solitude, which I often got. I couldn't forget a conversation I had witnessed between my Uncle Carleton and Aunt Winnie at my house years before when I surprised them by turning the corner of the hallway coming out of the bedroom: "Carleton, did you notice that the gift Catherine got for Peter this year is the same wooden puzzle we gave Betsy last year? It is very rude but she often does this. It's not like they don't have enough money," my Aunt Winnie said. They seemed a little embarrassed that I heard them but I was just a kid and paid little attention to it. Yet, I did notice the next time my mother re-wrapped a gift of mine from the previous year and gave it to one of the cousins. Aunt Winnie was right — it is a little rude.

There was always competition between the two brothers, Carleton and Hayward. Carleton was the one who worked out in the gym and had muscles; he was also very handsome, which brought a lot of attention from the women. He was a rebel that my father possibly wanted to be at times, yet would never risk the wrath of Grandpa Fred's disapproval. Uncle Carleton didn't seem to care what anyone said; he was going to do whatever he pleased.

There was also some competition with us kids, as I was the one who liked to eat nothing but turkey, gravy and rolls at these family dinners, while the cousins actually liked eating vegetables! My weight was a lifelong problem, but they enjoyed exercises and eating healthy foods; they all had normal weights. I felt judged by my cousins, although they didn't mean to make me feel bad. I remember being included in all the parlor games my uncle invented for us to play every holiday; there were prizes for the one who could make the most different words from "Merry Christmas," for instance. Uncle Carleton didn't play them, as it wouldn't be fair, but the other adults made certain they helped the kids rather than compete with us. My favorite game was the tray filled with at least thirty items, mostly household things like paper clips, spoons, maybe coins, etc, which we had five minutes to look at and memorize before the tray was taken away and we had fifteen minutes to write down every item we remembered seeing. Kids are often better at the game than adults.

One Christmas my world blew up. Patrick and I had been married five years and Matthew was almost four years old, keeping me very busy; so busy I often stayed in my bathrobe all day. The day began with promise — Santa Claus had been there for all of us, the dinner I cooked just for the three of us was delicious, as my cooking and baking skills were getting good. After dinner the phone rang. Patrick ran to answer it. I was doing the dishes and cleaning up when he came into the kitchen.

"Who was on the phone?" I asked. "A wrong number," he replied. "I have to go to the gas station to get cigarettes," he continued.

I was stunned, as I knew that was a lie, having seen a new pack of cigarettes on top of the dresser just that afternoon. Three hours later, long after Matthew was in bed, my straying husband came home and told me he was leaving. He had fallen in love with another woman, someone he had met through work. He wanted a divorce. I wasn't at all prepared for the anger, the shock. I was devastated. He left that night and went to her.

Good riddance to bad rubbish. My thoughts were not kind.

Chapter 29

"I thought you'd never get here," I said. "I know," he replied. "That's what took me so long."

Betsy:

I was still in shock four months later when we went to divorce court; it got worse, as he had a better attorney than I did and the court awarded Patrick a huge portion of my inheritance. Matthew was in kindergarten, so I improved my office skills and got a job supporting us. I had to decide what I wanted in the future for my son and myself. What I wanted was a log cabin in Vermont, in a small town where I knew no one. I wanted to be left alone, to recuperate from a devastating experience, vowing never again to trust a man.

And that was still my attitude five years later when I was eating breakfast one morning at Patsy's Diner, a place I often went to for lunch but seldom for breakfast.

"Hi, my name's Larry Mitchell. May I sit down?" His rugged, lumberjack-type looks and friendly manner got my attention, but I asked, "Why?" Larry laughed and said, "Okay, have it your way, but I'll be back." That really got my attention. Yet it took him five months of being friendly and non-threatening for me to trust him enough to go out on a date with him. And it took him maybe five minutes after the dinner date ended — where I couldn't eat a bite of food — before he got me into bed. That was definitely an eye-opening experience! "So, this is what orgasms are all about," I dreamily said, very satisfied with this man I had chosen to sleep with on our first date. "You've never had one before?" Larry asked, incredulous. Thus began an opening of our hearts and bodies to each other that I thought happened only in romance novels, and probably not even in those!

A few minutes later he was showing me what it's like to have multiple orgasms, full-body orgasms, orgasms that arise from every part of my body. And his.

After a few months of dating — well, mostly just having great sex — Larry moved in with Matthew and me in our cozy little cabin on twenty acres down by the river, where deer and other wildlife walked by the sliding glass doors in the dining room. Suddenly, the place was even more of a home for my son and me. Larry easily found a couple to rent his house. Larry wanted to marry me and adopt Matthew, but Patrick never would have allowed it; the adoption that is. I wouldn't have expected him to, as he was a good father, just not a good husband for me. He took Matthew on weekends when he wasn't doing a run driving the truck out of state. I had no interest in marriage, having tried it once too often.

"Betsy, I want you to marry me, and I will keep asking until you say yes," Larry said one night after an exceptionally passionate "romp in the hay." "Larry, don't keep asking or it will be over with us, okay?" was my final reply to a question he had asked many times. It was a few years before he asked again but eventually I knew I could trust him and we got married one late winter morning by the Justice of the Peace down the road from us. We went on a short trip, just the two of us, leaving Matthew with a friend for the weekend, enjoying the sights in Burlington, Vermont on Lake Champlain. But, mostly we just looked at each other, talking a lot. We were having a lot of great sex, of course. Isn't that why honeymoons were invented?

About six months later Cousin Penny came through town on her way back from spending the summer in Concord, New Hampshire. She had moved to Florida after her divorce but cooled off in New England each year.

"Hey, favorite cousin, how are ya?" Penny asked, as she came through the door of my office on a Friday morning.

"Hi, yourself; let's take a break and talk in the other room," I replied.

As we caught up on what's happening with her travels and latest lovers I told her Larry and I had gotten married. "Congratulations! That's great news — when did you do that?" she asked excitedly.

"In March, just a private ceremony with a couple friends and Matthew — no big deal," I replied, which was shocking to her. She wasted no time telling me.

"I cannot believe how differently you and I operate, Betsy. If I had gotten married I'd shout it from the rooftops. How long were you planning to keep this a secret? Were you going to tell anyone in your extended family?" she prodded.

I had no answer, but was thinking how private I am; I realized I'm secretive by nature. My life is no one else's business so why should I tell them what I am doing?

"What did you just say, Penny?" I asked, as something I heard broke through my thoughts.

"I said you can now go to the city of Portsmouth and get your birth certificate; adoptions are no longer sealed. Please go soon; she may still be alive!" Penny continued. "No excuses, Betsy, you've wanted this information for a long time and we both know it."

Damn! How does she always know when I am afraid of something? Yes, I was definitely frightened by this. Actually, I was terrified and unsure of what to do. I changed the subject; she caught that ploy, too, yet said nothing. She just gave me that look she has when she knows I don't want "to go there." She soon left to continue her trip back to Florida.

It took me a few years, but I finally did find the courage to go to city hall and request my birth certificate. It was much easier to get than I thought it would be, but very difficult to look at. My hands trembled; Larry steadied my arm while I looked at the words on the paper, known as statistics by others. But this was my life I was looking at: Ellen Rose Hill, maiden name Lavoie; she was twenty-three years old when she gave birth to me, her second child. "Oh my God, Larry, this makes her real!" I exclaimed. I read on: father unknown. "But, Larry, she must have been divorced or widowed, as she does not go by her maiden name, so that means she was married at one time or is using a fake name."

It really shook me to the core to read this but isn't it a relief to finally know the truth? This also explained the hospital bracelet that was in a small box of personal things Daddy gave me when I was young. "H-I-L-L" was on the tiny beaded bracelet the nurse put on my wrist to identify me when I was born. For many years I thought my parents made a mistake in the spelling of our last name because I was obviously Elizabeth Hill, not Elizabeth Hall, as everyone called me.

I spent the rest of the day thinking about my real mother, even during what was apparently a tasty lunch at a restaurant overlooking the Piscataqua River. I think the name of the place was Fisherman's Pier. By now, I was mature enough to realize there are valid reasons to put a baby up for adoption. It can be a very unselfish act for a mother to do that. I no longer resented my mother, as I felt she wanted me to have a better life. Now I was curious and excited. What if she's still alive?

One day, months after I'd gotten my birth certificate, Cousin Penny came for another visit. She was looking for land in Maine, hoping to replace the farm she had sold after her divorce from Rob.

"Look, Penny," I said, placing the legal paper on the kitchen table. It took a minute or two for it to register what she was looking at.

"Oh wow!" she shouted. "You'd have a lot of answers if you looked her up; even more when you get Uncle Hayward's hair analyzed using your DNA," Penny continued. She was referring to the lock of red hair from Hayward's first haircut at age one. Penny found it in a chest of drawers after her father died and gave it to me, saying I can find out the truth about who my father is with this piece of evidence. Apparently, some people in the family thought Uncle Carleton might be my biological father. Penny and her siblings might actually be my blood relatives.

I was really angry later when Penny searched for my biological mother. I no longer speak to her. *You are a pushy broad, Cousin Penny.*

Chapter 30

"Be kind whenever possible. Kindness is always possible."

The Dalai Lama

Penny, with my father, 2001-2002:

"Honey, it's okay; I'm not hungry," my ninety-year-old father said, as he lay dying. Dad had been admitted to the hospital in Florida after having fainting spells and being unable to swallow. By the third day of his not eating I was noticeably upset. The nurses assured me it was not a difficult way to go, that the body shuts down, and if he says he's not hungry he probably isn't hungry. I did ask that the man who was eating meals in the same room with Dad be moved and he was, just to save my father the trauma of smelling the food and wanting the comfort of eating.

He didn't always know I was his daughter, yet he knew I was his security blanket. Sometimes literally, as I often got clean blankets out of the warming oven to cover his thin legs. And when the doctors could offer nothing more than a PEG tube to force-feed him Dad said "no." But he answered "yes" to the question about trusting me, posed by the Hospice social worker when she interviewed both of us one day.

Dad was dying; he knew it and I knew it. Fortunately, the nurses knew it, also. I wish I could say the actions of the doctors showed they knew it, but they were forcing — until I made a big stink — respiratory therapy on him, along with other unnecessary, yet paid for by Medicare, procedures. I quickly learned that it doesn't matter if we have a *DNRO* — Do Not Resuscitate Order — and a *Living Will* signed by Dad many years before Dementia put a claim on his mind. The doctors and hospitals get the money, and plenty of it, often ignoring those of us with the legal medical power of attorney as long as they can get away with it.

We had lost Mom eight years before this; Dad lived on his own most of this time before beginning to fail, forgetting things on the stove, unable to clean house or cook. My sister had been paid to go to New Hampshire, living in her own home that he paid for and driving a truck he paid for. But Patricia was often asleep, hung over, when he needed her. So, I came to New Hampshire, newly-divorced, supporting myself by working early mornings in a bakery/deli, then spending time helping Dad each afternoon and evening.

"I see the man you left sitting there at the dining room table like a bag of concrete. I see the man you're going to; he's an athlete, an old love, a foreigner, who will visit soon," Sue, the psychic, said. I was having my first session with her. It was December 2001, and my divorce would be final in six months. Sue hesitated to say more about the "foreigner," whom I knew to be Simon, who was planning a visit in just a few weeks. He had sent me a letter in New Hampshire, getting my address from the Christmas card I sent his parents. He was divorced the year before and was interested that I was getting divorced. The plan was for him to come over in February for one week.

I had no doubt the "bag of concrete" was David. *Oh well, sorry he's suffering.* I asked her if the foreigner and I would have a permanent relationship, which made her shrug. She mentioned a few small things about me (which did come true, by the way), then said that after my father died my life partner would find me. He would be living near a body of water. Somehow he would be connected to Native American things. Our relationship would be intimate and spiritual; we would be able to make love from across the room, without even touching each other! She also said this was well worth the wait; it was everything I dreamed of — and more. It was mine to have, for certain.

Somehow, I always knew that. Even as a child. I will have a best friend, lover, and husband all rolled into one man. And he will be worth all the pain and frustration of the past.

Our relationship will be worth waiting for. I'm gonna hold you to that, Sue.

Well, Simon did come over from Birmingham, England in February; he stayed one week, as planned. When I met his plane at Logan Airport in Boston I was shocked at his short, stocky, dissipated appearance — the guy looked like an alcoholic. He grabbed me, kissing me in such an open-mouth, tonsil-scrubbing way that I almost gagged. I realized quickly that, unless he can learn to kiss well and soon, that sexually we will have nothing in common.

This is where having boundaries comes into everyday decisions for me; sometimes they are life-altering choices, impossible to reverse once in motion. The question I had thought about was this: *Penny, are you lonely enough to go with this guy with whom you have a child, a history, but nothing else in common? If you are, isn't going with Simon settling for less than the best you deserve?*

Heather and the two grandchildren, Billy and Carrie, drove east from Michigan to stay for a few days. It was good to see Simon with all three of them, especially our daughter. Heather acted quite upset, though. As I watched her I could see questioning looks, her sadness visible. I could feel her anger, directed at me, her thinking, *"Why couldn't I have this with my Dad while growing up? Whose fault is it?"*

If she had come right out with it, I'd have answered, "It's no one's fault; it just is. Be thankful for what you have now, before this moment slips away and you're too busy worrying about what you don't have to appreciate your blessings." That's what I would have said to my beloved daughter, whose insistence on being a *Victim* cast a pall, a veil of darkness, over everything in her life. Be happy, Heather, I wanted to say. It's a choice.

Later, Heather was totally pissed off at me for breaking up with her biological father, saying I owed it to her to stay with Simon. *Really now, you're serious, are ya?*

Meanwhile, I was realizing that, even if Simon and I had anything more in common than having a child together, which definitely was NOT true, his love for beer would have destroyed the relationship. As would his pathological lying.

Simon had told me via e-mails for months before this visit that he gave up drinking long ago. And that he no longer told "tall tales," two of the reasons for the split years before. He must have forgotten what he said in the e-mails because copious amounts of beer and other alcoholic beverages were present during his entire visit. I agreed to keep an open mind, giving him the benefit of the doubt, as all of us can change. I sure have. I was looking forward to the visit until I saw that he was still telling "whoppers," not just little fibs. That fantasy of his self-image began to unravel right away. By the last day before Simon returned to England — a sexless visit, by the way, because alcoholism ruined any chance of his having a hard-on — we both knew it was over.

Keeping the faith that what I wanted in a life partnership was mine to have, I drew a line in the sand with Simon, turning away, never to look back.

"Hello, this is your father's neighbor, May Carmichael. Carleton is yelling out the window for help." The phone came around three o'clock in the morning.

"I'll be right over," I said, and was on my way in minutes.

Dad said he couldn't breathe, but refused to go to the hospital. We sat and talked an hour or more before I thought it late enough to call my brother, as I had to get some relief in order to go to my job at 5:30 a.m. As it turned out Dad did go to the hospital with pneumonia that day. Next morning we went to the hospital to visit him and he asked where he was; at first we just thought he was confused, but he looked so at peace we thought we might be the ones who were confused. Edie said, "You are at the hospital; don't you remember coming here by ambulance yesterday afternoon?"

"No," Dad replied, "I was over there, and it was so nice."

Someone asked "Over where?"

"There," he said. "Can I go back?"

While Peter and Edie were talking with the nurses, as they had medical power-of-attorney for Dad, I held his hand and listened as Dad, the poet he has always been, began to eloquently describe a white mansion with lots of marble, flowers, and gardens. There was light everywhere. "Everyone is happy," he said. Dad said my mother tried to take his hand before he got sucked away, going back through a tunnel. "Winnie came to me and I almost grabbed her hand…"

Peter heard some of this as he returned to say that Dad's levels had dropped way down during the night — they had him on a monitor — so they had to administer oxygen. This revived him. Why didn't the staff honor the *DNRO*? Giving oxygen, thereby saving his life, resuscitates a person, right? We discovered later, after much detective work, that the admitting physician forgot to enter the *DNRO* into the computer. Don't these guys make more money by administering stuff, fussing with the patients, looking concerned while taking their huge fees from the Medicare office? We were disgusted, but the best was yet to come.

I've no doubt Mom really did come for him. I also know why he didn't go to the "Other Side" then: the profound lessons I was to learn in the next few months while caring for him would be a gift from my father. He had to do that for me first; it was a selfless act from a man who was selfish his (almost) entire life.

My father was put into a nursing rehab hospital, the best in the state. He got feisty with the nurses, pushing one back enough to make her fall on her butt, getting hurt. He was pretty much ignored, as they were afraid of him. He wore the same wringing wet diaper much of the day. When we came at lunchtime to feed him we managed to get his pants changed. Then he found a way to escape in his wheelchair so they put a monitor on him; it would beep if he moved away from a certain area. Of course, he was strapped in and hated it, so they put him on anti-psychotic drugs, which made him act totally psychotic. He cried each time we visited; Peter and I cried, too. Patricia stayed away as long as she could get away with it; Peggy lived in another state.

"Hey, Edie, Peter, I have this crazy idea," I said one day. "We move Dad to Florida where I take care of him 24 hours/day, 7 days/week." I popped out with this one day after being unable to watch my father in that awful place any longer. Dad's 5000 books — yup, I counted most of them — were moldy, causing Dad to use his "puffers" too often. We knew the books were a major problem, as all of us had trouble breathing when we'd visit him at home and couldn't stay much longer than one hour if we wanted to breathe. The nasty winters in New Hampshire, with very few people available to care for the elderly in their homes, made my idea sound better each day . At least there would be no snow or ice and we could go for daily walks with his wheelchair. And there'd be no books. He couldn't remember long enough to read now, anyway; or be read to. That "crazy idea" worked out well for both of us; he never had to use his puffer in Florida.

Dad flew to Florida two months later, accompanied by my brother. Peter delivered him to me before getting on the next plane back to New Hampshire. Meanwhile, Dad and I made the ninety-mile journey from the Tampa International Airport to live in the once-vacant house. I had arrived in North Port with only three days to get the house livable before my father arrived. I hired a neighbor to help un-load the trailer I pulled with my van, with all of our personal belongings from New Hampshire inside. There were no books, of course. Some pieces of furniture were borrowed from Edie, who lived nearby in the winter.

"Dad, don't open the door. What are you trying to do, get us killed?" I asked, a bit frightened, as he tried to get out of my van going 70 miles per hour. Fortunately, he couldn't figure out the seat-belt situation. I talked him down, beginning to realize the poor man was going "cold-turkey," withdrawing from the anti-psychotic drugs. I expected this, but didn't know exactly how it would happen or when. We got home safely; at midnight we were arguing about my removal of his adult diaper, which was heavily-laden with human waste material. He was not able to get it off, but not about to let me do it, either. I used every tool of persuasion I had, even joking that he had changed my diapers sixty years before (which I doubt he had), and now it was my turn to change his. For a second he remembered I was his daughter, but the stubborn old coot wouldn't budge!

"Dad, if I can't take care of you at home we'll be forced to put you back into a nursing home," I finally said, in desperation. BINGO, that broke through his foggy mind and he allowed me to change his clothes, diapers and all. The showers later became a battle when he was so seductive that I called Visiting Nurses Association about it. They didn't have workers to give home showers for the elderly. I soon learned that most of his bad behavior came from being a spoiled brat and not just a ninety-year-old man with Dementia.

Poor Mom — I am certain this was the type of behavior she'd had to deal with her entire married life.

Great! I had on my hands a spoiled upper-class Boston boy who was "discovering" his sexuality and thought I should marry him so he could have sex. A seductive ninety-year old who has the mind of a twelve-year old is not a pretty sight. He and I both laughed about it after I realized I had to make the transition from daughter to caretaker, which I did.

As previously planned, Heather flew in to Tampa, taking a few days of vacation in order to help me with Dad less than a week after he had arrived. We drove together to pick her up at the airport. Don't forget, he was still coming down from those drugs, so picking her up may not be my brightest idea. It was only 7 p.m., early for most people but late for Dad, who (as I was about to discover) couldn't handle being in public places once he got tired, which was probably after three or four in the afternoon.

I swear we were waiting at the airport only ten minutes, but it was early September in Florida. The humidity and temperatures were high and uncomfortable, especially if a person wasn't used to it. I had to wheel him from the van, which I parked on the third level in the garage, to the terminal quite a distance away. He was getting more pissed off by the minute; such a spoiled child. After a few minutes in the terminal I realized we couldn't find Heather. All of a sudden, he got out of his wheel chair (never did allow me to strap him in) and turned around, ramming me with it. He was very strong, a ninety-year old former body builder, and he was hurting me. Someone called the security guard, who rushed over; by now Dad was yelling that I was trying to kill him. The guy looked down; Dad had returned to sitting down, tired, I guess. He asked my father directly what was wrong and got an unintelligible answer. Then the guard looked at me with confusion when I calmly said, "My father has Dementia, and we are here to pick up my daughter who came in on a Northwest Airlines flight from Detroit. Can you page Heather Weston, please?"

Meanwhile, one of the ladies at the ticket-checking part of security came over, put her arm around me and told me she went through a similar thing with her elderly father. Dad was crying and apologizing, I was crying; even the security lady was crying! I'd venture to say a few of the hundreds of onlookers were also crying. Heather showed up after being paged and we all went home, exhausted.

That incident was an eye-opener for me: Florida, with all its thousands of elderly residents, doesn't seem to be any better equipped to handle the increasing problems of caring for "old people" than other places. I was surprised. I also noticed the lack of support and options available as we age and need more care. It will have to fall to the families. Nursing homes aren't cheap — Dad's cost over $100,000/year. They also, even the best ones, leave a lot to be desired.

The next evening Dad barricaded himself in his bedroom, apparently using a chair under the door knob. No matter what Heather or I said he was not about to come out. We heard him throwing stuff.

Did you ever hear the phrase, "When you cannot calm down a ninety-year-old man with Dementia, just calm yourself down?" Luckily, I had the foresight to buy a couple bottles of wine my first day in Florida, while stocking up on groceries.

That next hour was probably the closest my thirty-eight year-old daughter and I had ever been, as we closed the door to the Florida room, sat in rocking chairs next to each other, telling stories, gently rocking away, while demolishing a bottle of mighty-good-tasting Chardonnay that I'd had the intelligence to put in the refrigerator days before.

Eventually, he got tired of the game and didn't resist when Heather crawled through the bathroom window and proceeded to wash his face and hands to get him ready for bed. I went to bed, also, as I always went to sleep when he did; otherwise, I'd never sleep. Every night he was talking to my mother; sometimes his own mother showed up, both long-dead, of course.

I kept a journal, recording daily incidents with Dad, just in case someone in the family wants to know what Dad's last few months were like. Someone, someday, will get a good laugh out of it. And maybe have a better understanding of those who came before them.

"You're trying to kill me, making me eat all this junk," Dad complained one evening when he was devouring part of a sponge cake with ice cream on top. We had made a quick trip to Publix late that afternoon when I realized I had forgotten to thaw out meat for supper. Publix had good hamburger meat, which my father could easily eat without teeth. He spied a group of sponge cakes containing white flour and white sugar. So, the former health nut now demanded that I buy him at least one.

"Dad, you don't eat these. Let's get some fruit for me to make you a smoothie," I said, still being the health nut I am.

Well, you know the drill: he gets out of the wheel chair and tries to ram me, causing a scene. But, I am onto his game after the airport fiasco. I quickly get the cake, along with the sugary ice cream he wants, thinking to myself *you'd better die soon, you old pain-in-the-ass.* Of course, then I felt a bit of guilt, which disappeared when he harangued me at home later, accusing me of feeding him poison.

A good sense of humor got me through this and other strength-zapping moments. My sleep patterns were so disrupted after a few weeks of caring for Dad that it took maybe a year after he died to get back to sleeping normally.

Caretakers make a mistake when they concentrate so hard on helping the patient that they neglect themselves. In order to avoid that trap I hired a neighbor lady, Jamia, right from the first week, who just happened to work in a nursing home, of all places. She had Saturday mornings, 9 a.m. until 12 noon and Wednesday evenings, 5 p.m. until 8 p.m. available. That was it for my time off which I spent at the nearby hot mineral springs or Nokomis Beach, ten miles away. I needed to relax and keep healthy, as I was by now almost sixty-years-young.

I honestly could not have handled more than nine or ten months of this stress; I had been doing it only one month when I came to realize that fact. No matter how romantic or easy one thinks taking care of an old guy with Dementia is, it always is stressful. No way around it.

I called his doctor one day about Dad's talking much of the night or falling out of bed when he got up to wander the house, consequently giving me little opportunity to sleep, asking if it would work to give Dad a sleeping pill each night.

"That's not necessary, just get Tylenol PM," Dr. Johnson answered. Then he laughed, saying to take one myself if that didn't work and then I wouldn't care what Dad did. I thought that was funny, was glad to hear another sense of humor expressed, but I never did take anything for sleeping. I just don't agree with taking drugs, never did. Not even the legal kind.

After three nights of smashing the tablet between spoons and adding applesauce to make it easy to go down while spoon feeding my father I realized this pill not only didn't help him sleep, it actually made him jumpy and unable to sleep as much as before. I mentioned my observation to Jamia, who confirmed that it does the same to many people. She also confirmed that doctors know the anti-psychotic drug Dad was taking at the nursing home often causes patients to have psychotic episodes, but they give it anyway! I had known all along that's what happened to Dad. By now, after a few weeks of cleaning out his system, controlling the diarrhea with liquid acidophilus, my father was pretty much over the affects of those pills. Of course, what was left was still a very spoiled child.

"What happened to my brain, why am I this way?" my father asked me one day when we were out for a walk in the wheel chair. Since being honest comes naturally to me I answered the best I could, from the heart: "Dad, the doctors say you have Dementia; I think your brain cells got damaged when they gave you radiation treatments for skin cancer a few years ago." He nodded, as though my answer made sense to him.

I learned a lot from Dad those last few months. He showed me unconditional love and helped me help him pass on to the *Other Side*. It was really sweet how one minute he'd protect me like a father does, while the next he'd grab my hand and tell how afraid he was that he couldn't "do it right." I was given the gift of being able to listen to him, unafraid, and objective. Listening is often more important than talking.

One day, after being admitted to the hospital in Florida for his final stay, I saw that his restraints had been tightened; when I inquired about it the nurse's aide said he was afraid of falling. I quickly told her he was "up on the ceiling" looking for a way out and afraid of falling down from the ceiling, not the bed. She gave me a look that said it all: *What, are you nuts, lady*? I assured Dad many times that if he chose to come down from the ceiling he would do so the same way he got up there, gently floating.

One day Hayward came to visit — now mind you, he was long-dead — urging his baby brother Carleton to get ready to go with him soon, to not be afraid, he would help him "do it right." I could feel my father's sense of peace as he was telling me about the visit. I can't help wondering how lonely it must be to have no one to listen when one is dying and afraid. Of course, there are many who wouldn't discuss it even if we wanted to listen; maybe talking about death — or making out a will — are things that make death real and imminent.

"Grandpa, remember Alan Ryan?" Heather asked. She had made a surprise visit, flying in from Michigan for the weekend.

"Oh, yes, he just floated by here," Dad excitedly said. My older sister, Patricia, was married for many years to Alan, who had died two days before this visit, yet no one had told Carleton because we didn't even know ourselves until that very morning.

One morning I came to visit at around 9 a.m., my usual time. He was sitting up in a chair, dressed as best could be in a hospital gown, ready to do something interesting. Of course, he was bored, who wouldn't be? He didn't read because he couldn't remember the previous sentence, TV bored him (he couldn't see all that well, either), so we decided to go for a walk. But first, I had something to show him.

"Dad, let me help you out of this chair. I want to show you something," I eagerly said.

We walked to the window; I got the chair and helped him sit down. We then spent maybe a half hour watching a three-to-four-foot-long alligator playing in the puddle right outside the window. We'd had a huge rainstorm the night before and the yard outside the hospital had low spots in the lawn, which attracted birds after a storm. That is what the alligator was waiting for — a meal. My father, the "nature nut," got as excited as a ten-year-old boy would be seeing his first alligator. I had promised him an alligator for many weeks; we'd often go for drives looking for them, even once at night. But, this was his first. He was fascinated.

After he was through looking at that one he wanted to bundle up and go for a walk, looking for other alligators. We went around the hospital, which had a big pond, where I could see a pattern in the sand obviously made by the swishing of an alligator, much like a broom would make.

We went out for another walk later in the week, yet never saw another 'gator. I believe that lone critter was sent by the angels just to give Dad one last memory of this spot on Earth called Florida.

The night before Thanksgiving 2002 Carleton was taken by ambulance to a *Hospice House* to live out his last few days. By then he was being given a mild form of morphine under the tongue as a pain/fear reliever, so he wasn't lucid enough for conversation. His organs had failed to the point that they knew he would be gone very soon.

You know what I like about these *Hospice House* "angels" who care for our loved ones during their last days? They know what their jobs are and they do them well. No temperatures taken, or blood pressure readings, no IV's; no pretenses, just unconditional love for each patient. One nurse told me they often hear the patient talking to their departed loved ones and saying things like, "Oh Mom, that IS you; I am so glad to see you," or some similar statement. Only a few hours later the patient passes away.

Saturday morning I went for my usual visit and Dad's eyes were closed, as they had been the past few days. I held his hand and gently stroked his forehead as he tried to find the energy to speak. "That's okay, Dad, I know you want to tell me you love me; I know you can hear me. I love you, too, Dad," I quietly said. He squeezed his eyes tightly closed, then loosened the eyelids as if to open them but didn't. "See, Dad, I knew you could hear me!" I exclaimed.

I suspected this was our last visit on Earth together when I kissed his forehead and said I'd see him in a few hours after grocery shopping. I've no doubt he knew he had only a few hours to "do it right," as he was a private person who would never die in front of someone else.

When I returned at 1 p.m. his door was closed and the nurse met me to say he had just passed away. She held me as I cried and told her it was harder than I'd thought it would be.

My father had lasted only three months after being taken out of the New Hampshire nursing home, but I daresay they were some of the best months of his life. Somehow I was able to hold his fears and pain in my heart with no ill effects to myself. I was criticized by one of the more dysfunctional members of my extended family for not being "emotional enough" while caring for Dad. I got no answer when I asked the valid question: If you're dying and afraid who would you rather have caring for you — someone who is not afraid, who could sustain a positive energy for you, listening to your fears OR a person who goes around, wringing her hands, saying "Oh me oh my, look at the dark sky?"

Carleton, with all his self-absorbed actions causing much resentment with his wife and four children, had somehow managed to be an unselfish father to me those last months, showing me how to love unconditionally, teaching me compassion for others. I also found compassion for myself. *Thanks, Dad. See ya later.*

Chapter 31

"Love is a verb, not a noun."

Penny, and siblings:

"Well, we're all orphans now," we four siblings agreed as we got together in New Hampshire in 2003. Dad had died recently; it was a strange feeling being "orphaned," even though we were grown up and not dependent on our parents; hadn't been for many years.

"You know, Dad made a lot of progress those three months we were in Florida together," I told Peter, two sisters Patricia and Peggy, and Peter's ex-wife, Edie.

"At age ninety how much progress can one make?" Peggy asked. She was the most cynical one of the group.

"No, really, he cried and made me promise to tell Mom's relatives in Maine how sorry he was about the way he treated them; he even asked me to drive him there from Florida!" I exclaimed. "I told him he couldn't even stay in the van long enough to make the thirty-mile trip to Sarasota without taking off his seatbelt (which he soon learned how to fasten and unfasten) and threatening to open the door as I am driving along at seventy-five mph. How could he expect to last the week it would take to get to Maine?" I continued, as the laughing subsided. "He was afraid to die because Mom would be there and she would be angry about his many infidelities; he told me this. But she must be the one who convinced him it was okay because I heard him talking to her nearly every night, even apologizing for cheating on her. Toward the end he was convinced there is no anger on the Other Side, as I had assured him."

Dad spoke with such clarity at times I forgot for a minute that he had Dementia. He wanted to talk and I wanted to listen. The one thing he refused to talk about was Betsy's adoption, saying "Oh we can't talk about that," in a tone filled with conspiracy. So we never did.

My friend Sue, the psychic, is the one who told me about his trying to force Mom to have an abortion at the beginning of their marriage. He was genuinely shocked when I mentioned it. "How did you know about that?" he asked. So, I told him. He accepted my explanation. In fact, I believe the best gift I was able to give my father was to always be honest with him, to allow him to do his dying with integrity. *You done good, Dad.*

Now, the five-way conversation got more interesting: "Did you know about the baby Mom lost after I was born?" Patricia asked. This was news to us; apparently Mom told only Patricia. We never did find out how far into the pregnancy this happened but the baby was a girl.

"What does anyone know about Betsy's adoption?" Peggy asked.

"Maybe Dad had sex with Catherine and fathered Betsy," someone interjected.

"No, that can't be true," I said, "for a few reasons: Dad wouldn't be attracted to her; also, it wasn't Hayward who was sterile, it was Catherine. Mom told me so; besides, remember how Dad would hug us all goodbye and not want to let go? He never did that with Betsy; wouldn't he have done so if he's the father, even if it's a secret?" I asked. "You know what I think may have happened? Hayward had an affair and he and Aunt Catherine adopted the baby," I said.

"Or," someone interjected, "Dad's the one who had the affair with the woman and the baby was adopted by Uncle Hayward and Aunt Catherine."

Patricia piped up and said, "Dad did tell me one time that we have a sister somewhere but clammed up when I asked questions."

"Is it possible a woman was paid to have a child for them? That's done more often than people realize," Peggy added. She was the most detailed thinker of the group. She actually never said a word — not even Dada or Mama — until she was three years old, then began speaking with perfectly-formed sentences, adult-level words. She's our champion at Scrabble, the only person to ever beat my ex-husband, David, at the game. It's obvious she does a lot of thinking, absorbing knowledge along the way.

It was the next day that I read the diary my sister found in Dad's home when we cleaned it out to sell after Dad went into the nursing home in New Hampshire, later knowing he was going to Florida with me and wouldn't be returning. I knew of the diary's existence, but didn't get a chance to read it before this. My grandmother Lillian kept diaries, lots of them. They usually had mundane things in them like: "Went to Schrafft's with Margaret" or "Bishop drove us to the Algonquin Club" was another entry I sometimes found; most of these diaries were thrown away. This one had all those entries, yet one caught my attention, as it did for Peggy, which is why she kept it: "Met with Hayward to discuss his problem," written in April 1946, seven months before Betsy was born. Of course, now I am growing suspicious of what "Hayward's problem" could be.

❧

"I want you to be the executor of my estate. Will you do that for me, Penny?" my sister asked. Patricia called me one day in July 2005, right before our shared birthday. She would soon turn 69; I was almost 62.

She and her long-time fiancé, Jim, were living in Charlottesville, Virginia, renting a house while he returned to college. Jim was retired military, almost twenty years younger than her. They were a sweet couple, very much in love. But they both had health problems. Patricia had always been sickly, mostly "hung over sickly."

"Oh, Pat, you know how I hate even balancing a checkbook. Don't you have anyone else who can do this for you?" I asked, hoping for a yes answer.

"Penny, you're the only one who can handle my kids and all the crap they'll give you when I die. Please do this for me," she pleaded.

"Okay," I reluctantly agreed. "But only if you don't leave me a mess."

It was agreed that she'd get a lawyer to make out a will, medical power of attorney, and living will and send me a copy.

I called her many times, beginning in September. I must have left six messages in the next three months. There was never anyone home, never any return call from her.

In December I got an urgent phone call from Jim: Pat was in the hospital with leukemia. They both needed my help. I drove the nine hundred miles from my home in Florida, arriving two days after the call.

My sister looked disoriented. She obviously was very sick. They had put her on anti-psychotic drugs to calm her down, and she was acting strange. Her head was wrapped in a bandana in anticipation of losing her lustrous head of hair, her pride and joy, from the chemotherapy. They put her on it, even though the doctor said they gave her only a 20% chance of recovery. I guess 20% is better than zero percent.

Patricia had me call her lawyer, asking if he'd come to the hospital so she could sign the papers he'd spent many hours putting together. What? I'm flabbergasted to find out she never signed them! He agreed to come over on his lunch hour, bringing a legal secretary as a witness.

You'll never guess what happened next. The hospital administrator kicked him out, saying they would declare she's not in her right mind and they cannot allow her to sign legal papers in their hospital! Fuck! (That's my word, not the lawyer's — he's a devout Mormon.)

Mr. Scott says we have no choice but to hope she gets sent home soon and is well enough to sign papers when she's released.

I made two more trips to Virginia — one in January, another six weeks later, to visit her before she was sent home from the hospital, not exactly pronounced cured.

Now Patricia, no longer on drugs, but clearly exhausted by the hospital routine, is at home, resting peacefully. My changeable-as-water sister has yet to sign any papers.

"No, I can't sign these; I might change my mind," Pat said to the lawyer only two weeks before she died, without a signed will. It's called "intestate." Of course, there's no will. How could it possibly happen any other way? Patricia was true to her nature right up to the very end.

The call came on a Tuesday — Patricia had died peacefully in her sleep, at her home where she wanted to be, with the love of her life, Jim, by her side. I had recently sold my Florida home; Tennessee was a twelve-hour drive, rather than two days. I left immediately for Pat's home, having sad thoughts during the drive, interspersed with happy memories of my big sister.

My sister, that poor, lost soul, did leave a mess, and her grown kids did give me crap over her estate, but I survived the job. I sometimes think about my sister, how sweet and beautiful she was as a young woman, and I am thankful to have had her in my life.

Then, it hit me! Now, there are only three of us siblings. Surprisingly, losing our parents and later a sister just continues to make the remaining siblings closer. And that's a good thing.

Chapter 32

"When you are angry, you see the world with eyes of anger....If you are sad, you see the world with the eyes of sadness, and everything you perceive will be sad. But, if you have the eyes of love, you just see love wherever you go."

The Mastery of Love, don Miguel Ruiz

Penny, and dreams:

I am giving birth to Rob's baby. Even as I'm dreaming I actually know it's a dream. It was such a strange sensation. *Gosh,* I'm thinking, *this is me watching me dream.*

Rob and I are happily-married, living in our own little hippie home. He's encouraging me to push. We're about to have a baby. Our baby. The one I never had with him in real life.

I woke up, puzzled by what I saw. Little did I know at the time this was only the first of many dreams and nightmares I'd be having about my life with Rob, the man I had long-forgotten. I would learn later that I was beginning to do a lot of what is called "lucid dreaming."

That's the problem with reading self-help books: If you take them seriously you realize a bit of soul-excavation, often a lot, is going to happen soon. This latest book was about remembering dreams as a way to grow spiritually. The idea was to wake yourself up and write down the details in the journal next to the bed, as soon as you could. They usually fade within seconds.

This whole "excavation" thing began in September 2004 when I was wondering what to do with the rest of my life. Since I come from a family with longevity — many lived into their nineties and a couple even beyond one hundred years old — I figure the "rest of my life" could turn out to be one hell of a long time. Maybe time to have another life, to do what I want to for a change.

The question I asked myself was this: Will you use every means at your disposal to keep learning about yourself and life? I answered yes to that question, in spite of the temptation to be a couch potato.

Within weeks of making this commitment to my growth I began having dreams of Rob. And not all of them were pleasant.

PART TWO

Chapter One

"There's no coming to consciousness without forgiving our parents."

Marianne Williamson

Penny, searching:

As I approached the end of an hour-long, breathtaking drive through the Lake Winnapesaukee area of New Hampshire the slight nervousness began. This was unusual for me: I have no secrets so I'm pretty calm about seeking out answers, even when it involves someone else's hidden skeletons.

Betsy was no longer speaking to me, having made it clear I had no right to look for her biological mother. This was also my family history; there was conjecture in the family that my father may also be her father. We could be sisters. My curious nature was on fire; the Detective archetype in me was working overtime. I was a creative, intuitive thinker; not just a nosey person.

The day was lovely in a misty, gray New Hampshire sort of way. I felt fortunate the roads were not carrying the usual Sunday crowds; June was the beginning of summer's high-tourist season. Luckily for me, the rain and cold began on Friday, exactly as the weather forecaster predicted. Many tourists cancelled their plans, knowing this was a storm front that would last the entire three-day weekend. Only the already-reserved-lose-my-deposit kinds of tourists were moving north on Interstate 93 in Concord on Friday afternoon and by Sunday morning many had left the area, leaving the roads somewhat deserted. I took Route 28 north so I could "wave" as I passed by the road to my great-grandfather's house and cemetery in Barnstead, which was now owned by another family. I had previously gone to see the family house and was taken by a neighbor into the woods to see the gravestones of my ancestors, put there more than three hundred years ago, now covered by moss and pushed up in the grass by the huge roots of trees growing next to the stones. I was thinking how ironic that this was a field where crops grew to feed my ancestors and now the ancestors' bones are feeding the trees growing into their graves. I stopped at the family cemetery only when my genealogist-sister Peggy was with me.

God bless my sister Peggy. She is NOT going to be thrilled to hear I am searching for Kevin, the man I found on the Internet, one whom I believe to be Betsy's half-brother. She says this isn't my business; she's also the one who says my father's infidelities are not our concern. Wait a minute! What if he IS Betsy's father? Isn't that our business? If my perceptions of men and their inability to keep commitments are distorted because of my father and his un-zipped pants then it IS my business what he does — to my trust in him, at least. Fortunately, I have grown up and no longer need to look at my father as "Daddy."

Oops! I missed Route 171, the turn-off to the area of Ossipee that "Mapquest" told me Kevin Hill lived. After driving maybe five miles further I was at the road leading to his driveway. The directions were perfect: his house was just where the website said it would be.

Oh boy! Now I'm getting more nervous. *What if he asks me to leave, refuses to talk to me? What if he gets upset to hear that his mother had a baby — probably out of wedlock — and gave up his sister for adoption? What if he just doesn't give a damn?*

No one answered the side door near the driveway — I tend to knock too softly sometimes — so I went to the front door and knocked, calling out, "Hello, is anyone here?" *Well, it is Sunday morning and some people go to church or to their families for Sunday dinner.* As I walked away disappointed, I heard someone ask, "Yes, you knocked?"

Like the slightly nervous woman I was at the moment, half-dreading what's coming next, I spoke rather quickly, "Hi, my name's Penny Hall and I don't know how to say this so I will just come out with it: I'm searching for my cousin's brother whom I think is named Kevin Hill and she's mad at me because she's a very private person and loves secrets and I'm too open for my own good and too curious so I'm the one doing the looking."

He smiled and offered, "I'm Kevin Hill." All this time I'm thinking as any heterosexual, single woman interested in men might think: *He's rather cute.*

"Oh, great," I continued, gulping for courage. "Her mother was Ellen Hill who, according to my sister Peggy, the genealogist, was married to Parker Hill."

"Ellie was my stepmother and she married my father after her two girls were grown. You can't have the right Ellen Hill. Besides, my father's name is Lester," Kevin said.

Why did it never occur to me that I might have the wrong Ellen Hill; that the genealogy-nut Peggy got the information wrong? Or I did? "Would you like to hear a quick story?" I asked. He indicated he'd love to; after all, the allergic reaction to an antibiotic that was keeping him out of the sun wasn't a problem because he was told only to stay out of the sun and the sun wasn't out to "stay out of." His blue eyes were lively, curious. I noticed his sexy, six-foot-tall body and full head of hair, graying, of course, looking about sixty-years-young, same as me. I began the story of the family reunion at Hampton Falls, the photo of my brother's daughter who bears a strong resemblance to my cousin, Betsy. "We always knew she was adopted, but this reunion was one of the first times I put into words what had been gently nagging at me for years: that Betsy was probably not adopted 'out of nowhere' as had been assumed. That there might be a biological connection."

"My parents adopted out one of my seven sisters during the Great Depression of the 1930's and we found her a few years ago. Actually, I got a phone call from a woman who hung up when I answered, yes, I'm Kevin Hill, but it took her five years to get up the courage to call again. And by then my older sister, Brenda, began saying she remembered Mom being pregnant, then all-of-a-sudden there was no baby. With no explanation she can remember. There were ten of us in the family and my parents could barely feed us; we've assumed that's why our sister wasn't around when growing up. Brenda found her after a long search, but before she could call her my long-lost sister, Mary, called me again. It's wonderful having her at family reunions; we're making up for lost time."

181

His openness surprised me. I don't know why it should; I'm not the only person in the world who has no secrets. But men aren't usually this open.

"Kevin, have you any idea if there's another Ellen Hill in your family? Maybe an aunt, your father's sister, or a cousin, perhaps, who had a child born out of wedlock in 1946? Surely your family wasn't the only one with times so hard they had to give up a child for adoption," I said.

Kevin went into the living room and got his cell phone to call his sister. "Brenda, there's a lady here who wants to talk with you about Ellie," he said, handing me the phone. After a few minutes of speaking with Brenda I was satisfied that their stepmother, Ellie, couldn't possibly be Betsy's mother — she was from Massachusetts and moved to New Hampshire only to marry Lester Hill, a friend from childhood when she spent summers at her grandparents' cottage on Lake Winnapesaukee. Brenda said she'd ask the family for more information and we exchanged e-mail addresses before saying goodbye. We made a connection that got me thinking I would hear from her.

Underneath the disappointment that Kevin isn't Betsy's brother is excitement welling up inside me: *This Ellen Hill whom Peggy found died in 1988; if she's not Betsy's mother then isn't it possible the real mother, Betsy's Ellen, is still alive?* I thanked Kevin for his time and walked back to my rental car, thinking about our conversation.

Too bad he's married, was one of my thoughts.

Chapter Two

"A filthy enactment; I will not obey it, by God!"

Ralph Waldo Emerson, upon hearing of the passage of the
Fugitive Slave Law in 1850, which compelled Northerners to
return runaway slaves to their masters.

Penny:

"Hey Sis, now don't be mad at me but I looked up Kevin and he's not Betsy's brother. We don't have the right Ellen Hill," I said that night on the phone.

Since Peggy told me the previous summer that it wasn't my place to look for Kevin — it was Betsy's if she chose to do so — I wasn't certain how she'd take the news of my search. She has always played the role of the older, more grounded — sometimes bossy — sister, and rightfully so, as this is who she is.

"I'm not mad at all. I thought about it and realized this is our family history, also; not just Betsy's. So, tell me about the trip," she said. As I gave details of the visit I couldn't help but wonder how we're going to find this lady. And wouldn't it be great if she's alive?

"Peggy, I'm renting a cottage at Mendum's Pond in Barrington the middle of August. Why don't you fly to Manchester and spend time just hanging out? I'll go to Portsmouth City Hall and get the birth certificate information to work with. Wait, didn't you take down the maiden name and birth date of Ellen when I called you that night after I saw Betsy's birth certificate?"

"I have it here in my BETSY file. We don't need the birth certificate because I have all the information, but we will need to trace the marriage licenses in person at the courthouse in Rochester; they're not on-line, probably because of privacy issues," my genealogy-nut sister said.

This will be a fun vacation; hope I get to just hang out reading, cooking, and swimming. Gotta get my money's worth, as Dad used to say. I plan to do some sleuthing, but not too much.

❧

"How dare you have letters that belonged to my father? You shouldn't have read them, either!" Betsy e-mailed this sentiment to me one day right before I was to leave for the lake cottage. I had found more than one hundred letters from her father to his parents and to my parents, written beginning in the late 1920's and ending in the 1960's. Rather than throw them out, as Betsy had wanted to do the day we all went to my grandmother Lillian's after her death to pick out personal items, I saved them just as my father had while Betsy went around "cherry-picking" all the most valuable antiques. Her actions said "to hell with the sentimental stuff." My father was a packrat but also a history buff; I've no doubt he saved many things that day and over the years simply because he had respect for history.

Betsy could, at the very least, have thanked me for sending her the letters. So, I sent her this e-mail: "Gee, Betsy, you could have offered to reimburse me for the postage or at least said thank you. That's one advantage of being one of four children: learning to think of others. Is that the real reason you don't want to find your mother? Because you will probably find siblings and you want to remain the spoiled, only child of wealthy parents? Your behavior is ridiculous. With Love, Cousin Penny."

Chapter Three

"We are restless hearts, for Earth is not our true home."

St. Augustine

Penny, in Mexico:

"I was born in Cuba," Gretchen replied, in response to my asking where she was from. I had come to Mexico for one of many visits the year of 2006, a busy one, for sure. I was making decisions while building the little house, a "casita," which required my physical presence, even though my friend Hannah was managing things well. We were sitting around the table of my latest new friend Maria, who had been telling us how she and her husband, a musician and instrument-maker, had lived in Thailand, Costa Rica, and other equally exotic places, before settling into buying a beautiful home in my neighborhood in San Miguel de Allende, in the high desert region north of Mexico City. It took little time for them to decide that San Miguel is a "forever" place for them.

Our Colonial city is high in elevation (over 6000 feet) with much beautiful architecture. Some say it's the magic light that makes us want to stay. There must be some truth to that as artists and other creative persons discovered this inspiring place long before I did.

"My father came from Germany at age sixteen, orphaned, penniless, and speaking only Yiddish, German, and Polish, but no Spanish or English," Gretchen continued her fascinating story. "He worked very hard, earning money any honest way he could find. One day, at age twenty-six, he saw this lovely blonde girl come out of an ice cream shop and was quite smitten with her. He had to meet her! So, he walks into the shop and guess who the owner is? Isabela's mother. The girl was called Isabel in New Jersey, where extended family lived, but Isabela was her name in Cuba. Her parents brought her to Havana when she was tiny so they could have a better life. Havana was a lovely tropical city, right on the water, being an island, of course. And filled with the most delicious smells of food and, ah! the music, with hot rhythmic beats, coming out of every pore. My father struck a deal in Yiddish, as that was the only language he shared with Anna, my future grandmother. The mother said he could visit Isabela, chaperoned, of course, and if he wanted her hand in marriage he must bring the equivalent of U.S. $2000 or the bankbook proving he had that amount saved. This was 1929 — I was born in 1930. One day he came to the bank to deposit the money so he could show the bankbook to Anna and Robert, the future in-laws, before proposing marriage to Isabela. The bank was closed, as that's the day the stock market crashed and people lost everything — everything that was in the banks, that is," Gretchen grins, as Maria and I are shrieking with laughter and cheering the good fortune of the lovers. "They were married soon after and I was born nine months later. Later, we moved to New Jersey, where we lived with family members while my parents tried their luck at making a life in an area made even colder by comparing it to the tropics we had just left. We moved back to Cuba when I was three-and-a-half and lived there many years. By then, all three of us were fluent in English and Spanish, which comes in handy here in Mexico," Gretchen concluded.

There are many interesting people in Mexico, especially San Miguel de Allende, which has much "corazon" — heart — and much beauty. The place drew me in the first time I went there, arriving after a long, overnight bus ride through the mountains in the wee hours of a frosty January morning. I said to myself, *Penny, you are home*, knowing I had lived there in another lifetime, or many lifetimes.

The young Mexican girl began to move to her right as we encountered each other on the choppy sidewalks of San Miguel. Of course, she saw that I was a foreigner and allowed me to go right, as we do in the USA. Yet, as a part-time resident, I know tradition makes us go to the left and I began to move to the left. She and I laughed as we did the right-left dance common in San Miguel, which has a substantial foreign resident population, plus thousands of visitors every year. When in Mexico do as the Mexicans do and that includes carrying a roll or partial roll of toilet paper, a bottle of water, and small peso coins and bills, as there isn't much change in Mexico. During the first trip many years ago I learned to tip the bag boy at the tienda, the small grocery store, where tips are the only income for these kids. I also, after sitting quite awhile waiting for the check, realized one must ask for *la cuenta*, as it is rude in Mexico to give the restaurant patrons their checks before they ask for them, which I often do by making the scribble sign inside my raised hand. I love the fun of learning forms of etiquette in my new country. I also learned NOT to ask, "tiene huevos?" when I wanted eggs for breakfast. The one and only time I made that *faux pas* was on my first trip to Mexico and, after I had asked the question, the waiters were trying really hard not to giggle, covering their mouths. If you ask a Mexican man if he has eggs, waiter or not, he knows you're asking if he has balls or testicles, even if you don't know that's what you're asking. How do you expect him to answer that question? With a "no"? I don't think so. "Hay huevos?" is the accepted question for if the restaurant serves eggs. I have also learned since driving my car in Mexico that when I see a STOP sign I might be wise not to stop (unless there is a car coming) because I cannot assume the guy behind me will stop. The rules are definitely different there.

On one of these trips with my car I was three hours from the border of the USA, but it was getting late; I was tired and the mountains were pretty big all around me, outside Monterrey, so I took the exit for Saltillo, the next city to their west.

"And how long will you be staying, senora?" the young man asked, as I was trying to exit the first motel I came to at the edge of town. I had been driving through the courtyard, looking for an office, which I had yet to see; he ran after me, as there was no office to find!

"I need a room for one night only," I answered.

"Are you alone, senora?" I was puzzled by now but indicated I was alone. Then he told me they rent only by hours, six or twelve hours being the two choices. I laughed and asked who their clientele was and he told me "novios" — lovers. I bade farewell, thinking, *the place is deserted; wouldn't they make more money if they had a travelers' motel AND a lovers' motel all rolled into one, as we do in the USA?*

Soon I came upon the Camino Real, a fancy resort-looking place which required a gate pass to get inside. At the desk I gasped at the price of 1800-pesos, less than 180-dollars, but high for me, and the clerk gave me the deal he probably gives everyone who asks: $80 including breakfast buffet and taxes. That was pretty high for Mexico. The room was quite lovely, but the shower held a pathetic stream of water that any man without prostate problems could surpass in both force and warmth. I took a bath instead of a shower; *I know, Dad, gotta get your money's worth.* Only he was talking about staying awake all night in an expensive room. *Hey Dad, I got my money's worth by sleeping like a baby.*

While driving the 1900 miles each way from Tennessee to Mexico, then back to Tennessee another 1900 miles I had plenty of time to think. This was a time I was still being haunted by dreams of Rob, my first husband, the one I let go because he wanted to be elsewhere, even though he couldn't articulate it at the time. And I got to thinking about angels, how they are always with us and sometimes try to get a person to go on a more spiritual path. So, the angel comes to Earth on assignment, got to get Rob, for example, but he doesn't want to go with her, refuses to see the opportunity before him. Maybe he's supposed to be her helper, going away from the ego world toward the spiritual one. She knows the chosen ones are in for a pleasant surprise, a very happy life, yet what if the person cannot see that possibility? She also knows he has free will and it is his choice to make, not hers. This has nothing to do with her so she goes on to the next assignment, spreading love as she goes, as she knows for certain that love is a VERB, not a noun.

I thought of a recent conversation I'd had with Edie: "Hey, Penny, did you hear about two monks, one in training and one being the teacher? The student asks, 'Teacher, I see so many people drinking and doing wrong things while you and I meditate and lead a righteous life, yet they sometimes seem to be happy. We are happy, too. I am confused because I sometimes want the fun they seem to have and yet I am happy with this life. Which is better?' To which the older monk replies, 'Why, both ways are best, of course.' That is the way I look at the need we all have to judge others. Each of us will evolve our souls, eventually. Can't avoid it, no matter how we live," Edie said.

I had long-forgotten being married to Rob until those dreams began, maybe thirty years after we split up. In them he was always trying to tell me something. They showed scenes of our marriage — trips, feelings, making love — scenes I had wanted to forget, thought I had forgotten.

"Admit it, girlfriend, you're dreaming about him because you don't have a lover right now and you just want to have sex with him one more time," my sassy friend, Sonya, said. She definitely has a point, but it isn't about sex, it's about closure, apologizing, being curious. Okay, maybe sex, too.

The dreams became more frequent, more intense, to the point of hurting my ability to sleep. I had to know what was going on, why he wouldn't leave me alone. One night, with candles burning as they usually do when I meditate, I had an epiphany, a release of my will, a complete understanding of why I was having some of these dreams. The latest one was to show me my willfulness, a lifelong trait I had developed as a passive child trying to keep others from pushing me around. I realized that night, as I lay sobbing for what seemed like hours, but was probably minutes, that I may never get closure with Rob; he may not want to speak with me. I needed, instead, to concentrate on why I was attached to him or had the need to speak with him. I saw that he was too passive for me, that I had pushed him into marriage; I had been willful with him as I had been with everyone else. No wonder he was angry with me and had sent a bitter letter four years after the divorce saying he hoped I was happy that I had ruined his life; he was very unhappy and I had taken the best years of his life. At the time I was puzzled; after all, didn't he get all the dreams we had together — didn't he get them with her? Not if he refused to take responsibility for allowing me to push him into marriage, just as he allowed her to do. It is so easy to blame the partner, as it distracts us from looking at our own work. If I get the chance to speak with him I will apologize for my part in the failure of our marriage. He may be the same angry man, but it doesn't matter. Who am I to say he should have changed just because I have? Everyone's soul evolves no matter how many lifetimes it takes. There is a saying in Mexico: *Lo que es, es. What is, is.* NO blame, no judgment, just unconditional love.

We all have different paths. I wish nothing but the best for Rob and his wife. And the same for David. I love them both; have changed the love that turned to hate back to love again only because I have first learned to love myself. And for that I am eternally thankful.

Chapter Four

"With each choice we make, we either become more involved in the illusory physical world, or we invest energy into the power of spirit."

Anatomy of the Spirit, Caroline Myss

Penny:

On June 1st, 2006 I returned home to my fixer-upper south of Nashville. I'd been in Mexico for about a month, being a tourist in need of rest, although San Miguel de Allende is not the quietest place I've ever been. My beautifully-funky 1950's Cape Cod was almost finished; ready to move into. I'd been camping in a tent amongst the wildlife, including deer and unidentified critters trying to get inside my temporary home some nights. My friend John, fifteen years younger than me and wanting more than friendship, came to my house on his way from Florida to Las Vegas, the land of opportunity. I had bought him a new, deluxe air mattress, complete with Egyptian cotton sheets, down pillows and a lovely down comforter, as the nights were still a little cool for just a sheet. There were lots of options out west for John, whose master carpentry skills I admired. I wanted him to have the best for a good night's sleep. Especially since having sex with me was not going to be an option. He needed to earn money for the trip and I desperately needed his help.

We spent two weeks working day and night, sanding and staining original pine ceilings downstairs, even in the kitchen. We installed gorgeous maple kitchen cabinets, along with white Whirlpool appliances. The plan was to buy a front-load washer and dryer when I returned so he and I did what was necessary to expand the bathroom to add a laundry area. It was hard work.

"Penny, come with me; I really care about you. We can have a great life in Vegas," John said toward the end of the visit.

"John, I can't get past the age difference — you still have a child to finish raising, a career to work on, while I am retired and want to travel. I have to be free to do what I want with my time. It cannot work," I said.

"Penny, you're so full of energy and life; I don't see any age difference," he insisted.

"John, you're not listening to me," I said, emphasizing that last part. "I'm the one who can't do it; I cannot go backward," I firmly stated.

We hugged and parted as friends. He left a few days later for his trip out west and I went to Mexico. I wasn't resting as well as normal, mostly because dreams of Rob kept invading my sleep. They always left me tossing and turning, often for many hours.

What do I do when I am tired? Go on a trip, usually. I had spent much time in Mexico during the past few years because of a house I was building. But this summer I'm thinking, *what about Peru and Ecuador*? I hadn't been there in almost forty years, since right before I met Rob in 1967, when my father, Heather, and I visited Peter in Chile where he was stationed in the Peace Corps. I was anxious to visit Machu Picchu, a place I had seen in photographs.

After a few weeks in Mexico I was rested, ready to finish my new home in Tennessee; maybe I can now call it a "fixed-up" house. It was dusk as I drove my van into the long driveway. At first, I thought my eyes were playing tricks: there was no house! It took a few seconds to register that my house had burned down.

I don't know if everyone reacts this way, but I was in a state of shock and walked through the tall, damp grass to the house next door — not a wise thing in snake country, especially at night during the season when wild things mate and are more aggressive. Cathy, my new neighbor, whom I'd barely met a couple times, answered the door, telling me without my having to say a word that it happened the night before. It was a storm unlike anything they'd ever seen, and they've seen a lot of weather in an area with frequent tornadoes and wild lightning storms. The local furniture company burned to the ground only hours later because of the same storm system. I used her phone to call the sheriff, who told me some details, which I heard through my sobs.

Well, eventually they determined it was struck by lightning and the clean-up began. But meanwhile, after twelve hours of crying and not sleeping much at the motel I'd gone to in town, I'm thinking, *Penny, you'll be sixty-three years old soon. You must stop this crying or you'll get sick. You're healthy, but tired. Let it go.*

Gradually I did let it go. Fortunately, I had good insurance; but more importantly, no one got hurt.

When I had my birthday a few weeks later I thought, *here it is, that seven-year cycle once again.* I have a chance to look at this new time-line: nine times seven years equals sixty-three years, does it not? One can think positively about any incident; I call it "shifting perspective." I began to see the fire as a new beginning, burning off the old, so to speak. The "old" me was burned off in the fire, encouraging thoughts about the new person I was going to be. The one who is thrilled to find her life partner.

I began to question why I was in Tennessee, where I felt I didn't belong. The fire soured me on the area a little. The market had begun a downturn so it wasn't guaranteed I'd now make a profit renovating any house. I'd been in the Deep South for more than twenty years. It's time to stop speaking "y'all talk" and get back to my northern roots.

Yet, since my insurance company said they wouldn't pay me the full amount if I didn't re-build, I made plans to start a new house, figuring in a couple years I'd sell it and go north, for the summers, at least.

By now, I know my friend John is not a candidate for partner, but what about the rest of the men I am meeting? It's possible there is someone in Tennessee for me, but I'd have to appreciate a man chewing tobacco, then spitting it into a tiny can with lid that he keeps in his pocket. I don't think so. Friends keep telling me there are no men "out there." I'm finding a few, but am seeing that men in their sixties seem to be really old, as if they are already dying. Not just physically old, but living that stifling traditional role of man being the boss and woman obeying. Or looking for a "nurse with a purse."

Sorry guys, I've done the traditional thing twice; it won't be happening again.

My need for freedom and independence reared its head with both husbands and made me feel trapped by marriage. I do suspect, however, that being "trapped" isn't a problem if you're with the right person. The younger men seem to have no problem wanting an equal partner; even guys five to ten years younger than I have a better idea of what men-women roles should be. But, can the guys in their fifties break into a song and actually know the words to the music on the "Golden Oldies" station?

The war in Vietnam took many men of my generation. The 1960's was an exciting time to live but many of our men had to live — and die — in worse-than-hot, enemy-filled jungles far from home. Many who came back to the U.S. were so wounded mentally and spiritually they have never really come home. Come to think of it, Tennessee is a good place for these veterans to hide from the outside world: perfect climate, cheap land prices, people who mind their own business and think nothing of it when they see a guy carrying a gun. There are many very secluded parts of Tennessee, as I found out during my search for land in the summer of 2005.

I think many men see their fathers old by age sixty and think they, also, are supposed to be old. There's often an attitude of defeat and depression in older men; maybe they know they've been left behind and the clock's ticking. The women are leaving them in the dust. If they choose to examine their values and roles in society they might see an opportunity to grow. Yet, I haven't met many older men willing to open up and ask questions about their lives.

I spent the beginning of the summer in my new apartment, looking at the four beige walls. No colors to cheer me up. My dream of living in that 1950's Cape Cod I had almost finished renovating before the fire was now gone. I was a bit depressed, lonely, and bored. Finally, I began to remember what I realized after my divorce from David: that I know and love myself. I am ready for a partner whose growth is equally important to both of us, as mine is to him. All I have to do is continue embracing whatever the next seven-year cycle brings. And he will appear.

I want to tell you something I realized that day I visited Kevin, hoping he was Betsy's long-lost brother. I was aware of an attraction to him, briefly lamenting that he's married. Little did I know he was also attracted to me. And he was divorced.

One day not long after my visit to Ossipee I got an e-mail from Brenda, Kevin's sister. "Will you be coming here again soon? I want to show you some photographs and letters that Ellie's daughter has in her possession. It seems that our father, Lester, had a brother we never knew, one who fought and died in World War II. Dad never mentioned him, but now that I think about it, I do vaguely remember a faded photograph in the secret compartment of my father's Windsor desk; when I sneaked into it and asked Dad who it was he concentrated on bawling me out for getting into his private things. Then said it was 'no one'. Family's really important to me, but I guess the hardships of the 1930's and 40's gave people a different perspective. E me sometime. Your new friend, Brenda."

Well, the Detective in me was once again fired up and raring to go so I answered her, saying Peggy and I will be at the rented lake cottage in August. We will look her up.

Chapter Five

"Intuition is the ability to use energy data to make decisions in the immediate moment."

Caroline Myss

Betsy:

It's as if the lights are going out, I was thinking, as the excruciating pain gripped the back of my shoulder. We lived way out in the country but the ambulance was a better choice than the forty-mile drive by car to Brattleboro, Vermont. Larry called the paramedics within minutes of realizing I was in trouble. I almost passed out from the pain; it was unlike any I'd ever had before, something I hope to never experience again. The feeling of being unable to breathe was the hardest part, as it brought on a lot of fear. *What if I die out here?* Stubbornness and the fear of dying kept me going until the ambulance got there and the guys administered oxygen.

I had a lot of time to think about my life during the hospital stay. Many tests were taken and I was told I had a mild heart attack, but with medication and change of diet I should be able to control the problem. We worked at getting my blood pressure down to a more normal level. Then I went home to finish recuperating.

When one comes close to dying the ensuing enlightenment is hard to ignore. I was being given a second chance and planned to take advantage of it. I've always been an avid reader, mostly of fiction, yet now was attracted to self-help and spirituality. In more than one of these books I read that heart problems are often caused by one's heart being closed emotionally to others. I thought about that a lot. I became determined to open up and allow people into my life. I mended fences with my son Matthew, from whom I had been estranged, and eventually came to understand how fear can take over and leave little room in the heart for love and generous thoughts. I spoke with Larry about my fears; we cried together when we both realized what we could have lost, and became much closer because of my new openness. For this workaholic to take extra vacation days after returning home from the hospital was a shock to everyone, including myself.

Within a couple months of having the heart attack I began the search for Ellie, my biological mother. I had no clue where she was. I hired a private investigator; he had news for me within a few weeks.

Chapter Six

"Repression says 'if I don't look at you, you will leave me alone.'
To which the Shadow answers, 'I can do things that will make you
look at me.'"

The Book of Secrets, Deepak Chopra

Penny:

Since the terrorist attacks of September 11, 2001 it has become more
difficult to get information, such as birth certificates and marriage licenses
that used to be available to the public. I can understand why, as we now
have identity theft as the number one growing crime in America. However,
I do have to ask what we genealogy "nuts" are going to do about tracking
down ancestors. What we'll do is make our Detective archetypes work
harder visiting all the "old folks" we can find, recording information like
the "Foxfire" series of the 1970's. Or read the invaluable books by the
Delaney sisters, *Having Our Say* and the one written by Florence after
Bessie died at age 103.

Our "Delaney sister" was Harry Nutter, a ninety-eight year-old gentleman
with a terrific memory, who just happened to be the father of a lady we
met the previous summer when Peggy and I were looking for Camp
Cambridge. Jane turned out to be a distant cousin; and a new friend.

To digress a bit: In the early 1970's my father asked me to drive him to
Alton to find Camp Cambridge, which we found with no problem. Even
though the land and buildings no longer belonged to the original members
of the Lake Shore Social Club (the club no longer existed either), the
buildings were all there, intact. They looked just as they do in the old
photographs — minus the people in early 20th century clothing — and in
the old paintings I have found since.

During the summer of 2006 I took Peggy right to the place, which I
recognized from the look of the land and the island directly in front of the

house. Even though the water tower, the buildings, and the train were long gone, the railroad tracks were still there. Of course, the older sister had trouble believing the younger sister — I wasn't quite sure myself — although I kept coming back to the way the land sloped and the way we could drive onto it from the highway. The trees were no help as they had either grown in thirty years or been cut down, but the island couldn't possibly be a mirage.

As it turns out, I was right. We'd been driving along the shore, looking for historians to talk with, when we met Jane and her husband. Peggy and Jane made a connection right away. We spoke with her father, a man who grew up in the tiny town of Farmington, New Hampshire, Ellie's hometown. Mr. Nutter was a fascinating man, happy and full of information, not cranky like so many elders can be. We were having so much fun I almost forgot why I was there. The focus of my sister's visit was the Lake Shore Social Club, which Mr. Nutter didn't know about. But my reason for being there was to find out about Ellen Hill.

"Mr. Nutter, do you remember Ellen Lavoie from your hometown?" I finally got the courage to ask.

"Oh, yes, I do; she was a lovely girl, liked by everyone. She was always smiling. She married Parker Hill as soon as she turned eighteen, but he died in the war. She had a son; don't know his name or where he might be. You could look up Hallie Scruton; I hear she's still alive. She knew everyone in town. Ellie was a lot younger than me. Why do you ask?"

I hesitated and my sister encouraged me to continue, so finally I said, "We have reason to believe she is the biological mother of my cousin Betsy, who was adopted at birth. She was born in November 1946 in the Portsmouth Hospital."

"Yes, we did hear a rumor she had a child born out of wedlock right about that time," Mr. Nutter said.

"Dad, didn't you say she got married again, to a local guy?" Jane asked.

"Yes, his name was Thomas Lovell; I think he died. They had a son. Oh, I do remember they owned a country store near Rochester," he recalled.

I piped in, "How do we find out if that store is still around?"

"Oh, gosh, that must be fifty years ago; there aren't many country stores left any place now," he replied. Mr. Nutter was winding down, seemed to say most of what he knew on the subject. We visited another hour or so, then thanked them for their hospitality and said goodbye. We planned to keep in touch; after all, my sister had found a friend in Jane and she just happened to be our cousin. What are the chances of that happening randomly?

After leaving Lake Winnapesaukee we took time to visit our brother Peter, who lived in Concord, New Hampshire. He has just returned from the Amazon, where he spent three weeks with a shaman, who performed ceremonies using a root called ayahuasca, normally found only in the jungles of Peru and Brazil. Peter looked very healthy and happy, eager to tell us some of his experiences, even though he knew "straight" Peggy wouldn't approve.

I have always been a hippie of sorts, yet don't use drugs, not even legal ones prescribed by medical doctors. So, this was a foreign concept to me and one I wasn't really interested in until Peter mentioned a German woman he met there.

"Her body was riddled with parasites so bad we could see them under her skin and in her eyes. The doctors gave up on her, saying they had done all they could and she would die eventually, as the critters would eat through her organs," Peter began his story in a way that grabbed my attention. I was sitting at his dining room table, fascinated, while Peggy was not hiding her disgust, snorting a bit in judgment of both Peter and this woman.

"She thinks she got them in India, where she taught for fifteen years," Peter continued.

"Penny, you should re-think your desire to go to India," Peggy quickly interjected. I just looked at her, ignoring her comment, eager to hear the rest of the tale.

After three weeks in the jungle near Iquitos, where fourteen people from around the world slept in hammocks in open huts (there were jaguars in the village), ingesting ayahuasca in ceremonies four times each week, and eating no food except rice and plantains, she returned to Germany.

A few weeks later Peter got an exciting e-mail from her, saying the doctors could no longer find any traces of parasites in her system. I'm thinking, *of course not, they starved to death from the meager diet!* Well, the lady's cured. I was now hooked by curiosity. I wanted to remain healthy. Maybe this would help me.

Peter gave me the phone number of the coordinator of these trips and, before I had a chance to change my mind, I was committed to a seven-day session in the jungles of Mexico in just two weeks!

That evening, back at the lake cottage, Peggy and I went swimming, even though it's a bit chilly for me. I had arranged with Brenda, Kevin's sister, to meet her and a sister at Kevin's house the next day, Sunday. Since it was an hour's drive or more, and we'd had such a busy day, I went to bed early. Peggy got out one of her many books and stayed up for awhile, reading.

When I called Brenda a couple weeks before this to arrange the rendezvous, she gave me some news a friend had told her: "Penny, this is upsetting to me, but I must tell you something. Darren has just told me that when he did research for a book about adoptions he discovered there had been a "stolen baby ring" right here in New Hampshire in the 1940's," Brenda said.

"I have a feeling where this is going, which is something that never occurred to me," I replied.

"Penny, it is possible Betsy was sold by these people in the ring. Apparently, they often told the mother her baby had died; most of these women were alone, with no one to protect them. Then they had free rein to adopt it out to the highest bidder. It happened in the same time-frame as Betsy's birth; newborns were sold to wealthy couples out of state. When it was looked into by one of the now all grown-up "babies" the private investigator he hired turned up dead. It's a mystery. It looks like the ring was hushed up because of politicians and other powerful people getting a cut — maybe as much as $50,000 or more was paid for each baby, and that was a lot of money sixty years ago," she concluded, almost out of breath.

The news was a bit of a surprise to me; I guess I had this romantic notion that two people fell in love, couldn't be together for whatever reasons, and had a baby that the mother loved but could not afford to raise. She gave the child away so it could have a better life. The idea that my aunt and uncle may have bought a baby was not a nice one to me. But, we will probably never know the truth.

We talked for a minute more as she told me her sisters love to visit their brother and couldn't wait to meet my sister and me. At this point I wondered out loud if this might be an imposition for Kevin's wife.

"Oh, he's not married; they've been divorced quite awhile," Brenda said.

Come to think of it, I had assumed there was a wife inside the house when we met; it was a pretty big house for just one person. And there were three vehicles in the driveway. *Wait, Penny, you own three vehicles and have some serious living space, or did before the fire, yet you live alone.* Never assume anything. Ever.

Sunday arrived and I was excited for obvious reasons: Finally, we're going to get some more pieces of the puzzle. I was at the beginning of a new friendship with Brenda, which is good. Of course, there's always the question of Kevin: Will his eyes still twinkle when we see each other again? Does his home have the lived-in look of a bachelor? Does this genealogy stuff fascinate him, also? All kinds of questions, mostly about Kevin, but the main one was: Is Ellie still alive?

As we gathered in Kevin's neat and clean, yet lived-in, living room I couldn't help but notice the electricity between him and me; I was sure we hid it well, though.

Brenda began with the reason we were all there: "I have these photos of our father's brother, Parker, whom we never knew. He died in World War II. Here's also a photo of a young woman whom I believe to be Ellie."

"Look at those big, dark eyes and curly hair!" I exclaimed. "That must be Ellie; Betsy looks just like her!"

Brenda continued, "According to a letter sent to Dad, written by Ellie, she and Parker had a son, but Parker probably died without knowing about his son's birth. In those days there was no e-mail and often there was a delay of many weeks between letters. Two letters from Ellie were in Lester's personal affects. In one she wrote about ice cream and gaining weight. In the second letter she wrote of the birth of her son named Kevin. They were given to his mother, our grandmother Lily, after his death."

"Here's the photo I saw when I was little," Brenda said, handing it to me to pass around, "but Dad wouldn't talk about it."

"Does anyone know the name of this son or if he is still alive?" I asked.

"Sis, I'm going to contact the Veteran's Administration; since I'm a Vietnam vet they might be able to help me. After all, we're talking about my uncle and cousin," Kevin said.

I was looking at Kevin, thinking, *God, how that man's eyes twinkle and not just when he's talking to me. He's a happy soul.* That reminds me of the advice I gave my daughter when she was a teenager: Look for a man who can whistle while changing a flat tire in the rain. She didn't take my advice; but then, neither did I. If the Universe gives me another chance at a loving relationship with a man I'll jump in with both feet if he is a totally happy soul.

The afternoon went by quickly. Kevin had made iced tea and lemonade and bought cookies. *Oh wow! I just love a man who cooks.* It was a fun day, a productive time. Brenda said we should do this again sometime. I agreed. We promised to keep in touch. Kevin asked for my e-mail address and roared when he saw the part of "hell" and "wheels," saying, "You get a lot of speeding tickets? We car nuts sure have a lot in common, don't we?" He said he'd e-mail me when he got information about the missing cousin.

As we were leaving Kevin asked if I could help bring dirty glasses into the kitchen; the others were chatting outside on the lawn.

"Penny, I'd like to see you again. Would you go out to dinner with me next week?" he asked, smiling, of course. I gave him my cell phone number and asked him to call, indicating I'd love to have dinner with him but needed to check with my sister to see when she was flying back to Seattle.

Kevin and I hugged each other that lovely afternoon. And I did notice the sun was out, shining brightly, something New Hampshire often does well.

Chapter Seven

"Challenges are the fuel for our spiritual growth."

Trust Your Vibes, Sonia Choquette

Penny, and love:

I've been thinking a lot about the love-that-turns-to-hate. Did you ever watch elderly, long-time married couples in a restaurant? Actually, some aren't so elderly, just married too long. I'm a curious person, a people-watcher, and I've seen many couples sit together in public with nothing to say to each other, not even communicating silently, telepathically. It's just that they were no longer interested in each other. Is it because they've said it all, with nothing new left to talk about? Since our cells are renewing every few seconds we humans must have the capacity to change ourselves many times over. And, if we do, we are sharing these changes with those closest to us. I don't think it's a matter of having nothing to say or having said it all. I think it's a matter of having too much they want to say, yet leave un-said. Maybe too much anger is between them; too much of their living is in the past.

Since women are usually more in tune with relationships than men are I'd venture to say it's mostly women who haven't said what's on their minds. And, of course, the men who don't want to hear it.

It's all so perfect: Those of us who truly want to learn the lessons we came here to Earth to learn actually do learn them. But I guess what they say is true: At first we get a whisper of truth in the ears and, if we don't heed that warning, the baseball bat comes out. I was so stubborn I sometimes got hit by a freight train! That should give you a clue as to how dense I was. Advanced lack of awareness, I call it. I guess the Universe has to get out the big guns for those of us who are really stuck in the trappings of the ego world, throwing us into a situation so adversarial that we have no choice but to look at ourselves.

We make choices every day, during each encounter with another person or situation, choosing an action any time our conscience emerges and says no, you don't want to do that. Or maybe it keeps quiet and allows us to make that mistake, which may not be a mistake, after all, just part of our need to learn the lesson. I've realized the trick is to live in the present moment — not always so easy — as this is truly all we have. The past is in the past, and the future has yet to arrive. The present is where our conscience resides.

Living in the future is like saying, "Okay, when he stops being mean to me I'll be happy." Excuse me! Maybe when we stop allowing him to be mean — and sometimes that means we have to leave him (or her) and allow that person to wallow in his own meanness — we'll develop personal integrity. We'll develop a strength within that says "don't mess with me," yet conveys the meaning without anger. That's where our strength is: seeing the truth without being angered by it. Discerning rather than judging.

I was married to a man who didn't really care to know who I was, or whether or not I was happy, as long as his needs were met. How could I expect him or my kids to respect me if I didn't truly love and respect myself?

But I have learned my lessons well. It's a choice I have made. Actually, the power to choose is probably our greatest gift from the Universe.

Having lived the life of an angry woman for many years I can say that often a person who's filled with anger is just looking — not consciously, of course, as a conscious person isn't angry — for someone to be angry at. A target makes her feel powerful; she can get energy from the victim.

It's something to think abou; a challenge for sure. If I can change, anyone can change. I am no different from anyone else. No smarter. And no dumber.

Chapter Eight

"At what time do the vortexes open?"

A question asked at the Sedona, Arizona Welcome Center

Penny, and feminine energy:

"Hell hath no fury like a woman scorned." I used to think of that phrase as women being vengeful and filled with anger. Some women are. But lately I have come to a wiser conclusion, a deeper understanding of the angry woman.

Women become angry when we're not understood. We need to talk things out; that's how we arrive at a conclusion, a knowing of the truth of something. And when our man talks to us he is showing we are loved. But, when he doesn't... well, you know the rest. Of course, most men talk to us when they are courting us; after all, they want us to fall in love and know that if they tell us about their past, what they want, and how they feel they pretty much have us, don't they? After the hunt is finished and the guy has "bagged his quarry" the challenge is over.

Women also put on their phony faces for seduction. And maybe later on they run around in their bathrobes all day. Or find other weak men to seduce.

"You know, Penny," Edie said one day when I was visiting her in Florida, "when Peter and I were splitting up, yet talking about getting back together, I told him it's easy to get someone to fall in love with you; the trick is to stay in love once the bloom has worn off. The trick is to keep the woman once the 'warrior has shot the deer,' and is tempted to just lie on the couch. The trick is to keep the bloom and this "bloom" is all about communication. When a woman is talked to she feels loved; when she feels loved she glows and radiates feminine energy and the guy basks in it. He stops talking 'cuz he already has her. She stops shining and becomes demanding and the guy is wondering what the hell happened."

I often think about that conversation with Edie. One reason the movie, "Something's Gotta Give," is popular is because Jack Nicholson's character "gets" the woman played by Diane Keaton. She marvels that he's the first one to ever get her. She's finally understood by someone. Her feminine energy is allowed to just BE, probably because the male character's masculine energy is so present, so "in the moment." She's not put into a tiny box, made into his fantasy (at least not right now) of the "perfect woman." You know the rest: Diane Keaton's lady falls in love with Jack Nicholson's guy. Of course.

I was moody and filled with a huge amount of passion and energy as a child. When I'd get upset I'd sometimes go to my room and slam the door, almost always wanting one of my parents or siblings to knock on the door and try to talk to me. To persist in their understanding of me, to not abandon me, leaving me with this anger I didn't understand. Instead their attitude was "she'll get over it." My parents missed many opportunities to teach me lessons; I missed the same with my own kids.

The truth is I didn't get over it. I carried that sense of abandonment, of not being loved, into two marriages. Of course, I chose two husbands who had no clue of the beauty of the passions of a wild woman; in bed they seemed to appreciate the lust while not understanding the woman. Hell, I didn't "get" myself; how could they?

David Deida writes in *Intimate Communion* that a woman is able to fully surrender her passions to her partner only when she trusts his masculine energy more than she trusts her own masculine energy.

Now, I am very aware of my own energy, both feminine and masculine. And I clearly see that a woman filled with rage is not a very feminine one. She may wear make-up, dye her hair, and don the latest fashions in plastic surgery and clothing, but that doesn't mean she exudes a lovely, feminine energy.

A woman filled with rage becomes hardened inside to her own sexuality and, consequently, her partner's, which energetically pushes the man away from her. That lack of acceptance for the man and his penis can have major implications with the sexuality of both men and women. In being pushed outside of the woman during sex he becomes de-sensitized to her sexually and emotionally. I suspect this rejection of each other can be the basis for much of the sexual dysfunction we see in society, like premature ejaculation or lack of women's orgasms.

Soon after this conversation with Edie I went on one of my many trips, this time to the Southwest, wanting to check out Arizona and New Mexico and visit friends along the way. I was in a motel room in Arizona when I turned on the TV.

"Electric Orgasm"? What on Earth is this, I'm thinking, yet too fascinated to change the channel. I had detoured through Lake Havasu City on my way from Sedona, where I rented a room for two months in order to have a base for explorations. I was on my way to see a friend in Bakersfield, California, whom I'd met in Europe and had not seen for twenty years. I also wanted to walk across the London Bridge, the same one Joy and I had walked in 1960. Only then it was in London, England.

I was on one of my *Vision Quests*, and now in the line of my vision was a documentary filmed in England about three couples who are having trouble with the women's orgasms, or lack of them. At first, just looking at the title, I suspected it was a cooking show where we can learn the secrets of those yummy rich brownies called "Chocolate Orgasms" that we used to buy in Fanueil Hall in Boston. The best brownies ever; I swore they had marijuana in them like the ones hippies ate. *Well,* I'm thinking, *why shouldn't these couples with sex problems be from England, the country that gave us our Puritanical views on sex?*

I sat there, stunned, as this was not what I envisioned my *Vision Quest* to have in it. I'm thinking *I've seen everything* when the doctor surgically inserts electrodes into each of the women's spines! Excuse me, I need to vomit. I guess the woman can push a button on cue and get a shock that will cause her to "enjoy the moment." Wouldn't a class in sex education be less painful? Or a session with an Energy Healer?

As I watched the dynamics between the couples, I noticed the resentment two of the women had for their husbands. Did anyone else notice this? It seemed so obvious. Most women are aware, on some level at least, that most men feel responsible for their sex partner's orgasms. What if a woman feels powerless (and an angry woman does feel powerless; that's one reason she's angry), yet discovers she has power over her husband in this one area? Denying her partner the satisfaction of giving her an orgasm would give her pleasure, wouldn't it? Or at least make her feel powerful.

Maybe that's the key: Don't stay with your partner long after your body wants to leave.

As I watched TV I was thinking *I left my husband when the time was right, but I did feel stuck in neutral toward the end.* A few well-meaning friends (even my husband's own sister) pushed me to leave earlier, and they may have been right. Yet, it wasn't the right timing for me. So, who's to say when or IF we should leave? All I know is we need to own our power and stop giving it away to anger. There'd be more happy sex, don't you think? Maybe even a lower crime rate.

Chapter Nine

"I have learned not to judge others (or myself). After all, I could be wrong."

Penny:

When Kevin called me it was decided that he would meet us at the lake cottage and drive Peggy to the airport in Manchester to catch her late afternoon flight to Seattle.

Now, don't tell the hard-core feminists, but I was glad to have Kevin take over and do the airport thing; his goal-oriented, masculine energy was comforting to me. Sometimes this world can be a tiresome place for a woman alone.

I was able to give Kevin pretty good directions, as the cottage was owned by friends from high school. The original cottage was the summer home for their family and had been the setting for many class picnics the day after the big bash on Saturday night. Plus, I knew Kevin had the street smarts to find his way to any place. He didn't get lost, and arrived on time.

After Peggy left on her flight Kevin and I ate an early dinner at one of my favorite restaurants, "C.R. Sparks." He declined the wine offered by the waitress; he even ate all his salad and veggies. *Here's a guy who eats healthy. That is sexy.*

"Kevin, in answer to your question, I also do not drink wine or alcohol. Want to hear a true story?" I asked.

"Of course, I do," he replied with enthusiasm.

"A few years ago I took my grandson, Billy, with me to Mexico for part of the summer. He was ten at the time. The first night we ate at one of my favorite places, "El Pegasso," and I ordered a Corona to go with my spicy food, enchiladas, I think.

'Nanny, you don't drink,' he said, questioning my order.

'Well,' I replied, 'I am having hot food and just want to cool off my mouth.' He just looked at me and shrugged. I drank less than one-third of a bottle of beer. The next day I had a headache, one that wouldn't quit all day.

Billy looked at me, shaking his head, saying, 'Nanny, you don't drink.' Kevin is chuckling at this point. "Go on," he urged.

I continued, "We had a great three-week visit, and at the end of it I was celebrating buying land to build my new house. We went to 'El Pegasso' for steak. I had the filet mignon — less than ten-dollars, by the way — and ordered a glass of red wine.

'Nanny, you don't drink,' Billy reminded me.

'Well,' I said, 'I thought I would celebrate buying the land; red wine goes well with steak, don't you think?' Of course, Billy shrugged again, being a non-judgmental ten-year-old.

"For TWO days I was sicker than a dog, liver congestion, sinus headache, nausea, all-over awful feeling. Billy looked at me the second day and said, 'Nanny, I TOLD you, you DON'T drink!'"

"Out of the mouths of babes," Kevin said, roaring with laughter at the finality of Billy's words. I was thinking, while watching this man whose eyes twinkle: *Oh, wow! I have a thing for happy eyes.*

We left the restaurant fairly early — maybe 7 p.m. — and there was the usual long waiting line, which we had avoided by eating early. I'm lost in my thoughts: *I'm not crazy about waiting lines; what I make at home is better than a restaurant can offer, anyway.*

Kevin interrupted my thoughts. "You don't like waiting lines, do you? Me neither." I just looked at him in amazement, feeling the beginning of an understanding between us. Maybe this guy actually gets me.

It just popped out: "Kevin, would you let me cook for you tomorrow night? It's my last night at the lake cottage," I said. It turns out he'd love to and he'll bring dessert, if I don't mind. Mind? I love a man who cooks!

The August evening was getting chilly, something New Hampshire does really well. Kevin helped me with my jacket. His hand brushed my face and a chill ran through my body. I turned to look at him and I could almost hear his mouth saying, "Not tonight; I'll refrain from kissing you tonight."

Okay, I'll wait.

Chapter Ten

"If a problem has a solution, then what is there to worry about? If a problem does NOT have a solution, then all the worrying in the world won't solve it. So, why worry?"

The Dalai Lama

Penny:

The next day I knew I had to make a quick trip to Farmington to find Hallie Scruton; my intuition was telling me she'd be an invaluable source of information.

I knew Hallie lived on Meaderboro Road because Mr. Nutter had talked about her being neighbors and friends with Professor Meader and his wife. My mother had also been friends with them, often visiting their farm, taking me with her. Walking around the experimental plots as Dr. Meader explained his life's work was a treat for both Mom and me. We all shared a love of horticulture and nature. My mother was raising a pair of his Reliance peach trees, which were ready to bear fruit around the time of her death, when my parents' farm had already been sold.

After two stops to ask directions in the area of Professor Meader's home, I found Hallie's house. He had passed away years before, not long after Mom died, so I know they're growing flowers and veggies together in Heaven. I softly knocked a few times and was getting ready to knock louder when I heard the scrape of a chair inside.

"Yes, what is it?" she called out.

"Hello, my name is Penny Hall and Mr. Harry Nutter told me you're the town historian," I replied.

Hallie opened the door and said, "Please come in, dear. You have an honest face." Of course, my sense of humor, which has to stay hidden at this time for obvious reasons, was begging to come out to ask if Ma

Barker ever looked honest. She and her son, what's-his-name, had to look somewhat honest at one time in order to lure people in and do all that bad stuff on their killing spree many years ago. I stifled the devilish little humor bug in me for the moment, as even I knew the inappropriateness of that question.

"Mrs. Scruton," I began...."

"Call me Hallie, dear; what's your name again?" she asked.

"Penny Hall," I answered.

"Hallie, Mr. Nutter said you might remember Ellie Lavoie," I continued.

"Well, of course, I do. Poor thing lost her husband, then she re-married and he died last year — or was it the summer before then? Oh well, she's still living in the old family homestead right up the road a piece. She has a son nearby. I believe the younger one is out west."

"She's still alive?" I was surprised. I guess I kept in my mind not to get my hopes up, that she was dead; by now I was almost in shock, wondering, *Okay, Penny, now what?*

Ellie has two sons, apparently no daughter besides Betsy. That explains the genealogy confusion: both brothers named their sons Kevin. I wonder if Lester ever knew of his nephew's existence when he named his last son Kevin. Maybe he didn't. He certainly never told his kids of Parker's existence, which goes beyond the word "private" for me, but it is how some people operate.

Hallie and I spoke a little longer about town history, about my mother — a "lovely lady," to use Hallie's words — who gave away and sold organic lamb and chickens, along with vegetables from my parents' farm. Their quality foods certainly helped me develop discerning taste buds. With fresh corn, for instance, we used to put the water on to boil, run to the garden, pick corn, husking it into the compost along the way back to the kitchen, then plunge the corn into the boiling water for only a few minutes before eating it; didn't even need butter or salt.

After Hallie gave me directions to Ellie's house it was time to say goodbye.

"It was a pleasure to meet you; you're a kind lady. Thank you very much for your help; I appreciate it," I said to Hallie as I left.

"Come again, dear. And good luck in your search," was Hallie's goodbye wish for me.

Well, now I'm running low on time; got a hot date with Kevin tonight. But, I'm going to see Ellie before it's too late.

Chapter Eleven

"Consciousness is the ability to release the old and embrace the new with the awareness that all things end at the appropriate time and that all things begin at the appropriate time."

Anatomy of the Spirit, Caroline Myss

Penny:

As I drove up the driveway of the modest home where Ellie lived as a child and now is living out her "golden years," I couldn't help feeling like my cousin, Betsy, would feel in this situation: overwhelmed and excited. Ellie is alive! I guess I didn't expect to find her alive; I'm not sure I even expected to find her at all. I thought it was possibly too late. I have no clue what Betsy will do with the information I'll give her, but that is no longer an issue with me. Peggy was sort of right: this was Betsy's quest; only part of it was mine.

I softly knocked on the door. No answer. I heard a noise in the yard and turned to see a lady with flowers in a basket hanging on her arm. Her curly hair was now gray rather than almost-black, but it was definitely Ellie coming toward me. *Oh my gosh, it's really Ellie.*

"May I help you, dear?" she asked, as she stopped near me before moving toward the door to open it.

"I'm looking for Ellen Lavoie Hill Lovell; my name is Penny Hall," I said.

"Hall?" she asked.

"Yes, Hall," I replied.

She said softly, taking a quick breath, "Please come inside so we can talk."

We talked at length; she reminisced about Hayward. She asked me about Betsy, so I started from the beginning, telling what I remembered from family reunions and Christmas gatherings, little impressions of the kind of girl Betsy grew into being. I was surprised at how open she was, easily discussing an event in her life that must have been painful to remember. It was as if she just had to tell someone who she was; she wanted me to know the truth about her life. Keeping secrets close to one's heart must make a person want to talk, eventually spilling all.

The truth is on that bright, almost-autumn Friday afternoon my heart became filled with compassion and love for this gentle lady. She could have become bitter by the hand that the Universe dealt her; after all, she was a victim at one time, wasn't she? Giving up her only daughter for another woman to raise could have ruined her life; instead, she has become as gentle a woman as I have ever met. Extraordinary lady.

She wanted to talk and I wanted to listen. I also wanted to tell her story.

I realize now that my gift to Ellie was Betsy, similar to the gift she gave to Hayward and Catherine. I re-created her daughter from start to the present time, leaving out anything negative; she didn't need to hear about sad parts of the life her long-lost child had endured. Now, I understand why I had to do this.

Before I left Ellie's home she gave me her phone number and asked me to call Sunday so I could speak with Kevin. Kevin, the three-year-old boy, who loved to hug the knees of the tall man he knew as "Uncle Hayward;" Kevin, the boy who became a young man wondering what happened to Hayward and then being denied recognition when he saw him years later. Kevin, Betsy's big brother.

Many months later, after Ellie moved to a nursing home, Kevin found letters addressed to Betsy, along with some for him. She wrote about her love for Hayward, saying she had no choice but to give Betsy to him, as the child deserved a better life than Ellie could provide. She wanted her daughter to have two parents, a good home, the education Ellie never had. Ellie gave up Betsy because she loved her, not because she didn't care. These letters also showed that the deep love between Hayward and Ellie never stopped, even though she had found love again with another husband and son. Ellie wrote about her hopes and dreams, revealing who she became as an adult apart from being their mother. These adult "children" found out who their mother was as an adult, now knowing they no longer needed her to be their parent.

This was a gift Ellie left for her children. A gift of unconditional love.

Chapter Twelve

"The relationship you have with yourself is reflected in your relationships with others."

The Four Agreements, Don Miguel Ruiz

Penny:

I pulled into the convenience store parking lot a few minutes after leaving Ellie's house in order to call Kevin to let him know I'd be late. He was already at my lake cottage, having arrived early, enjoying the scenery from the rocking chair on the porch. I could hear his smile when he said he knew I hadn't forgotten our date. I apologized and told him I still had to buy an organic chicken to roast. He detected in my voice a need to talk about Ellie, so he said, "Penny, we can find something here for supper; no need to take longer if you don't want to. Don't stop at the store on my account; we can talk when you arrive and eat later."

Oh God, I'm thinking, *I love a man who wants to talk to me — and listen, of course.*

When I arrived forty minutes later I saw that Kevin had found some pumpernickel bread and spread goat cheese on top, adding thin slices of tomato and black olives, all items I usually have in my kitchen. They were just coming out of the oven and the smell was making me hungrier than I'd been in a long time.

Meanwhile, Kevin was assembling the salad; I reached over, put my arm around him and kissed his cheek. He was pleased. "Thank you, Kevin," I said. "This is really kind of you."

"We have to eat, don't we?" he casually asked, but he was grinning from ear to ear.

We talked and ate and talked some more. Our impromptu supper was yummy, made even better by our team effort. He was as excited to hear about Ellie, Hallie and his cousin Kevin as I was to tell him. He asked about my travels; I told him about my house in San Miguel de Allende, about trips I want to take to South America and Turkey, how I miss New England and may move back if I can find affordable land, but I can't stand the winters. He told me he wants to return to Vietnam as a tourist — I want to go there, too. We agreed he could be my tour guide as I don't want to go alone. I invited him to visit my home in Mexico.

Conversation flowed between us, something I had missed while being married to David. His power plays had made me wonder if it is possible for a man and a woman to speak, to be together, without seeking control over the other. Talking with Kevin made me know for certain there are men who can be equals with their women. No power plays, no trying to control the woman. Such joy!

"Wow! Look at the time," I exclaimed at two in the morning. No wonder I was beginning to wilt. "Would you like to sleep on the couch, rather than try to drive home this late?" I asked.

He accepted my offer; we hugged, and went to our beds. By dawn the weather had turned really cold in this un-insulated summer cottage, something New Hampshire does well in August. So, I had a choice to make: look for extra socks and sweaters to put on, as I had given Kevin my extra blankets, OR go to the couch and see if he'd move over and make room for me. And keep me warm.

The only thing I'll say about that is this: it had been a long time since a man had held me and kissed me. It was definitely worth waiting for.

Oh, I almost forgot — Kevin brought dessert. He looked for watermelon but it was out of season. He also loved to spit out seeds in the sand, trying to go as far as possible. But he did buy organic grapes, which he washed and served for breakfast the next morning. Actually, it was the same morning, but who cares? Kevin said he didn't know grapes could taste so good.

I do love a man who can cook.

Chapter Thirteen

"Fear creates a dark reality . . . every prophecy is self-fulfilling."

Alberto Villoldo

Penny:

When Sunday arrived I was impatiently waiting until it was late enough in the morning to call Cousin Kevin at his mother's home. I'm such an early riser I have to watch the clock, remembering the time I called Peggy at 6 a.m. from my new home in Kentucky — problem is she lived in Washington State which is two hours earlier than Kentucky, not two hours later, as I had thought. She was not amused; I don't know why.

"Hello Kevin, this is Penny Hall. Ellie told me I could talk with you today," was the slightly awkward way I opened the conversation. I didn't really know how receptive he would be, but I needn't have worried.

"Oh hi, Penny, Mom did say she enjoyed talking with you Friday," he replied. "And that you might call."

We talked about Hayward and Kevin said how much he cared about him and that he wished they could have spoken honestly that evening at Sparhawk Hall. I told him all about Betsy — his mother had told him of her existence after Ellie's husband, Thomas, died the year before, but there were blanks for me to fill in. He said how eager he is to meet his sister, but agreed to my sending her his information after I told him how private she is. He said he can be patient and wait for her to come to him. He's retired and loves to putter around the farm, fixing things; goes fishing a lot. He has a small homestead with a stocked pond near his mother's home. We talked about his brother, Eddie. We also spoke of Thomas, the man both boys called Dad. It sounded to me as though Ellie did a good job raising them. My Kevin had asked me to give his new-found Cousin Kevin his cell phone number, hoping he was open to a meeting. I knew they'd hit it off and want to make up for lost time. Even though Ellie had shared what she knew of Parker, Kevin's father was still a bit of a mystery to him so he was eager to meet others in the family who knew more about Lester and his long-dead brother, Parker.

My job is done. I told Kevin I'd call him back in a couple weeks to see how things were going, although I have no doubt my Kevin and I would be in close communication with one another from now on.

I did follow up with a couple calls to Ellie's home in the next few weeks but no one answered. My Kevin had met with his Cousin Kevin by then and called one day to say Ellie was in the hospital with pneumonia. No one seemed to know if she'd be going home or to a nursing home after she got well. She was becoming a little frail and her sons were concerned about her ability to live alone now.

Yes, I did send Betsy a letter telling her much of what I knew about Ellie and Kevin, along with his phone number and address. Of course, she never acknowledged receiving it.

❦

"My dearest baby girl"… the letter began. My Kevin's cousin, the other Kevin, found it in his mother's chest of drawers after she was admitted to the nursing home. She would never return home.

"My dearest baby girl, I want you to know I have always loved you, that I gave you up for adoption so you could have two parents to love you and give you an education. If I'd had schooling to help me support myself I would never have given you away. It breaks my heart to this day, many years later, to have to say that. Not a day goes by that I don't think of you; I pray every day that you are loved by your father's wife. I know Hayward loves you very much, just as he loved me. I understand why he couldn't find the courage to leave Catherine; it just wasn't done in those days, in his circle of friends," Ellie wrote in 1985.

Ellie wrote many letters to her "baby girl," always referring to Betsy that way. Her last known letter was written five years before she left home to live out her last days in a nursing home.

"Baby girl, I held you in my arms when you were minutes old and you looked up at me with eyes so big I know they were filled with wisdom, even then. I checked your little body, unwrapped for a minute while I marveled at how beautiful and healthy you were. The time I was allowed to hold you was too brief; the nurse came to take you away as you nuzzled at my breast. She had to pry my fingers off your blankets. Don't let anyone convince you that it is impossible to die of a broken heart; a part of me died that day as I cried and softly protested: 'No, no, don't take my baby girl!' Even in my darkest hour I wanted to do the proper thing and try not to disturb others in the hospital ward," Ellie wrote.

"I don't know if you will ever read this letter or the others I have written to you, but I wrote a letter every year on your birthday, sharing my thoughts, my love, my life, with you. I am hoping that somehow — just somehow — you know who I am and how much your father and I loved you. He was so lucky to have watched you grow — he told me this many years after taking you home to raise. Baby girl, I did see you that foggy morning on the Marginal Way in Ogunquit. I'd have known you anywhere. Did you know it was me, that lady you smiled at as we walked past each other? It was also the last time I ever saw your father; he didn't have to tell me he was very ill. I knew then that I would never see him again. But, I will see him when I enter the gates of Heaven. I know I will. Oh, how I wish I could see you one more time and say how loved you are. Please forgive me for giving you up. I had no choice. I wish I'd had another option. Your Mother, Ellie."

Chapter Fourteen

"We are not held back by the love we didn't receive in the past but by the love we're not extending in the present."

Marianne Williamson

Betsy:

The call came on a Thursday morning: "Hi, Betsy, this is David Stevens, your investigator. I've got news for you — are you sitting down?" he asked.

My heart skipped a beat, maybe three. I quickly found a seat and plunked myself down, afraid of what I would soon hear. "Okay, David, I'm sitting," I quickly replied.

"Your mother, Ellie, is in a nursing home with pneumonia and is not responding to treatment. The doctors say she may not have long to live," he continued. "She's eighty-three years old now and suffers from Dementia, but was living on her own until a few months ago. She is failing fast."

A sense of urgency filled my being. "David, please give me the name and address of the nursing home. Can I just go there unannounced?" I asked.

"She's in a private room; just tell them you're her daughter. And good luck," he said as we hung up after I wrote down the information he gave me.

I've wanted this moment to happen for sixty years, but now that it's here I am terrified I can't handle it. Even as a small child I remember thinking, *I'll fix Mother, I'll find my real mother and she'll love me more than this mother does.* What if that same anger shows up again?

Betsy, I told myself, *you're a grown-up. Just go there. Try to call Larry, but he's probably out in the field, not in the office at this hour. Come on,*

Betsy, you can handle it alone; just go! Leave a note for Larry. Do it before it's too late. I urged myself to act quickly on this news. My mother's alive, but maybe not for long.

I don't remember driving to the nursing home in Dover, New Hampshire, but it was almost three hours from my home in Vermont so my mind had to have been swirling the whole time: *Will she know me after all these years? Is she conscious? How old was I in the last photograph she saw?* "Oh, God, please give me the strength I need today." The last one I said out loud to the Universe.

What I do remember is what happened after they showed me to her room because it's burned into my brain and into my heart: Ellie was in a hospital bed, an oxygen mask covering her mouth and nose; her eyes closed. She looked small and fragile. A nurse was nearby, monitoring her vital signs; she indicated that I may touch Ellie. My mother. I was finally touching my mother! Tears rolled down my face as I held her hand, speaking softly: "Mother, it's Betsy, your daughter."

I could say I'll never know if she heard me or recognized my voice, but that wouldn't be the truth. What she did next proved, to me at least, that she knew me: she slightly squeezed my hand. *She knows me, I am sure of it!* I rejoiced silently.

I stood there a few minutes before noticing that, in the curve of her left arm, on the other side of the bed, was a baby doll, wrapped tightly in a receiving blanket, swaddled as they do with newborns. She never forgot me.

Bless the nurses for being so understanding of what Ellie needs. I need it, too.

I whispered, as I bent forward to kiss her forehead, "I love you, Mom. I will never forget you."

Chapter Fifteen

"When love beckons to you, follow him Though his ways are hard and steep."

The Prophet, Kahlil Gibran

Betsy:

After that day in the nursing home I was filled with a sense of peace, a calmness I'd never felt before. I brought out old photos and letters, souvenirs of my life, things that reminded me of my father and Catherine — my other mother, the woman who raised me as her daughter. I put a lot of ghosts to rest.

Larry took me there to visit her one more time, but she was so frail and far gone that I felt I needed to say goodbye to her that day.

One morning soon after this final visit the nursing home called to say she had passed away. My mother had died. I cried for Ellie, for my father, for Catherine, and I guess I even cried for myself. Only then was I able to look at the information both Penny and the investigator had sent me about Kevin.

The next day I decided to go for a drive, back to New Hampshire — this time Farmington. I wanted to see my brother alone; I needed to do this. Larry was working, as I had asked him not to go with me, but he was there with me in spirit, giving me strength. I drove up the driveway to my brother's home. My brother! I can't believe I have a brother.

I knocked on the door. Kevin opened the door, smiled, and said, "Hi, Sis, what took you so long?"

Chapter Sixteen

"He who knows he has enough is rich."

Tao Te Ching

Penny, and ayahuasca:

I flew home from New Hampshire on a Tuesday and kept busy getting ready for the trip to Mexico, as I had just one week to take care of business in Tennessee. The builder I chose had such a good reputation that I just put it all in his hands. He said he'd be breaking ground on my new 1500 square-foot Ranch-style home while I was gone, but not to worry. I had seen many examples of the quality he built so I concentrated on choosing the upgrades I wanted: oak floors, ceramic tiles, and an unusual bathroom vanity. The lights I chose were different and more expensive than what he usually installs. I was getting excited by the possibility of having just what I want, choosing fourteen colors in all for the interior. The house had cathedral ceilings, an open space right off the dining room, and there were French doors going to a lovely, wooden deck, overlooking my land, in itself a treat.

To fight boredom in my beige apartment I had bought an eggplant-purple, suede sofa, a really striking piece of furniture, with a loveseat to go with it, the upholstery a deep gold brocade with small terracotta and purple-colored flowers. That, along with oriental rugs I'd inherited from my grandmother, and a couple special lamps, made the apartment more comfortable, yet still not a place I wanted to be. I knew the furniture I had chosen would be spectacular in my new home.

A week later I flew to Mexico City. It was so good to be back where I felt very much at home. Mexico was no more a "foreign country" to me than Tennessee or New Hampshire. Even though my Spanish wasn't all that great, the language spoke to me, and my ears loved hearing it. Of course, I practiced my language skills on every unsuspecting Mexican I encountered — taxi drivers, hotel clerks, people serving meals in restaurants.

The bus ride to Puerto Vallarta was long, maybe six or seven hours, going to Guadalajara first. The scenery was okay, but not fascinating. Toll roads are pretty much the same all over the world. A good time to sleep and think, which made me remember the first time I'd come to Mexico. I was on an overnight bus from Laredo, Texas, heading toward Monterrey in the late afternoon, with a raging rainstorm outside. The windows were getting all fogged up. A small girl, maybe eight-years old, was using her fingers to make designs on the window near her seat. For some reason, I was fascinated. I guess it's because I see so many kids in the U.S. picking up their handheld electronic devices whenever a split second of boredom hits them. This child, who may never earn as much in a year as the average American kid, doesn't have the distractions of "toys," and therefore uses her own resources, her imagination. That gives me concern for the American child, who is closing many windows of learning opportunity.

I'm usually the only non-Mexican on buses in and out of Mexico. That gives me a chance to see Mexican culture, or part of it, close-up: mothers holding plastic bags filled with tamales, ham sandwiches, tortillas and beans, whatever they have at home to eat along the way. Coca Cola is the most popular drink. The Mexicans drink more coke per capita than any other nation, which I find appalling. I'm alarmed at the flabbiness of teenagers, many of whom have "spare tires," even before they've had children. Diabetes is on the upswing there, as are all major illnesses. Oh well, I can't change others, only myself.

One trip I made, I think it was from San Miguel de Allende to Chiapas, was a very steep mountainous ride. We were going uphill, around a curve, at night of course, and the driver tried to pass a truck, believe it or not. Another bus was coming right at us. I looked around and saw I was the only one concerned. I looked at the Virgin Guadalupe, the sacred mother of Mexico, hanging from the driver's mirror, and said to myself, *oh well, Penny, these look like nice people to die with.* Of course, we didn't crash, but now I sit about six rows back, no more front seats, and I try to sit on the same side as the driver; I know if there is a correction to save a life it will be made to protect the side the driver is on.

Back to Puerto Vallarta: There I was, on an early bus in order to spend a couple days in Puerto Vallarta, a place I'd heard so much about. I sure don't know what the attraction is; the timeshare sales people/vultures almost ruin a person's walk down the street. I don't like the place, but I do get to go "canopy-jumping." First, I pray. Second, I get a harness on, to which a zip line is attached. I pray again before sailing on a cable across the jungle, looking down at the river a few hundred feet below. I am flying through the air going to the next platform from which to launch myself (there are fourteen platforms in all). It is a good thing to scream; people will think you're having fun. Just kidding. I told friends you just have to be a writer so that if you actually survive a fall it will make one hell of a good story.

Early the next morning I left Puerto Vallarta by bus, arriving forty minutes later in Sayulita, a surfing town with good restaurants right at water's edge, and a laid-back atmosphere. I was ready to find the small resort which was to be my home for the next week, knowing I would have my own little straw *palapa*, without doors or windows, just an open space for any critter who decides to walk in to do so. We were meeting that day and starting activities the following morning.

It was a bright, uplifting morning in the jungle near Sayulita where we gathered for a meeting before going to the first ceremony. In the dining room of the retreat right on the Pacific Ocean, waves crashing below, the shaman poses this to us: "Picture yourself part of a group that falls overboard with only one life raft and room for half the people who were onboard the wrecked ship. Tell us why you should be one of those saved." As I'm listening to each person say all the good things he has done in his life I am wondering why we ALL can't be saved. When my turn came I said just that and here is my solution: "The stronger ones link arms with the weaker ones and form a circle in the water, other weaker ones being in the raft, and we all are rescued because we are looking out for each other." The shaman just nodded when he heard the translation from English into Spanish from the group leader. It didn't matter to me that he didn't say anything; I wasn't looking for his approval.

A few minutes later, the shaman, Don Augustus, was walking behind me on the narrow path to the straw-roofed ceremonial house; he put his hand on my shoulder. I energetically covered his hand with mine; not physically, just telepathically. We understood each other. I felt encouraged to continue my journey. During the first ceremony — they each lasted about 6 hours before we were "awake" enough to go back to our huts — I began singing the ancient chants I heard coming from Don Augustus. Somehow I knew the words. I felt someone's eyes on me and opened mine to see the shaman laughing and looking at me. He was so filled with joy it was infectious. I got a soft giggle going inside.

The taste of the potion was a cross between mud and molasses, barely potable yet quite powerful. It took about one hour for me to feel the "vine" crawling through my body, going sometimes where I asked it to and sometimes where it knew I needed help. Each ceremony — we had one every other day — produced some vomiting with the men, and some crying, mostly women. At one point a member of the group was having trouble being calm and the shaman walked over to him, chanting to invoke the aid of his helpers, the spirits. I soon realized I was also helping, giving healing energy to him. I looked around and saw a couple others doing the same.

Someone asked me later how it felt to be taking what "everyone knows" is a hallucinogenic. I replied that I'm not so sure it is one; I see ayahuasca as a spirit-helper that opens us up in order to see what is inside. Nothing comes up to be looked at that isn't there. I also realized I have no need to repeat the experience.

The next day was Sunday; I walked to town with others in the group, but kept feeling someone "unknown" was with me. That night, as I lay in the half-asleep, half-twilight state before full sleep, I saw the love of my life, a shaman, on top of a mountain in what looked like Peru, and he said to me that we would soon be together, to keep the faith. I cried and whispered how much I missed him. I got the message that he and I had been married in a previous life and we allowed the ego to interfere with our ability to help others, thinking we were better than "our subjects." We had to find out the hard way in subsequent lives just how ONE we all really are, that he and I were no better than anyone else. Arrogance certainly doesn't belong in the healing world.

It was on this *Vision Quest* that I allowed the Goddess to come into my heart. Tuesday, the day after the second ceremony, some of us went into Sayulita to shop and eat a light lunch, knowing we needed to stay on a pretty strict diet with no alcohol, meat, or dairy. As we passed a gift shop I noticed a beautiful, young, blonde painting something near the door; it looked like an abstract. She obviously painted by inspiration. There was a statue of Buddha in the window, which drew me inside.

"Go ahead, guys, I'll meet you at the restaurant," I said to my new friends so I could spend time in this fascinating place. I walked to the center of the store, heading toward the desk where a man was seated. He said, "Hi, I'm Jeffrey," and I introduced myself. Out of "nowhere" came a golden beam through the window at the top of the ceiling, a clerestory of sorts, bathing us with light. I couldn't tell you what either of us said, just small talk, but the feelings were like I had never before known. I knew, even at the time, that the last of my angry, non-feminine energy was gone, leaving room for the Goddess. She came into me right then and there. I moved with a poise and calmness I had never experienced.

"Wait, how do I reach you?" he asked, as he ran after me when I said I had to leave, walking out the door. I just said I'd be back. Of course, when I went back a few days later he wasn't there. I also noticed the light coming down from the window on the roof wasn't anything special, just a tiny bit of light.

It wasn't my imagination that there was a "presence" the day I met Jeffrey. She, the Goddess of feminine energy, has never left me, even a few years later.

The first night in my *palapa*, having put everything of value (including passport and credit card) under my pillow because of "little thieves" called coatamundis who take what they can to store in their jungle homes, never to be seen again by unsuspecting tourists, I heard two critters walking into my open *palapa*. Because we had no electricity the resort supplied us with many candles, one of which I was burning. That enabled me to see these guys, to whom I said in English, "Go away, this is my home now." After they left I realized the *palapa* had been built right in the middle of their path to other places. They never returned, possibly because I burned a candle all night long the remainder of my visit. Or maybe they understood English.

Chapter Seventeen

"Hello, if you are the same Robert Warner who used to know Penny Hall many years ago, please contact me. . . "

Penny, in Mexico:

We are on a boat that begins to speed up and Rob falls backward into the ocean after trying to find out why the engine is going so fast. I clearly remember this dream where he is yelling that we are caught on an anchor. Huh? Wouldn't that make us stop?

I'm back in San Miguel de Allende, feeling very peaceful, right with the world after spending a week with ayahuasca. There are a lot of subtle changes in me, yet I know it's too soon to totally realize just what's happening with me. One thing I know is that I'm still having dreams of Rob. Dreams are funny — a strange mix of fantasy and reality. This latest one is no exception.

Rob disappears from sight while I watch the water come through the boards in the floor. I'm terrified, not of drowning, but that I'll never see Rob again. How's that for an obsession? I just want to be with him. I yell for help before waking up, actually sweating even though it's chilly in the early morning hours in San Miguel de Allende, the high desert region of Mexico.

When I awoke from that dream, the latest of many, always about Rob, I cried for a long time, saying out loud, "it's so real." I was afraid to go back to sleep because I just knew the dream would continue. *Gosh, Penny, I'm thinking, it's only three o'clock; why don't you find something to do?*

Enough is enough, Penny! While drinking a few cups of tea that morning I decided to find Rob.

By 8:30 that morning I'm walking through Parque Juarez, then onto Calle Aldama toward "La Conexion," my mailbox — service place, marveling at how beautiful my adopted home really is. It never fails to take my breath away, no matter how many times I go there. I am getting sleepy while waiting for the place to open at 9 a.m. I'm not used to getting up at 3 a.m.

One of the benefits of having a mailbox at "La Conexion," besides daily mail delivery by truck from Laredo, Texas to San Miguel de Allende, is the free use of new computers and the Vonage phone for making free calls to the USA and Canada. I would come here each week to call Kevin and firm up plans for our visit together in January.

This morning the Internet search produced nothing — no Robert or Sandra Warner in the entire state of Maine. Heather hadn't heard from him in a few years so I knew it was possible he had moved. At any rate, there was no phone number listed.

Then I got a bright idea: The state of Maine must have a listing for each Geologist working for them. Bingo! Believe it or not, I found his e-mail address after a tedious search and was even able to read a paper Rob had written about soil contamination, recognizing a few words that he misspelled as being "so like him." He was always smart but not a spelling champion; not good with words or writing letters.

Here's the e-mail I sent to him: "Hello, if you are the same Robert Warner who used to know Penny Hall many years ago, please contact me by phone or e-mail. Thank you, Penny Hall." I added the information he'd need to reach me in Tennessee, as I was going back home after a trip to Peru and Ecuador.

I continued the finishing touches on my creative, cozy home, one I'd been building for more than two years. *Manana* is tomorrow in Mexico, but it also means later, often much later. That job kept me busy, choosing colors and painting the walls, meeting with the electrician to put up the colorful ceramic light fixtures made right in San Miguel, and buying things to make this place artistic. Hopefully it would be ready to move into during my next visit. I could finish my little home as I had the money to do so. I was staying in an apartment I'd rented right in "el centro."

"Penny, I've known you for over five years and you've never mentioned being married before; I thought David was your only husband. That's odd, don't you think?" my friend Jeanie asked me one day, when I told her about the dreams of Rob and our life together. These dreams were beginning to occur more frequently, sometimes every night, penetrating my memory bank, pulling me into the past.

"I'm sorry, Jeanie," I said, as I touched her hand. "I totally forgot Rob. I can't explain it. Maybe it's the only way I could have gone on with my life and been happy. He and I took different paths. For some reason he's coming back into my life now — at least in my dreams. It's helping me to face a lot of my own truth that I wasn't ready to see until now."

Some dreams were more disturbing than others. Yet, all of them showed me how careless we had been with the gift we were given many years before.

And that alone is enough to make me cry.

Chapter Eighteen

SEEKER: Thirst for wisdom and truth wherever they are. Shadow side of the Seeker: Inability to commit to a path once found.

Sacred Contracts, by Caroline Myss

Penny, in Machu Picchu:

"Oh, Hannah, what a glorious day for traveling to Quito," I babbled at 4 a.m., an ungodly hour for Hannah yet, being a morning person, it was the hour of golden opportunity for me. Hannah didn't say much, never does 'til about 10 a.m. after she's had a couple cups of coffee.

We were in Mexico City, having come here from San Miguel de Allende the day before and spent the night at Hotel Rioja, paying a whopping 250-pesos for two beds. That's less than US$25 in a major city for a spacious, clean room with TV and hot showers.

The 24-hour café across the street served us a hearty breakfast and we were off for the airport in a taxi we'd reserved the night before, knowing we can't count on taxis going by on the street at 4:30 a.m.

Hannah and I just looked at each other, giggling with excitement. It was a long-time dream of mine to go to Machu Picchu. I'd been in Peru when my parents took Heather and me to visit my brother in Chile the winter of 1967, just a few months before I was to meet Rob, the man who changed my life so drastically. Peter was in the Peace Corps, living for two years in the tiny village of Melipilla, one hour by direct bus from the capital city of Santiago. My parents had gone on to Machu Picchu but Heather and I had to return to New Hampshire, as I was the sole support of her and me, and needed to get back to earn money.

I swore that someday I'd get to Machu Picchu and Lake Titicaca, and that day came closer to being a reality when I said to Hannah a few months before, "Hey, want to go with me to Peru?"

We arrived in sticky, hot Panama with one hour to change planes. I thought back to the 1967 trip when we were on a ship going through the Panama Canal, with the other part of the "lock" at one point being so much higher than we were. I know Heather's eyes were as big as saucers; I'd bet mine were also. It was an unbelievable sight.

The plane arrived in Quito, Ecuador in the early afternoon. It took us awhile to locate a hotel, the first one listed in the guide book was permanently closed. The taxi driver finally found our second choice, "Grand Hotel," which was in its heyday sixty years ago, THE luxury hotel of Quito, where diplomats and celebrities stayed. The two sisters who inherited it from their parents may not have been able to replace the leaking roof or sagging beds, yet they exuded a show of graciousness and hospitality that will encourage me to stay there on my next visit. After all, I have yet to see the Galapagos Islands and need to return to Quito and take that trip someday.

But for now, let's see Quito. The first night we spent $2 each on two huge dishes of freshly-made Chinese food and quickly learned to share one dish.

I have to tell you, spending the U.S dollar in another country — and getting them as change — spooked me a bit at first. So, I asked a college-educated professional guy we met at the hotel this question: Has the conversion of their currency from "sucre" to U.S. dollar been good for Ecuador? He answered unequivocally yes, saying that at first older people, un-educated ones out in the countryside, were confused by the hundreds or thousands of *sucres* needed to buy U.S. dollars when the change began in the year 2000.

One day we decided to find the Equator, being in Ecuador. By taking many buses to find *El Mitad del Mundo* the trip took all day, even though it's less than twenty miles from Quito. That experience was definitely a highlight of the trip for me. Hannah and I took photos of each other with one foot in the continent of South America and the other in the continent of North America: we are truly in the "middle of the world."

We left Quito after three days, being tourists while getting adjusted to the altitude, having gone from 7000 feet in Mexico City to over 10,000 feet in Quito. Both of us were advocates of magnet therapy, so we bought tiny magnets embedded in adhesive and stuck one behind each ear on the mastoid bone and one at the top of the breastbone in order to increase the oxygen available to our bodies. We replaced them every five days with new ones and never had a problem with the altitude. However, once we got to the top of the "altiplano" in Peru on the way to Lake Titicaca by bus we were chewing coca leaves just like the natives, who have no difficulty with the high elevation, even over 14,000 feet. It's all what you're born to and live with, I guess.

We learned by the second day of taking five-hour long trips on buses with no toilets or pit stops that flying may be wiser. Dehydration is especially serious at these altitudes; it's made more difficult when one is over sixty years of age. Like most people I have to pee after drinking water.

The horribly tawdry, sticky port of Tumbes (the armpit of hell, I say) is where we decided to fly to Lima, Peru, normally a 30-36 hour trip by bus. The flight, which stopped in Cajamarca, took less than two hours. We never regretted spending the extra money.

Lima's big, an unpleasant city to us, but only one hour by air from Cuzco. We arrived in Cuzco late afternoon on a Wednesday, six days after leaving Quito to be sightseers. It was only ten days since we'd left San Miguel de Allende and gone to Mexico City for the first leg of the trip. We had seen a lot of Ecuador and were now going to see some of Peru.

Cuzco's a fascinating, high-Andes city, the place where most visitors to Peru are going to have problems with the lack of oxygen. Not everyone has a problem. The tourists were mostly Europeans who've flown sixteen, maybe twenty hours and are, understandably, jetlagged. They go out for a heavy meal; of course, they're really hungry! Have you eaten airplane "food" lately? They drink alcohol, which is a dehydrator of the body to begin with, celebrating the start of their vacation, probably staggering to bed in the wee hours of the morning — if they make it that far.

Rules for avoiding hospitalization in high altitudes, number one through four, have just been broken: 1) Rest the first day 2) eat lightly, especially after 2 p.m. 3) NO alcohol 4) drink extra water, lots of it — 2-3 liters the first twenty-four hours. Fortunately, there are coca leaves for sale legally on every corner in Cuzco, as they are un-related to processed cocaine. Most hotels and restaurants have oxygen available — the owners know how unruly tourists can be.

"What hotel are you folks staying at?" Hannah asked in her native language, German. We had met a couple in a café in the village of Ollantaytambo, where we came by taxi directly from the Cuzco airport in order to get acclimated in the lower elevation of the Sacred Valley. The lady's a nurse and the husband's a lawyer, both from Switzerland, where they routinely hike in mountains over 7000 feet in elevation. Should be used to altitude problems, right?

"We're staying at the hospital, where they brought us by ambulance our first night in Peru two days ago," the wife said. Her husband collapsed in the street in Cuzco and the doctor sent them to recuperate in Ollantaytambo, a quaint, authentic Peruvian village; also the starting point for the train trip to Machu Picchu. This is why Hannah and I were there, along with most other visitors. After a delicious meal, including the ever-present quinoa soup, we left them to continue his recuperation, probably a couple days longer, and headed for the train which leaves a few times each day, this one being a one o'clock departure.

It has gotten expensive to visit this place, now designated a World Heritage site. The government knows a captive audience when it sees one and it now costs more than 400 *soles* (equivalent to $140 U.S.) for each person to visit Machu Picchu. One could opt to take a bus all over, up and down and around if they didn't want the convenience of an eighty-minute train ride along the river, in the mountains, with great scenery. Our simple hotel in Aguascalientes, the village nearest Machu Picchu, was only $7 for two beds and cold showers, right next to the train station, which did have a few trains coming into and out of the place all night.

Needless to say, it was easy to wake up in time to catch the 5 a.m. bus that goes up the mountain twenty minutes to Machu Picchu.

It definitely deserves the distinction of being a World Heritage site. The mist coming off the mountaintop, along with many stone steps needed to get to the top in order to look down into the ruins, takes my breath away.

Literally. I almost cry being overwhelmed with the beauty of the place, the sacredness I feel here. My dream from more than fifty years before is coming true. My dreams often come true. But this is a BIG dream. Hannah and I pinched each other to make sure we were awake (one is never sure with Hannah that early in the morning), then separated, agreeing to meet in an hour at a certain spot, one near the llamas. Actually, there are llamas living all over the place, but this was one area we had agreed upon.

By 10 a.m. Hannah and I were ready to leave. The sun is pretty intense high up like that. We had the mistaken idea that, being September which is off-season, there'd be few tourists, yet our bus was one of eighteen. Lots of other tourists had the idea of getting up early to "beat the crowds." They start making the trip up the mountain at 5 a.m., continuing until after lunch, then more buses are at the top to take the people down to the village. Thousands of tourists EVERY DAY visit Machu Picchu all year-round! Hopefully, this gives the locals a decent way to survive financially. It was fun buying tiny figures to attach to a black "bowler" hat I had yet to buy, as they are worn mostly by the women in Puno, and we hadn't gotten there yet. My idea was to make a mobile with the hat as a starting point. The owner of the hotel told us where to buy souvenirs; she also said all the locals know the secluded mountain paths to get into Machu Picchu free of charge. They visit it frequently. I would hope so. They seem to appreciate the sacred beauty of the place. I sure know a miracle when I see one.

We returned to Cuzco, this time to be tourists rather than to just fly into the city and leave. I bought incredibly-soft baby Alpaca sweaters, skirts, and shawls. We visited old markets that were in business before Pizarro and his soldiers came to conquer the country. The people are still selling items in these markets, long after Pizarro has left the area. After a couple days it was time to leave for Puno.

A six-hour bus ride took us over the high plains, the "altiplano" of Peru, where alpaca graze in the fields. We were excited about the possibility of seeing Lake Titicaca. Time seemed to have had little or no effect on the customs and land of these hardy people. It's an ancient, authentic "tourist spot."

"Penny, look at the 'cuy'; they're all over the place," Hannah said, as we were walking along the waterfront in Puno. She and I, not being raised in Peru where cuy is a delicacy, didn't dare order it even though most restaurants serve it. Guinea pigs, they're called in most of the world, and are raised as pets in the United States. But, we did eat alpaca that night, which tastes similar to lamb, tender and not "gamey," like mutton can be.

"And where are you ladies from, may I ask?" a guy said, turning to Hannah and me after introducing himself, saying he's from France. We're on a ferry-boat early the next morning, going to the islands in Lake Titicaca. Hannah said she's from Austria and lives in Mexico. When my turn came I said I was from the United States. "Well, nobody's perfect," he said.

Now, wouldn't it be sad if this arrogant man were the only contact I'd ever had with people from France? Wouldn't I be tempted to think all French people are rude and boorish?

Fortunately, I have traveled all over the world, clearly seeing that people are people, most being nice; only a few are creepy. So, I calmly smiled and moved on with the conversation as there were eight others on the boat, some from Peru, and who knows if I am the only "American" they've ever met? The ferry-boat had an enclosure inside which is where all of us stayed, out of the intense sun. We were on our way to Uros, the floating islands, which have been in Lake Titicaca, the largest freshwater lake at this elevation of more than 13,000 feet, for thousands of years.

The magic of this huge lake, with its islands known for their spiritual nature, really speaks to Hannah and me. I remember saying silently to my parents, "Dad and Mom, you were right about this place. It is beautiful, beyond word." I knew they were with me in spirit.

Uros consists of eight or more islands, each one usually belonging to one or two families. Each is built on 6-10 feet of "totora" reeds, thick and buoyant, that grow in the shallow part of the lake. As the foundation of their "land" rots away from underneath they pile more reeds on top.

"Hannah, did you see the toilet we just used in that shack?" I asked, with amusement.

"Yes, it has a flush like a regular toilet but isn't connected; it all just goes down into the lake, don't you think?" she marveled. We agreed it was ingenious to use a regular toilet. It warranted a photograph, but out of respect for their way of life we chose not to take pictures. We chose to be appreciative that we had ANY place at all to pee, as we were drinking lots of water, serious about keeping hydrated.

We seized the opportunity to ride in one of their reed boats — sized larger than four canoes — for the equivalent of one-dollar each, three "soles." What fun! The fourteen-year-old young man who rowed us to another island where the ferry would pick us up told us about life there. Each child goes to school when he or she turns five. After age twelve they go into the city each day for high school. They begin to learn English, but are already exposed to it in the island schools. They all speak both Spanish and Aymara; some also speak Quechua, left over from the days when they traded with other isolated communities. These people are so organized that they require each ferry-boat to go one day to the first island (they often go to three or four, but they have to go in succession to be fair to everyone); the next day they begin with the second island. This gives each artisan a chance to capture the bulk of the soles spent by the first wave of tourists. They speak Spanish with the tourists, yet among themselves it is Aymara. I believe they are one of the last places in the world to speak this ancient language on a daily basis.

Hannah and I fell in love with Puno, a small, laid-back city at the water's edge of huge Lake Titicaca. It has a spirit of being real, with no hustling going on in the streets. Because of the altitude we chose to take bicycle cabs, especially when going uphill back to our hotel late in the day. It was three *soles* well-spent.

Time to return to Mexico; we'd been gone more than three weeks. So, we made our way north, reluctantly leaving Puno, and headed back to Quito to rest and sightsee a few more days in our favorite hotel with the friendly sisters.

"You know, Hannah," I said when we arrived, "when my parents and I were in Quito almost forty years ago it was called 'Quito,' not 'Old Quito,' as it is now. There was no new Quito; it was just a tiny town, quaint, not spread out like it is now."

"I know, Penny; I guess we can always count on things to change, can't we?" she asked. "I cannot wait to get back to Puno; it really got to me. Maybe that's where we met in another life."

I laughed and agreed anything is possible. We then toasted our glasses of wine to celebrate a great trip, one which will remain etched in our minds and hearts forever.

Chapter Nineteen

"By forgiving people who mistreat us, we don't absolve them from personal responsibility or condone their actions...Learning forgiveness is essential to our spiritual path."

Sacred Contracts, Caroline Myss

Penny:

We returned to San Miguel de Allende on a Wednesday, totally refreshed and happy. It was a wonderful trip, one we both were eager to repeat as soon as we could afford it. We especially wanted to return to Lake Titicaca in Puno. It spoke to both Hannah and me. That town is different from other tourist spots, probably because it is so high in elevation and far off the beaten path. Especially for people from the United States; most of the tourists we saw were young Europeans with backpacks, like the ones who used to travel in Mexico before it got more expensive.

Mrs. Rodriquez said she'd had a cancellation and the apartment was mine for all three months: December, January, and February. Kevin planned to spend two weeks with me in January, but the remaining time I set aside to do nothing except healing work like Rolfing, massages, naps, and simple food. I wanted to get back to the simple life of the hippie I'll always be.

Mexico isn't for everyone, some say it is too macho, yett I have noticed the Mexican people seem to feel the differences between the feminine energy and masculine energy. There's no political correctness, just an appreciation of the sway of the skirt or the curve of the lady's body. I mentioned that to a taxi driver who has lived in the U.S. and he said that is true, but as a taxi driver he still has to very careful not to act at all inappropriately — and he means even a little flirting — as her brother or father will hunt him down. And not just to talk. A couple of years before this trip I was thrown from a horse and broke a finger holding onto the reins. I had my left hand in a cast for eight weeks and all the waiters cut my salad or meat without my even asking. Please take me to a restaurant in the U.S. or Canada where the waiters do that. I'd like to see that happen in either place.

I returned to Tennessee on a beautiful Sunday; it was quiet on the highway as I drove my car from the "self-park" parking lot to my home an hour south of the airport. I bought food before going home to an empty apartment. I had no real friends there, except for a couple neighbors who were friendly. I had a brief moment of loneliness before catching myself and saying, "Penny, you are alone, but not lonely." To combat this feeling I got back into my routine of daily walks, Pilates exercises, and Tai Chi to remain calm, centered and healthy. Yet, I was still being haunted by dreams, having trouble getting back to sleep when I awoke each night from a disturbing scene of my past life with Rob.

I was also bothered by no phone calls or e-mails from Rob. There was no response from my e-mail to his work address. Didn't he care to speak with me?

One night, after an especially disturbing dream, I had an epiphany which allowed me to cut off some of my strong attachment to Rob.

"Please Rob, leave her; it's killing you," I pleaded one night in a dream. We were sitting on a rock wall next to the lovely home he had built on 100 acres in Maine after he married Sandy. She was a control freak, an angry woman filled with fear, and this negative atmosphere was toxic for Rob, a man who just wanted peace and harmony in his life. I could see he was soon going to be very ill.

He looked at me, obviously in a lot of emotional pain, yet not knowing what to say to me. His body was tight, movements stilted; certainly not a happy man. Rob started to say something when we heard a car approaching, which soon appeared in his driveway. His look became guarded — Sandy was returning home.

"What do you think you're doing here?" Sandy yelled, as she got out of the car and walked over toward us. *Well,* I'm thinking, *the bitch has the same nasty tone she always had — no growing up for her, I guess.* "He doesn't have anything to say to you; can't you see that?" she continued.

In my dream I got up to leave, saying nothing. I've found in my time here on Earth that when a person is trying to pull a power play on me the best response often is no response, not even quiet resentment. I just looked at her calmly, knowing power-hungry people want our energy because they have none of their own.

Rob didn't acknowledge my attempt to hug him when I left. I drove away, feeling a little sad for him.

I woke up from the dream, crying out for help with ridding myself of this obsession, this need to rescue Rob. A light came into my room, calming me, and I got the message that he'd be okay, and that I can now let go of him. For my sake, I need to let go. He's a grown-up and so am I, and that means to me that I must stay within my own realm; the realm he lives in is not my business. A big lesson for me, yet one I learned that night. I was finally able to release him. Maybe I felt he didn't need or want to be rescued, but I clearly saw the folly of trying to rescue anyone.

Yet the one "sticky wicket" staying around was my wanting him to fall in love with me once again, as he had forty years before.

I had contacted a Realtor by Internet and followed up with phone calls. Nancy's office was in the town of Madison, close to the farm in Maine that Rob and I used to own. I knew he was someplace nearby. I also knew I loved it there and wanted to return to New England, where I had been partially-raised, a place of my ancestors. When the snow starts Penny leaves for Mexico, of course. *Good plan*, I'm thinking.

October and November were spent making decisions about the building of my new house. I was semi-enthusiastic, although having it just the way I want, with lots of art work and colors, was appealing to me. That, and a lot of reading and writing, took my mind off the boredom, along with the anxiety I was feeling from having these dreams.

I left Tennessee the first week of December, the roads being crowded with Mexicans in overloaded cars and trucks going from the U.S. in order to visit family in Mexico. I was bringing my brand new Honda CR-V (I named her Harley) to Mexico, figuring it's possible it will get damaged on the bad roads but it isn't going to get me stranded, as an older vehicle might. She is loving every minute of this 530-mile drive through the mountains and desert, roads with plenty of gasoline for sale but very little food worth eating.

I found a safe parking space near my apartment and walked to the market to buy food — papayas, avocadoes, pineapple, lettuces, and other salad fixings, and a chicken already cooked so I could have a quick supper. The stores were getting ready to close but I did manage to buy a half-kilo of freshly-made corn tortillas to go with my purchases. I had left some items in the apartment, like un-opened jars of salsa, honey, and peanut butter in hopes they would still be available for my use. They were in the cupboards. I wanted to settle in before going to my casita to check on it and make a list of what I needed to buy before moving into it. I hoped to move before returning to the U.S. the end of February.

I had a hard time sleeping that first night in San Miguel de Allende. I saw visions of Rob running into me at the supermarket in Skowhegan and refusing to speak. Or maybe just not recognizing me. In the dream I looked great, healthy and young, tanned and fit; yet I began remembering the feelings of insecurity I had when he returned from Antarctica and no longer loved me. I cannot understand how people "fall out of love." How is that possible? What did I do to make him hate me? And why did I care if he ever loved me again? The last time I saw him, thirteen years ago, I had gained weight, my hair was now gray, and I didn't look so good. But he was no prize, either — he still couldn't communicate, was getting a beer belly and losing his hair; his actions showed he was still emotionally-repressed, as he had been when we were married. Is this dream just another trick to get me to become attached to him again? At least I no longer feel the need to rescue him.

"Hey, Penny, it's good to see you!" my friend Karma yelled. She was also here for the holidays. She walked across the street to talk with me. I was surprised, as she normally isn't in Mexico for Christmas.

"Karma, what are you doing here now?" I asked. She looked at me with her "eagle eye" and zeroed right in on my state of emotions.

"Woman, I am here because you need me. Come with me," she said, grabbing my hand. "I'm taking you to my apartment; I'll do some energy work on you. You look like hell," she commented.

"Gee, thanks, I need that vote of confidence."

"Penny, seriously, I can perform a secret ceremony on you. And some Reiki. Talk to me about Rob; it's getting worse, isn't it?" she asked with empathy in her voice.

"Karma, I have made much progress in dealing with these dreams; have even tried to find him, but there is no phone listed. I found his e-mail address at his place of employment for the state of Maine, but he has yet to answer my e-mail from three months ago, so I'm back to square one," I spilled it all out to her, as she is a good listener.

"I don't know how to tell you this, but I could care less about Rob or what he does or doesn't do; I do care how this is affecting you, though. Let's work on that," she said.

Over the next three hours, Karma performed a cord-cutting ceremony on me, saying Rob is not on my path and let's let him go. With chants and energy from her hands she calmed me down, finally doing some Reiki and covering me with a comforter, leaving me on her bed to sleep while she read a book. When I awoke we went out to dinner, and I gladly paid for hers. I was starving, hadn't eaten much all day. But before we left her apartment she got out her pendulum, telling me to ask a question out loud to assess what the pendulum will do when the answer is yes; for instance, "Is my age sixty-three?" It could only be an obvious yes. For no I asked "Am I in Tennessee?" Each pendulum is different so we needed to find out which way it will swing for a yes or no when I ask real questions I need answers for. After seeing that for "yes" it swings front-to-back and "no" is right-to-left, I ask the first question silently. Karma doesn't need to hear what I want to know.

The first question I asked the pendulum was this: Will Rob and I ever make love together again? Surprisingly enough, it indicated "yes" with no hesitation, swinging from the front to the back and back to the front again. The second question was: Will Rob leave his wife? It was an impertinent thing to ask, but one coming from friendship, wanting to help him. It was not a totally romantic question. Well, this next reaction was a new one for Karma and me. The crystal pendulum sat and sat and sat some more, more than a minute, maybe more, without moving. Then it moved from right to left and back, continuing to swing for a few minutes.

The answer was no. Rob was not going to leave his wife.

Karma and I spent time together during the next few weeks, as we usually did when she was there visiting for part of each winter. We met a few years before when sitting near each other in the *jardin* (another village might call it a *zocalo*). She's a retired school teacher, one who supplements her Social Security payments with substitute teaching in the public schools in Bend, Oregon where she owns an 1890's Victorian home. With her help I began to calm down, able to sleep better at night, but still needing naps.

Over the Christmas holidays I got invitations from a few Mexican friends, which I turned down because dinner begins at midnight Christmas Eve, ending by 5 a.m. or later. I'm in San Miguel de Allende to rest, usually going to bed no later than 10 p.m. My idea of a nice way to celebrate is to invite a few friends to eat dinner with me, sharing good conversation, music, wine, maybe playing cards or games like "Mexican Train." But always something more intimate than having lots of people around, listening to loud "ranchero" music all night, and drinking more tequila and beer than should ever be consumed.

I stayed home in my apartment New Year's Eve, acutely aware it is a celebration more for couples than for a woman alone. Oh well, maybe next year my partner will show up. The first thing he'll say to me is this: "I've been waiting for you to settle down and stay in one place long enough for us to meet."

Chapter Twenty

"As we let our own light shine we unconsciously give other people permission to do the same. As we are liberated from our own fear, our presence automatically liberates others."

Marianne Williamson

Penny:

On Wednesday, January 31st, I met Kevin at the airport when he arrived on the noon flight from Boston to San Antonio. We had almost three hours to take the shuttle downtown, find a good meal, and get on the "Americanos" bus to ride overnight to San Miguel de Allende. I had gone from San Miguel de Allende to Texas to meet him because there were items I needed to buy at "Lowe's" in Laredo. The bus ride was simple for me; since I traveled light I found it easy to walk across the bridge into and out of Mexico. The plan was for me to take him by bus a couple weeks later back to the airport so he could fly home.

When we last saw one another I'd had no clue when the next visit would be, but we did keep in touch through phone calls and e-mail. I considered us to be "friends with benefits." I felt he was getting interested in something more than that; I wanted it to be "shallow and casual" as a bit of role reversal. Women often want something more than sex, while for men sex is frequently enough. Deep down I did eventually want more with the right person; it was just too soon to know if Kevin was the one.

"Penny, I do believe this is the most beautiful sunrise I've ever seen," Kevin said, as the bus had been engulfed in a mysterious, peaceful fog for two hours since we had turned off the main highway headed out of San Luis Potosi. The narrow road carried heavy traffic, yet our seasoned driver maneuvered the huge Mercedes-Benz bus expertly.

"Well, Kevin," I said, "you did ask where the sun was hiding; here's your answer." Kevin was as wide awake as I was, both of us getting a decent night's sleep, having our own seat after most of the passengers got off at San Luis Potosi. We glanced at each other with that special look that lovers often have.

We arrived in San Miguel de Allende around eight o'clock in the morning. *"Gracias, senor, que le vaya bien,"* I said, as I carefully descended the steps of the bus with my two small pink duffle bags in tow.

"Por nada, senora, igualmente," the driver replied, telling me I was welcome and to also have a nice day.

I whispered in Kevin's ear that I love the way his eyes are as big as saucers, taking in all the sights, sounds, and smells of San Miguel de Allende. I feel the same way each time I come home to San Miguel. Now I am here with a new lover, a man whom I care about, in a city I have loved for many years, a place that still makes my heart sing while my eyes are absorbing everything.

The bus ride to El Centro took ten minutes and four-pesos each. The brief walk from the stop on Insurgentes to "El Pegasso" increased our hunger, as neither of us had eaten since 1 p.m. the day before in San Antonio, Texas. *"Con permiso,"* I said, as we moved around people on the narrow, stone sidewalks, always carefully watching for large holes in the walkways, San Miguel being the place of more than a few broken ankles. There's even a term for females who hurt themselves walking: The Fallen Women of San Miguel, not a group I'd care to join unless it involves sex. Just kidding.

"Buenos dias, senora," Rafael greeted me with his usual smile. "I see you have a friend with you," Rafael said, as we entered the restaurant.

"This is my friend, Kevin, who is here for a couple weeks. He's never been here before," I said.

"Mucho gusto, Kevin," Rafael said.

"Mucho gusto," Kevin replied. Wow! I love it when a man doesn't skip a beat; he's definitely a fast learner, picking up Spanish quickly.

During our breakfast of coffee and tea, fresh papaya, *huevos a la Mexicana*

— eggs scrambled with tomatoes, onions, and jalapenos — and frijoles with freshly-made corn tortillas, we made plans for the day: "First, we take our things to the apartment, which is a fifteen minute taxi ride, ten if the traffic is light, then we decide about filling the refrigerator, visiting friends, sitting in the jardin, or whatever," I said.

"Sounds perfect," Kevin replied, his eyes twinkling.

After getting settled in my apartment we walked to the restaurant, "Nutra Verde."

"*Hola*, Patty, how are you, girlfriend?" I greeted my friend as Kevin and I walked into her vegetarian restaurant.

"Penny," she squealed with delight, running to hug me. We hugged and, after introductions, she said she must have known I was coming today because she had frozen some squash blossoms in October and was now cooking them, one of my favorite foods in Mexico.

"Hey, Patty, we're going to buy food and candles. Need anything at the *mercado*?" I asked.

"Nothing, thanks. Where did you find Kevin; he's quite a hottie," Patty said, winking.

"Has that expression gotten to Mexico? I thought it was a gringo saying," I said, laughing at her openness.

"Yes, he definitely is a hottie," she continued. "Are you going to the *Alborada* tomorrow night? Here, help me with this table, okay?" As we moved the tables to straighten out the seating arrangement for the large party to come in soon, she told us about the *Alborada*, as I'd never been to one before: "The procession starts at 3 a.m., with people on stilts pretending to be giant puppets — *mojigangas* — and carrying cellophane and tissue paper stars. The stars represent the Virgin of the Light; the festival began with textile workers from Salvatierra who came here for factory jobs in 1925. They brought this tradition with them," Patty said, as she continued with preparations for her group.

"Kevin, the noise of the fireworks and the crowds can be a problem," I wrinkled my nose in mock disgust, "but we can go if you want," I said. "I'll go just for you; after all, you're a Mexico virgin," I teased him. We kissed Patty goodbye, promising to return soon for lunch, and went off to buy stuff on the list in our heads.

"Hi, Penny, you're here," Hannah said, as she hugged me in the street. "Hey, I'll be home by six; I'd love to see you both," she said, as I introduced her to Kevin. They hugged the Mexican way giving a kiss on only one cheek, not the European way of both cheeks, where Hannah had been raised. "He's even cuter than you said in your e-mail; mind if I flirt with him a little?" Hannah teased.

"He loves it, loves women; a very friendly guy. Can you picture me with a grump?" I asked. We all laughed.

"You're smart not to come in September, Kevin," Hannah said, "as we have many festivals, the worst one being the *Sanmiguelada*, "Running of the Bulls"; I was told it was a nightmare, with shit in the streets, sex right on the sidewalks, drunks vomiting, horrid, yuk! Two people were shot, only wounded, but we've never had guns here before. The previous year 20,000 people were here and that was bad enough. This past September we had over 50,000 people; can you believe that? Good time to leave San Miguel or just stay home. Or go to Peru. It's easier now that we have MEGA, the new supermarket. Don't need to go into town for much now. September is one entire month of partying, non-stop," Hannah said, wrinkling her nose.

"Someone told me that if we have it again and the same thing happens we may not get our designation of World Heritage Site; is that right?" I asked.

"As a tourist spot we have to keep down crime and meet very strict standards. It's worth millions to San Miguel and Mexico to earn this designation and, once lost, impossible to get back," she replied.

"I saw the towers being set up for the *voladores*. Do you suppose 'Attencion' has times listed for the men to fly?" I asked.

"Probably, but you know what 'Mexican time' means," she said. "See ya later?"

"Yes, we'll be there."

"Good! Looking forward to opening a new bottle of wine to celebrate meeting Kevin. Bye, hasta luego, amiga," said Hannah as she reached to hug and kiss me goodbye.

"Bye, Hannah, see ya," we said, doing the hugging and kissing routine as we're leaving.

Friday afternoon I wanted to take a nap because we planned to stay up all night for the Alborada, so Kevin stayed in the living room, reading a book. When I awoke late afternoon we went out to dinner at "Hecho en Mexico," another of my favorites, but it was so crowded with weekend visitors that we walked back home and just had a snack for supper.

"Kevin, I've got enough pesos for the taxi home tucked into my secret pocket in my slacks; is your money secure? These festivals bring out pickpockets and con artists; it can happen no matter where you are."

"Yeah, I'm good. Let's sit and listen to the music and watch the dancers," he said as we approached the jardin, the driver dropping us off as close as he could to the action across from La Parroquia, the tall-spired, pinkish-tan Catholic church that dominates the area. By 10 p.m. I am wilting in spite of the nap because I'm an early-to-bed, early-to-rise kind of person, always have been even as a child. But for now listening to the music was keeping me awake.

"Honey, the rockets are about to go off; wake up," Kevin said as he moved his arm that I'd dozed off on, gently nudging me. I guess he thought I could sleep through fireworks, and sometimes I can.

"What time is it?" I sleepily asked. "Can we go home?" Just then my question was interrupted by the first large rocket being exploded. The noise was deafening and I could feel a slight headache starting so we left the jardin before the other 6,000 rockets and fireworks went off.

Surprisingly, we had no problem finding a taxi and got home ten minutes later. I found on my first trip to Mexico that if I'm looking for peace and a quiet place to vacation Mexico is not the spot. Especially San Miguel de Allende, with its cock-fighting roosters crowing all night in practically every neighborhood, even downtown; these roosters then set off the dogs, who set off other dogs barking and howling. You get the picture.

Kevin and I sleepily made love about four in the morning, right before the sun was to come up. I had really missed sex, but turned down opportunities with guys who just weren't right for me. Kevin's example of how a man should love his woman began early when he watched his father always respecting both his own mother and his wife, Kevin's mother. This placing a woman in a position of honor was consciously remembered by Kevin.

As for my example, I saw an angry woman in my mother and a spoiled, selfish child-man in my father, who cheated on his wife every chance he got. The examples my parents set for me were of a love-that-turned-to-hate. I did a lot of work improving myself over the years, yet harmed my children with two "bad" marriages before understanding how not to do it. Now I had Kevin to help me understand some of the subtleties of respecting the opposite sex. I was enjoying what we had: a lovely friendship. I was enjoying the good sex, too.

Hannah invited us to dinner for 6 p.m. Saturday night. Conversation was great, as usual. Kevin fit right in. The meal consisted of baked chicken, roasted potatoes with fresh rosemary and pumpkin seed oil (she's from Austria and that is a delicacy she gets from there when friends send her care packages), and broccoli and carrots.

"Hannah, you are one of the best cooks I know. Thanks so much for dinner. And I have always loved your collection of music," I said, slowly pushing myself away from the table, groaning from eating too much. About 9 p.m. we got up to leave.

"Hannah, we're heading to the *jardin*; I know you don't want to be a tourist and go with us, so we'll see you tomorrow," I said, as we hugged and kissed goodbye. "I'll cook for you soon," I promised.

A few days later we were walking along Calle Reloj and Kevin spied a jewelry store — "Let's go inside," he said, grabbing my hand to follow him. The owner greeted Kevin as if he knew him; they even spoke Spanish to each other. What? Kevin speaks Spanish? When did he learn Spanish?

So, I decided to have fun and asked the man if the ring I'd ordered was ready yet — just joking around, really — and I winked at the man, a little smirk on my face.

"*Si, si, senora, esta lista,*" the man played along, obviously enjoying the moment. Now I'm not in competition with Kevin but that little bugger never told me he knew Spanish; he speaks it better than I do. I found out later that, after surviving Vietnam, he spent the following year in South America. He needed to be alone and heal. His parents understood when he came home for a brief visit before leaving again.

Kevin then asked the owner to bring out his gift to me: a gorgeous, turquoise ring, obviously made by a local craftsman. Now it was my turn to be surprised. "Penny, you should know I care about you; I got this ring so there'd be no mistake about my feelings," he said, as he handed the ring to me. "I designed it just for you, with the help of Senor Ramirez, of course," Kevin continued, as I stood there, speechless, a bit sick to my stomach. *God help me, I am not ready for any commitment other than being friends.*

Finally, I spoke: "Kevin, it's a lovely ring, but I can't accept it, knowing the meaning is different for you than it is for me. Please give me time, okay?" We stood there a couple minutes, saying nothing. We hugged. His eyes twinkled. "May I ask when you found time to order this? We've been together every day," I said, when I was ready to talk again.

"Penny, you fell asleep the second afternoon we were here. Remember you said that you needed to adjust to the altitude; it always makes you sleepy the first week? You needed to rest up for the *Alborada.* I left a note that I was going for a walk and discovered this place. I tore up the note when I returned and you were still sleeping.

A couple years before this trip to Mexico I was visiting Edie in Florida and walked into the dining room one day to find her writing a long list of something. I was curious, as I'd seen her write notes using only small bits of scrap paper, and this was a new, full sheet. I asked what she was doing.

"I'm making a list of what I am looking for in the perfect partner," she laughed as she told me.

"You can do that?" I asked, dumbfounded, as it never occurred to me to do so.

"Of course; I have columns for each of the three male friends I spend time with, listing each quality I want and checking off when one of them has that quality," she continued.

"Any luck finding one with all the qualities?" I ask, incredulous, as I had lived my life — so far, anyway — just taking what was handed to me, never realizing I should tell the Universe what I want in life.

"I'm getting close, Penny; it will happen, I know this," asserted Edie with much confidence.

I kept this encounter in my mind over the next couple years, making my own list of qualities I seek in a life partner, the first one being committed to spiritual growth, both his and mine. He has to be totally honest, with himself as well as with others. He also needs to be generous financially and sexually. Money isn't all-important to me, but how a man handles his money is an indication of how he handles his life. And a selfish sex partner is, well, a selfish man. He also needed to have a similar amount of money available as I do in case we go on a trip together; I'm not paying his way. Once in awhile I'd add something, like "a carpenter would be nice" when I was busy with a difficult renovation project, or I'd remember I wanted a man interested in his health and eating right, while being open to alternative health care rather than the conventional medical stuff offered, and I'd write that down. Right before this trip happened I had written in the margin: "a gourmet cook would be nice," smiling as I did so, knowing we might as well just ask for it all. We may just get it.

The next night I had a disturbing dream that Rob was very sick, dying in a hospital, and his wife wouldn't let me see him to say goodbye. I woke up, crying, which awakened Kevin.

"Penny, who can help you find him? Are his parents still alive?" Kevin asked, after I told him about the dream.

"You know, Kevin, I honestly never thought of that. Heather hasn't kept in touch with his parents throughout the years, but she probably would have mentioned it if they had died; if she knew, that is," I replied, getting excited at the possibility of talking with Rob's mother for the first time in years.

The next morning I walked to La Conexion to clear my head before calling Dora. I got a brainstorm and called my daughter at work after I couldn't get information from the Internet.

"Sure, go on 'zabasearch'," she said; then seconds later gave me the number, as she had done her own zabasearch while I was on the phone. *Oh, the Internet sure is awesome.*

"Thanks, Heather," I said, as I hung up, now a tiny bit nervous. *What if she doesn't remember me?*

"Hello," I said, as a woman answered the phone; I recognized Dora's voice, even though it had been thirty-four years since we had spoken. "My name is Penny Hall; I used to be married to your son."

"I remember you, you were married to my Robbie!" she exclaimed. "How are you, dear?"

I told her I was thinking about Rob and wondering if he was okay.

"Oh yes, dear, he's now divorced; he left his wife for another woman, then she left him for another man." That made me sad, as I was hoping he had learned something about fidelity, being over sixty years old now. Dora continued, "He's retired from the state of Maine, was forced to retire at sixty and has spent the past couple years doing a lot of fishing. You knew he was a scientist, didn't you?" she asked.

"Yes, I knew that, but always felt Rob didn't give himself credit for all he's done: going back to school on the G.I. Bill with a new wife and two babies before graduating, which was a lot. Then building his house? Heather told me about it when she visited one time."

"You're right, he is very smart and doesn't seem to know how much he has accomplished," Dora replied.

Before hanging up I asked if she thought Rob might want to talk with me, as I needed closure. She asked me to write her a letter which she would give him when he came to their house a couple weeks later for a visit. I agreed to do that and she reminded me of their address. It was good to hear her voice. We had always liked each other.

After I hung up the phone from speaking with Rob's mother I stumbled out to the street and made my way to the *Parroquia*, which attracts tourists from all over the world. The tall building seems to be reaching for the heavens and always calms me, just as candles do, when I need to calm down. San Miguel de Allenda has many Catholic churches but this is their most formidable one, built after Spain conquered Mexico in the 1500's.

An acquaintance of mine waved to me, indicating he wanted to come over and sit with me. I didn't want to appear rude, but the last thing I wanted was to talk with someone. I looked away, but not before I saw a puzzled look on his face. I was aware enough to know that my suffering was from long ago: re-living my divorce from Rob was taking me to the source of my pain, asking what was wrong with me that my husband could fall out of love with me after just a couple years of marriage. Was I so terrible then?

All I can do when needing to talk to someone is open my heart and allow it to speak for me. I am going home to speak with Kevin, from the heart. I abruptly got up from the bench, walked to the opposite corner from where the acquaintance was still standing, and hailed a taxi. Honesty is urging me to let Kevin know why I cannot go further with him emotionally. I will find the right words.

He was waiting in the kitchen, drinking our favorite vanilla hazelnut tea, calmly smiling as he greeted me with a questioning look.

"Kevin," I said, "I don't know where to begin. Rob's mother told me he's fine and enjoying his retirement, doing a lot of fishing." I stopped and looked at Kevin. "But that's not really what you're asking to hear, is it? Rob's divorced," I continued, noting Kevin's understanding look, his compassion, his calm demeanor, which made me burst into tears. He said nothing; just held me while I cried. *Gosh, how many tears can a person possibly have inside? Where on Earth do they come from?*

"I've always loved Rob, and that's why I hold myself back with you," I finally blurted out.

"I was wondering when you were going to realize that," Kevin quietly said, with the sweetest, most loving smile I'd ever seen on a man's face. "I felt the excitement in you last night when you talked about Rob. I knew then that you couldn't give your heart to me — you've already given it to Rob."

"You know me well, don't you? I'm so lucky to have a friend like you; do you know that?" I asked Kevin, as I hugged him. With a kiss on the cheek I continued, "I never meant to hurt you; I really do love you. You're an amazing man. I need to sort this out. I never was good at leaving unfinished business."

"Penny, if we truly live in the present time we know each moment is precious, sacred. I know you don't worry about the future any more than I do. I'm okay with this, really," he said, as he touched my cheek. It made me start crying again.

Sometimes I cry just for the pure joy of it. For being overwhelmed by an act of love that touches me deep inside.

The next week went by quickly, as the days were filled with meeting the electrician and plumber and getting a hot water heater installed, among other needed items in a house I would soon be living in six months of the year. Decisions were made that would need to be made no matter where a person is building a house. We managed to have a lot of fun with all of this activity in spite of the fact that our relationship had changed. We now just kissed each other on the cheek when going to bed. I didn't miss the sex; I realized from this experience I am really not a "shallow and casual kind of gal." It is time to know that about myself.

"Too bad we have to leave here in a few days, but the bus ride is easier going north as we leave at 7 p.m., arriving in Nuevo Laredo, Mexico at 6:30 a.m., having slept most of the night. A short taxi ride takes us to the bridge where we walk across the Rio Grande to the United States before getting the Greyhound to San Antonio," I said one day to Kevin.

"Penny, if you think that's the easy way I'd love to see what you think of as complicated."

"Well, at least we don't have to swim across, maybe drowning in the process," I said in defense of my "easy way" to the USA.

"I know how lucky we are, Penny. I have decided to go alone by bus, if you don't mind," Kevin continued. "I was paying attention on the way down and know it will be no problem for me to do this alone." I began to protest, wanting to be the good hostess. "Penny, it's okay, I am fine with this. I appreciate your hospitality and feel lucky to have seen this place you love so much. You're a good woman, Penny," Kevin said, with a tiny bit of sadness. But his eyes continued to twinkle, as always.

"Let's go to lunch," he said, getting up from the dining room table, taking my hand. "I'm hungry, aren't you?"

"Okay, I'm ready. We can go to Patty's; you like her squash blossom soup," I said, as I got my sweater, knowing it got chilly after sunset.

Kevin did leave, alone, just in time for me to celebrate Valentine's Day, alone. I was happy to stay in San Miguel de Allende, a place of healing and comfort for me. I was feeling thankful for meeting a good man like Kevin, one who is working on finding his more spiritual side. Hopefully, we will remain friends. I had only a split second's lack of faith about giving up the possibility of having him as a life partner. He had so much love inside, and knew how to express it. But there will be no "settling" ever again. If he isn't doing some earth-shattering thing to my heart he isn't the one for me. I know many women who would tell me how foolish I am but they have their way of loving and I have mine.

I finally know what is best for me.

About two weeks later I was driving back to my home in Tennessee; the five-day trip gave me time to think. I thought back to the time I was visiting Edie in Florida and walked into the dining room, where she was writing in a notebook. I asked her what she was doing and she said she was making a list of all she wanted in a partner.

"You can do that?" I asked, dumbfounded, as it never occurred to me to do so. So far, I had been living my life thinking I had to take whatever was handed to me.

"Of course," Edie answered, laughing. "I have three columns for each of three male friends I spend time with, listing each quality I want and putting a check mark when one of them has that quality."

"Any luck finding one with all the qualities?

"I'm getting close, Penny. It will happen; I know it," a confident Edie said.

I kept this encounter in my mind over the next couple years, making my own list of qualities I was seeking in a life partner. He had to be committed to spiritual growth, and be honest, with himself, not just others. He also had to be generous financially and sexually (and good lover), and have enough money to go on trips with me. Once I added "a carpenter would be nice." Or I'd remember I wanted a man who was interested in being healthy, but seeking alternatives to the standard medical options. Right before the trip to Mexico I added, in the margins because the page was full, "a gourmet cook would be nice." We might as well ask for everything. Who knows? We might just get it all.

I like driving alone. It gives me time to think, as I crave solitude as a way to heal. I love my adopted country of Mexico, something I think about a lot. I remember being in San Miguel de Allende when the World Trade Center twin towers got destroyed by terrorists on September 11, 2001. The borders were closed for much of that day and I had a brief moment of panic thinking I might not be able to get home to the U.S. Then, I remembered how much at home I felt in Mexico and calmed down. Of course, then I thought of my family back home and hoped all was well with them. I love both my countries — the United States and Mexico. There's a saying in Mexico: "Los Estados Unidos tiene el dinero, pero Mexico tiene el corazon y necesito los ambos." The United States has the money, but Mexico has the heart. I need both.

I'm a very lucky woman. I am thankful for what I have and don't worry about what I don't have. I call that a perfect life.

A week after returning home I was feeling maybe Dora didn't get my letter; after all, I hadn't heard a word from Rob. So I sent him a letter, getting his address from Heather. If he was in the same house, that is.

"Dear Rob," I wrote, "I am not certain how you feel about this intrusion in your life so I will keep it brief. I have much to say to you, but don't know if you are the same angry man you were many years ago, not wanting to hear from me. After the letter you wrote to me in 1978, saying you hoped I was happy, that I'd gotten the best years of your life, that I ruined your life, I was puzzled by your anger. Didn't you, after all, want to leave; didn't you get all our dreams, yet with someone else? Shouldn't this be the best time of your life? I wrote this in a letter to you way back then, but Sandy may have opened it and torn it up without your even knowing I had written to you. Rob, I want to apologize and explain something about myself: I was a passive child who became willful to keep others from pushing me around. I am really sorry I pushed you into marriage. If I know anything at all about you it is this: Above all, you want peace and harmony. And no confrontations. Ask any military man and he will tell you we often have to be willing to go to war in order to preserve peace and reach a harmonious state. I also longed for peace and harmony, but have found that in order to have it in a relationship I must first have it inside myself. Maybe apologizing for my actions will help others on their way to healing. Only goodness can come out of forgiveness. Much Love, Penny."

About two weeks after this letter was sent to Rob I received a phone call, one I was half-expecting, yet it took me by surprise. "Hello, Penny, this is Rob; I got your letter. How are you? Can we see each other and talk in person?" he asked.

I held my breath, as I replied, "Hi, it's good to hear from you. I would love to talk in person; let me call you before coming to Maine the end of June. I'll be taking the grandchildren to York to a beach cottage I rented, okay?" I asked. At least, I think that's what was said. I had no sense of time; I felt suspended in space during the entire call, which could have been one minute or ten.

"I would like that," he gently replied, almost whispering.

We said goodbye. I slumped down on the sofa and cried, relieved to know the sleepless nights were probably over. I could go on with my life wherever it took me. It was good to hear his voice.

That night I had no dreams and slept peacefully. Maybe Rob had gotten his message across and didn't need to bug me anymore. It would be good to see him for the first time in many years. I knew during the next few weeks that, even if we never saw each other again, I'd be okay. I had already gotten some closure.

Yet, I also knew we both wanted to.

Chapter Twenty One

"Do unto others as you would have them do unto you."

The Golden Rule

Penny, buying land:

The following week after Rob's call I was talking to Nancy, the Maine real estate broker I'd been in touch with since before Christmas. I got a bright idea while listening to her description of a ten-acre lot overlooking Wesserunsett Lake: "Penny, the stand of pine trees has been managed well; it is an absolutely breathtaking piece of land, a perfect spot to build a home. It even has a year-round view of the lake, although no frontage. It came on the market this morning; Mrs. Tupper's home was sold separately with only five acres of land. This is next door to her house but has quite a bit of road frontage so you'll have privacy. It is in your price range, too," Nancy said.

"I'll get a flight tomorrow, if possible. Southwest Airlines goes to Manchester, New Hampshire and I can rent a car and be in Skowhegan tomorrow night. I'll call you tonight," I said, before hanging up.

So, that's what I did, arriving before noon in Manchester, then driving to Skowhegan in my rented Impala, a trip that took maybe three hours or so.

That, in itself, was an emotional journey. This is the area where Rob and I had owned a farm, where we dreamed of homesteading and living the simple life of hippies. We knew people there, shopped in the local stores, and knew which roads went where. Of course, now I'm not the only one who has changed a lot; so has the town.

I found a cozy motel, "The Holly Tree", settled in and called Nancy. We agreed she'd pick me up the next morning. I slept well that night on the pillow-top mattress in this simple room with knotty pine all over, including the ceilings. The windows opened, allowing me to breathe in the fresh

Maine air. Maybe it was the deep-breathing, the freshness of the area that made me dream that night. It was a peaceful one, a loving one. Rob and I were sitting down together, eating a meal, smiling at each other, very happy. No more anxious dreams, no more nightmares that he is ill; just sweet dreams.

Before I had left Tennessee I e-mailed Rob, saying I'd be in Skowhegan, here's my cell phone number, call me if you want to talk or get together. In the few dreams I'd had of Rob since our phone conversation I envisioned us able to talk to each other, which was a pleasant surprise. That's all I thought I ever wanted from him: to have a real conversation, to have closure.

Okay, I'll admit some were sexual, often orgasmic; he turned me on, even in my sleep. Rob always brought out the passion in me in a way no other man ever had. We were extremely compatible as lovers, and even as housemates; yet we proved that two people can love each other and still not be able to live "happily ever after." Not that we set out to prove it, for sure. I began to occasionally have hopeful dreams that we could be together, realizing I have always loved this man; he was the one that got away many years before. Boy! The ego sure likes to get involved in our lives, doesn't it? It didn't seem to matter to my ego that I may not want him now — after all, I hadn't seen much evidence of older men being great catches. Most of them had too much anger and seemed disappointed. They certainly didn't appear to be interested in growing and finding their Higher Selves. The ones who were open and happy already had partners.

Rob and I had exchanged a few brief, not-too-deep e-mails over the past few weeks. I kept mine friendly and short while saying to myself, "Penny, if he's the same selfish, emotionally-repressed guy he was forty years ago you don't want him, anyway; maybe not even as a friend." I took the wait-and-see attitude.

I am very thankful to be an active person, happily renovating houses, going to lunch with friends, traveling. In other words, I have my own life. Now I'm looking for the guy who can provide the frosting to put on the cake I have been baking "forever." My need to control the outcome is over. Edie always said, "Penny, we must be interested, yet not invested, in the outcome."

Yet, I somehow knew that "sticky-wicket" was still hanging around: My wanting him to fall in love with me again, as he had forty years ago. I guess I had been lying to myself, thinking I was looking only for closure.

It was for this very reason that the Universe did not allow Rob to contact me those few days I was in Maine. I never heard a word from him.

Chapter Twenty Two

"Whoever says they will take you to God is a liar, because you are already there."

The Four Agreements, Don Miguel Ruiz

Penny:

I decided to treat myself to some body work; it had been a rough year, and I needed help with relaxation and overall well-being. Peter, bless his heart, recommended that I go to his favorite hot mineral springs resort near Boulder to loosen up before my appointments with a lady named Shar, who has taken on teaching the lost art of Tibetan cranial work. She discovered it in Nepal, sitting for many days at the feet of one of the last masters alive before he called her up to the table to work on a client who had walked for miles to receive his help, free of charge. She got whatever training she could from this man before going home to Colorado for nine months to continue training — intuitively — on her own. By the time she had a chance to return to Nepal the master was dead, as was the only other man who knew the technique. She was on her own. And that was twenty years ago. She now spends a lot of time and energy training other body-workers to carry on this very effective healing technique.

I was intrigued and eager to receive whatever help she could give me.

The mineral springs spa was heaven; I doubt there was an ounce of tension left in my tired body. A deep relaxation took over my entire being.

"Penny, when you talk about Rob your whole body gives off this phenomenal pink glow; did you know that?" Shar asked halfway through the hour-long session.

"Shar, it doesn't matter how much I glow if he doesn't feel the same or if he's not someone I want to be friends with now. It's totally out of my hands. And that's good.".

The visit to Boulder, with massages, Rolfing, cranial work, and mineral baths, was nothing more than sheer indulgence on my part. I loved walking and driving all over Boulder; I even visited the Celestial Seasonings factory, now outside of town. The first one in Boulder, in the 1970's, was small and unique; Mo, the co-owner and co-founder, had given us the tour himself. Many herb tea companies followed, but they were the first one. Now, they are owned by a big corporation but I still got a kick out of taking the tour in the much larger facility. I loved buying tea to enjoy in my luxury motel room, with the down comforter and pillow-top mattress.

Peter, you were right. I deserved this treat.

Shar and I really clicked and loved talking to each other. One of the stories she told me was about a friend who's looking for a life partner so she empties out half her closet to accommodate his things; then she begins sleeping on the same side each night, using only half her bed instead of all of it. The most interesting part, to me at least, is she now put out an extra place setting, complete with silver and napkin, each time she ate, moving from the island counter-top (where I also was eating, never having sat at my table) to the dining room table.

I know you may not believe this, but it's true: Her partner, a man even more fabulous than she had imagined, came to her in thirty days! It really happened. And that impressed me.

You see, I had known from the time I was quite small that I was destined to have that "special someone" as my partner for life. Sometimes, I even felt I had already been with him. Sometimes I even knew it was Rob, my first husband.

Oh well, sometimes I'm wrong.

Chapter Twenty Three

La diosa no sigue a los hombres; los hombres sigue a la diosa.

Penny:

I came home from Boulder on a Monday afternoon. Immediately, I moved to the Master suite, having told my friends when I bought the house that I had no plans to sleep there without a partner and, therefore, had been living in the guest bedroom. Time to change the plan — from now on I'd have one of the two huge closets in the master suite and I'd try to sleep on one side only of my comfy queen-size, pillow-top bed.

During dinner that evening — eaten on the dining room table for the first time — my brother called; when I told him about the extra place setting he begged me to tell him I hadn't gone so far as to put food on the plate.

"No, Peter, no food," I said with a laugh, "but I know this will work. He's going to be here soon; I'm positive."

"Where are you off to next, Penny? Aren't you coming my way soon?"

"I sure am. I'll be in Manchester Friday; I'll rent a car to go north to Maine for Memorial Day weekend. The real estate closing is on Tuesday and then I'll own my ten acres. I'll start building a small summer cabin after I sell the Tennessee house in a couple years," I answered him.

"You miss New England, don't you?" Peter asked.

"Yes, I do, but not in the winter. That's when I'll be in Mexico," I said.

"I know, I know, no winters for you. See you after Memorial Day, then?" Peter asked.

"Yes, right after I sign papers I'll leave for New Hampshire. My return flight to Nashville is Sunday, June 3rd; I am hoping to see you. I'll call you, okay?"

"See ya, Sis; bye," Peter said, as we hung up.

I was diligent during every meal, putting an extra place mat, bowl and spoon when I ate granola for breakfast; even another mug for tea. I'd look across the table and picture the "unknown him" with me. One time I laughed out loud when I had a mouth filled with salad and was being sloppy — I actually started to say "sorry" before I caught myself.

Friday morning I flew to Manchester again. Since Rob had not contacted me when I was there about six weeks before to find the land I decided not to e-mail or call him. There had been no contact at all since the initial phone call and e-mails. He's obviously not interested. Maybe he went back with the woman he left Sandy for and was just too busy to give my need for closure a thought. When my daughter Heather decided not to let the kids go to Maine with me because she wanted a family vacation with them in Florida I cancelled the beach cottage for the last week in June; no reason to be there if the grandchildren aren't. And that means there probably will be no seeing Rob at all.

"No, Karma, I'm not going to call him," I said, when she called me Friday evening on my cell phone. "La diosa no sigue a los hombres; los hombres sigue a la diosa," I told her.

She laughed while translating, as she's fluent in Spanish: "'The goddess doesn't chase after men; men chase after the goddess.' I know you don't call men, but Rob isn't 'men' so you need to call him," she insisted, but I cut her off.

"I'll call you tomorrow night, okay?" I asked. "You'll be home?"

"Penny, call me after 6 p.m. my time, which is 9 p.m. your time; I'm going out for the day. Promise you'll call me." I promised before I hung up.

The next morning I drove my rented car, this time a PT Cruiser, along the back roads, looking for Rob's house. I wanted to see the house I knew he'd built with his own hands. I had the address but couldn't seem to find the place. Damn, I'm lost.

Lo and behold, there's a parade going through town; it looks like I'm in

Madison. There's the old paper mill. I decided to park the car and walk around, being a tourist. The American Legion was having a flea market which drew me in. Of course, I don't need more stuff.

"There are some good deals here, don't you think?" the man across the table said to me.

I was looking at an antique plate for sale but put it down, saying, "I've got dishes at home I don't even use; I guess I don't need to buy another. I hope they sell all this stuff — it'd be hard to pack it all up to take back home."

I looked at other things for sale but didn't buy anything. I'd skipped breakfast and my stomach was urging me to eat lunch. I left to find a restaurant.

After lunch I thought, *it's a nice day, spring is in the air*. I drove out of town and, before I even knew where I was headed, I found myself in familiar territory. My body was so relaxed and satisfied from eating lunch that I needed a nap. I pulled over in a driveway near the land Rob and I used to own. It felt good to be there; I realized then just how much I'd missed New England. I also had an idea that my partner was a northerner, a "Yankee," as the guys in Tennessee called me. In some places the Civil War is still going on.

With windows open — probably to invite mosquitoes and black flies inside — I put the seat back and dozed off. I don't know how much time passed before I heard a crunch of shoes on the gravel driveway and abruptly woke up.

"Are you okay, Miss? I heard a man's voice. As I got out of the car to talk to him I recognized Brian, no longer a young man (my age actually), to whom I'd sold the farm many years before. It was so painful to own the place after Rob and I divorced I knew I'd never live there; when Brian, a friend of a neighbor, approached me about buying it I gladly sold it to him.

"Brian, is that you?" I asked.

"Penny, you look the same; good to see you," he said, as we hugged.

"So, how are you, Brian? Are you and Valerie still together?" I had heard from my neighbor Lily that they had split up, but didn't know if it was true. The first time Rob and I met Lily, a four-feet-six-inch wisp of a woman, maybe seventy-five years old, weighing eighty pounds wringing wet, she got tired of watching us struggle to lift the 100 lb. sack of feed she'd sold us onto the back of our Ford pick-up truck. She shoved us aside and hoisted the bag, effortlessly I might add, onto the truck. Rob and I stood there, dumbfounded, before all three of us roared with laughter.

"Valerie and I split up more than twenty years ago; she moved back to Oregon, taking our son Jason with her. I lost track of him for awhile, but we're close now. He's an accountant; would you believe this old hippie has a CPA for a son?" Brian said, laughing. "How about you?" Brian inquired.

"I'm divorced after twenty-two years with David; you never met him, but then you didn't meet Rob, my first husband, did you?" I asked.

We had a really nice conversation, which ended with an invitation to come over soon to see the house he built. *Well,* I'm thinking, *Brian definitely has some of the qualities on my list.*

I got back to my motel room around 6 p.m. I went for a walk, skipping dinner because I was still full from lunch. It was a perfect end-of-May evening, not too hot, not too cold. The black flies apparently don't come into town.

I had a couple books, which I tried to concentrate on reading when I got back from my walk. Soon it was time to call Karma. I didn't realize until the phone began to ring that I was a bit nervous about calling her. She was always nudging me — what direction will her huge energy force take me tonight? Funny thing is I trust her intuitive "nudges" almost as much as I trust my own intuition. That's quite a recommendation, I'd say.

"Penny," she answered. "Did you see Rob today? I just know you saw him — he is mostly bald and wears glasses and has a slight beer belly. I can see him, Penny. Trust me. You have to call him, please!" she urged me on.

"Karma, I don't call men; if he wanted to talk he would have called," I insisted.

"Penny, hang up, call him, then call me right back. Now!" the little bitch school teacher ordered me. When was the last time I argued with a teacher?

So, I called and got an answering machine. Phew! Gosh, it's almost ten o'clock at night; he must be out with his girlfriend. I hope this call doesn't cause problems for him. Maybe they got back together and that's why he hasn't contacted me. I left my number and asked him to call me at the motel.

When I called Karma it was getting late so we talked only ten or fifteen minutes before I hung up to go to bed. The last words she said to me were: "I have a good feeling about this, Penny; I really do."

The next morning, before 8 a.m., the phone rang. Of course it was Rob; no one else has the number at the motel. He sounds the same as he did in March, which was also the same voice from forty years ago.

"May I buy you breakfast, Penny?" he asked. We agreed on a restaurant near my motel. I looked through my luggage and found the Meerschaum pipe he had left at our home when we separated. It was one he bought in New Zealand on the layover before flying to Antarctica. I had saved it all these years. I wrote a note to him and tucked it inside the pouch: "Rob, have you ever really listened to the words to 'Forever Young'? That is what I wish for you. Love, Penny."

I got to the restaurant early and sat there reading. I was aware of Rob before I actually saw him out of the corner of my eye, coming toward me. I wouldn't have recognized him. Karma was right: he is almost bald and wears glasses, and has a slight beer belly. But, he looks good to me. I looked up to hear him say in a voice trying to hide his excitement, "That was YOU yesterday!" Now, I've been single long enough to know when a man sounds interested. However, I'm noticing within a few minutes that he is wearing a wedding band. I wonder how his wife feels about this meeting. Or if she even knows about it.

Soon our conversation is flowing; we are talking to each other in a way we never did when married. It is free, without a trace of anger, with no hesitation on either of our parts. I'm feeling really sexy thanks to my size 8 mid-rise "Lucky" jeans and low-cut turquoise top.

"Penny, I saw you yesterday talking to a man at the flea market; I was a couple tables away from you. I can't believe I didn't recognize you! You had on black slacks and a purple top and sandals with purple nail polish on your toes. Am I right?" Rob asked, with a laugh. "Your beautiful white hair was swept up in back, just like today," Rob continued.

He was right. Can you imagine not recognizing someone you used to be married to?

"Rob, why didn't you answer my e-mail six weeks ago when I said I was coming up here to buy land?" I asked, after a few minutes.

"What e-mail, Penny?" he asked.

"I e-mailed you before Easter, saying I'd be up here and gave you my cell phone number in case you wanted to get together and talk," I continued.

"Penny, I never got any such e-mail; which address did you send it to?" Rob continued.

"Why, the "a-j" one, of course," I answered.

"Oh no, I'm really sorry, Penny. I had to close that account because of a lot of spamming which made me delete hundreds of messages at a time. I have another address; don't you have that?" he asked. We agreed he'd give me the address later when I could write it down. And he told me he figured I just wanted to wait until we saw each other in June to talk, so he thought nothing of having no messages from me.

"And you were keeping it light, just in case I was fat and old-looking as I had been when we last saw each other thirteen years ago, right?" I asked, with a giggle.

"Yes, you may be right; but more importantly, I wanted to see if you were still angry," Rob replied.

Finally, after about twenty minutes, I told him that I noticed he was wearing a wedding ring — did he re-marry? No, he just hadn't taken it off since the divorce over three years before.

"Do you remember you wore my wedding ring for six months after we separated, not taking it off until Sandy was pregnant?" I asked. He had no answer to that. "What does it symbolize to you that you can't let go of?" I asked in my impertinent, yet gentle, way.

"Believe it or not, it keeps women away," to which I replied that I know many women who are relentless in their pursuit of so-called eligible men. He agreed it was a sad thing to see some women behaving as if desperate to be loved. A year ago he received a card from a woman saying she was sorry, had to refuse his proposal of marriage. He barely knew her; didn't think it was funny. Of course, that doesn't explain why he kept mine on years before. Some people have trouble letting go of something or someone; accepting change isn't easy for everyone. I dropped the subject, knowing it was his to look at, not mine. I also knew I wouldn't be getting involved with him if he kept wearing it. I found it a bit creepy.

So, he's not married. This excites me. But you want to know what makes my heart sing the loudest? We're talking, really talking, for the first time ever. And it feels wonderful.

"Rob, your mother told me on the phone from Mexico that you left Sandy for another woman, but then she left you for another man. Is that right?" I asked. Rob was quiet for a minute then said that his mother was almost eighty-five and got things confused easily. "Did you cheat on Sandy when you were married?" I continued.

"No, never; I learned my lesson from our mistakes — remember the damage we did to one another, Penny?"

It isn't easy to face our past, especially when it has been so painful. But that day, in a small diner in Maine, trying to eat part of a breakfast Rob and I were sharing, neither of us hungry, we began the process — together — of forgiveness. I knew we'd be okay no matter what happened from here on.

The luncheon menus came out; it's obvious after three hours of breakfast conversation we need to take this outside. As we are walking toward my car, which just happened to be parked right next to his truck, our hands grabbed each other and held on. Who knows whose hand started the movement toward the other? It's as if they had their own agenda. It was good to hold hands for the first time in over thirty-four years.

Chapter Twenty Four

"None of your stories are true — they're just scripts you've created."

Alberto Villoldo

Penny:

Monday, Memorial Day, arrived; it was one day before my real estate closing which will, once again, make me a land-owner in Maine. I would own ten acres, rather than one-hundred-fifty acres like Rob and I used to own.

I realized early that morning I had forgotten to give Rob his Meerschaum pipe. It was a good day for a drive and I made a plan to find Rob's house so I could give it to him.

I ended up near Dexter — don't ask me how. I often get turned around. This time I was carrying a map of Maine; isn't it time to open it up and look at it? I was on Route 152, having an idea by looking at the map, that if I made a left onto Route 154, then another left onto a dirt road, un-named, that I might find Rob's house near Cornville.

"Sir," I asked an older man standing in his driveway watching me pull up, "I'm lost. I'm looking for a friend of mine who has just a box number for an address. Can you help me?" I asked,, as I got out of the car.

"Who are you trying to find?" he inquired with a welcoming smile and tone of voice.

"Rob Warner; do you know him?" I continued.

"Of course," he said, as he proceeded to give me clear directions. "If you don't find him, come back. My grandchildren are here for a visit and we're having a cookout. You're welcome to join us; don't need to bring a thing, just yourself."

As I thanked him for his kindness I was struck by how friendly people are, especially up here. Were they always like this? Or am I now more friendly, thereby attracting the positive energy of others?

Rob was just sitting down on his sunny deck to eat lunch as I drove into his driveway. The house and land looked similar to the homestead in one of my dreams, the one where Sandy came home to find us talking and began yelling at me.

"Hi, Penny, I was hoping to see you today. Want some lunch? Ever eat partridge? I'm eating leftovers from Saturday night; my friend Pete has a group of us over every year after hunting season," Rob said as he showed me inside his house, filling a glass with water from his well. "Just a minute," he said as he grabbed a sprig of fresh mint sitting there on the counter and put it in the water.

"Thank you, Rob. Do you have enough partridge to share?"

"Of course I do." He made a fresh salad to put on my plate. He then cut the bird into pieces, as if searching for something.

"Pete uses a different shot than I do — cheaper and not as good for the environment; I try to dispose of it properly. At any rate, I don't want you swallowing shot of any kind so I'm searching for it," Rob said, amazing me, as this is a whole new experience.

The weather co-operated, the lunch was especially delicious, conversation even better. The black flies even stayed away. The Universe seemed to be bringing out the "big guns" to make certain we caught the magic that was seeping into each moment.

By three o'clock, maybe four, I don't know because I don't carry a watch or keep on my cell phone, I knew I was in trouble. I was starting to fall in love again. I wasn't fighting it, though. I got a clear message from somewhere that it would be okay. No harm will come to me, only good stuff.

"Rob, do you remember when you were in Antarctica and called me via phone patches?" I asked after lunch.

"Yes, it was difficult for both of us, wasn't it? No spontaneity, just one person says something, then 'over' so the other could speak. It was harder for you than for me, I know," he continued, looking at me with understanding in his eyes.

"The few letters I received were kind of impersonal. That hurt. I was working long hours, trying to be a good mother to Heather, and, when not working, staying home behaving myself." I hesitated a second. " No, that's not exactly true. I had an affair with a married man. I was never going to tell you, but we must be totally honest with each other, don't you think? He and I saw each other a few times the last six months of your tour of duty. Believe it or not, even though it was sexual, I spent time crying over you, missing you. I felt so abandoned. He was a life-saver for me. I'm sorry, Rob."

Rob said nothing for about a minute before quietly replying that he was glad he didn't know about it then. He didn't know what he would have done.

"Rob, you would have left me; you did leave emotionally. I knew when you came home you no longer loved me, yet you kept telling me everyday for the next four years how much you loved me. Remember I finally called you on it and told you to stop saying it and start showing it?"

"This was when we discussed separating, wasn't it?" Rob looked at me with a kindness I'd never witnessed in him before.

I burst into tears. My bare feet were propped up on a chair next to him. He grabbed my feet — I'm sure they were clean — and began to massage them, saying nothing.

Through my tears I managed to ask why he stopped loving me. I couldn't understand; was I that terrible?

"No, Penny, I'm sorry I hurt you. I was intimidated by your life experiences; you seemed to have it all together and I was just floundering. I didn't know how to be a husband. I had been raised in a very sheltered environment, with three brothers, no sisters. I felt so much younger than our few months' difference in age," Rob continued.

"Is that why you had sex with the fifteen-year old at Joe's party? Trying to be a teenager again?" I asked cautiously, as it was a very painful memory. After all, it seemed obvious to me at the time that a man who loves his wife doesn't have sex with someone at a party and flaunt it. It was as though he was getting even with a strict mother.

"Penny, I was in shock, couldn't believe I actually did that — still can't — but I have no excuse for it. I am really sorry, though," Rob said.

"I knew you were sorry and even told her father that. Do you realize you may not have had a career as a scientist if he had pressed charges?"

"We did really stupid things, didn't we?" Rob asked, with sadness in his voice. "Being grown-up is rather nice, isn't it, Penny?"

That day, with honesty bonding us together, will be etched in my mind forever. We shared the need — and the ability — for forgiveness and love. It was the day a deep understanding and friendship began between us.

Yes, being grown-up is rather nice, I think. And so is having a good friend in my ex-husband. I am also now able to be his good friend. His mother told him when she heard about us that it's always good to have friends.

Yes, it is always good to have friends. And sometimes friendships turn into something more.

Chapter Twenty Five

"I promise you, Penny; I can do that," Rob said.

Penny:

On Tuesday morning I was checking out of the motel when the phone in the office rang. The clerk handed it to me — it was Rob. Could we meet after I closed on the land? Would I have time to show it to him? Maybe I could stay longer? We agreed to meet in the title office after the 11 a.m. closing.

I realized something interesting when I saw Rob walk into the title office as we were finishing with the paperwork: Most women are quicker to grasp a situation when it involves relationships. It's just an observation. Wouldn't that explain why I clearly saw that we were becoming more than friends, yet said nothing to Rob? My feminine energy was definitely keeping an eye on things, as I let him do all the chasing, and didn't even have it in my mind to chase him. The viewpoint of the goddess is that it's his loss if he lets me go.

"Penny, you made a good purchase; this is a gorgeous piece of land. I am saying that as a Soil Scientist, but also as a friend," Rob said. We spent about two hours walking around the land, looking at Wesserunsett Lake; we had seen the other side of the lake from the farm we had owned together. I had washed my hair in it, bathed in it, and made love in the lake with Rob. We stood there with arms around each other. When he kissed me I didn't expect it. We were friends, but not lovers, so it took me by surprise. It was a pleasant one, of course. And, I obviously had a responsibility to give the kiss back to him, didn't I?

"Will you stay here with me for a few days? I have a guest room which you are welcome to sleep in," Rob said, after kissing me. I told him I can stay one night only. And sleep in the guest room.

I fell asleep that afternoon on his couch, but awoke when he came in to cover me with a blanket. I quickly got up from the couch. He smiled — we both knew why I got up from the couch. I was avoiding any move toward sexual involvement.

Dinner that night was wonderful — fresh salmon, baked potatoes, and salad. Actually, Rob put the salmon on top of the salad, something I'd never thought of doing. After dinner Rob showed me his catch-all, a spare room that was just a mess. I made the comment that it wasn't *feng shui* from what I could see. All that clutter and trapped, dead energy in his house was not good. That comment made us both tell the other of visions we'd had as children.

"Rob, I learned very young not to share things I see because I would be called crazy; was called crazy, as a matter of fact. One day, when I was around eight years old I was staying home from school to help Mom because she had been having a lot of trouble with asthma attacks — she needed me to make my 'super-duper-salad' for her. I heard commotion on the canal — we lived in Phoenix then — and went to investigate. The police were hauling a body out of the water. They told me to leave, so I moved a few feet back. What I saw I never told anyone, as I knew better by then. The man had foam coming out of his mouth, but I saw his body, or a vision of his body, moving upward, out of its own body. It didn't scare me, just fascinated me. I didn't have many visions after that, at least ones that I remembered, until many years later when the fog was being lifted from my soul by meditation and clearing of the mind. Does that sound crazy to you? I did have a nervous breakdown later, so who knows, maybe I was always crazy," I said.

"It's not at all crazy," Rob assured me. "I saw my grandfather's body or felt his presence. I've never been sure, as the image was out of the corner of my eye. I was working in their lake cottage after they both had died, cleaning out things, when he told me he was fine and it was good to see me. It was more of a telepathic connection, not actual voices. I can't explain it."

"You don't have to explain it; this is how I see things — telepathically. I think I always felt that about you, that we both had seen stuff we were trying to forget. What we did forget was to share it with each other. There was no trust, maybe?"

If you don't know yourself you can't possiby totally trust yourself, as you cannot trust what you don't know, can you? Rob and I didn't share ourselves out of a lack of knowing, not a lack of caring. Of course, it turned into a lack of caring, didn't it?

As I was getting ready to make the bed in the guest room Rob came in and just told me, straight out, "I love you, Penny. It's been a long time since I've said that to anyone."

I was stunned; I honestly didn't expect it. I just quietly told him I'd never stopped loving him. Then I began to cry and told myself I wasn't going to be afraid of him this time. I said it out loud and Rob told me I didn't need to be afraid of loving him this time. After I stopped crying I said to him that he loved me now, but for how long? There's that trust thing again.

Let me explain something about the early 1970's that some people just don't understand. It really was a time of the sexual revolution. It wasn't just hippies who were professing "free love;" there were many others wanting to break loose of the old Puritan conventions about sex. Our wanting to not be possessive, to experience life to its fullest by having other lovers, wasn't as odd as it may seem now. Of course, it hurt us and destroyed our marriage, but something else would have come along to do that, anyway. It just is the way it is. We were together for a reason. Then it was time to move on.

Rob's kisses that night were not filled with passion, just a friendly cautiousness. Without talking about it we both knew sex would come later, not on this trip.

The following morning we spent time doing things in the garden, taking a walk around his land, waving away the black flies as we went about our business. He cooked for me again. I finally told him about some of my dreams of him. He told me he was relieved when Sandy left him for another man, that things had not been good for a long time; she had cheated on him before, early in their marriage. Being a kind man he wasn't about to say nasty things about her.

"We need to honor our former spouses, don't you think, Rob?" I asked.

"Why?" he asked, as if he thought I wasn't thinking clearly.

"You and I wanted nothing more than peace and harmony. We also wanted freedom and independence. Those are some traits we've always had in common. Wouldn't you agree?" He agreed with that assessment so I continued, "We had no trouble giving freedom and independence to each other; gave too much as I remember. But, the peace and harmony couldn't come without each of us having it in our souls. And we didn't. We had anger. You had passive-aggression. I just had aggression. So, we could not be the ones to force the other to look at him ,or her self; it wasn't in our nature to slam the other against the proverbial wall and say, 'you WILL look at this.' That's why we had to find Sandy and David. They are twins, did you know that? Both bullies, control freaks; they both abuse power, trying to steal it from others. Without their intervention, which took a lot out of them, maybe we would still be complacent and psychically-lazy."

"I never thought of it that way," he said after thinking a couple minutes. "It really doesn't matter if the evolution of our souls came out of adversarial relationships; all that matters is that it happened. Is that what you're saying?"

"That's right. I don't like the personalities of either, but I do respect what each of them did for us. And you wouldn't have Cathy and Andrea without her. We just weren't meant to have our babies together. And I wouldn't have Benjamin, either, so it all worked out well, didn't it?" I asked.

The last comment made us both cry; sometimes a person cries for sadness, sometimes for joy. That day we just cried together. Healing was taking place in both of us.

That night, as we sat across from each other, eating another yummy meal cooked by my friend, Rob, the gourmet cook, I told him what I did in Tennessee, moving to the Master suite, sleeping on one side of the bed only, and putting out an extra place setting for my unknown man. He told me he had envisioned a partner for him during that very time-frame I started doing the thing in Tennessee.

"I sat right here a few nights last week and saw my life partner across from me, sitting right where you are. It surprised me, as I am not lonely and didn't even know I was looking," Rob said, still a bit surprised at what he had seen. He wasn't the only one who was stunned by that revelation. We both sat there with our mouths open. Of course, we then had to fill them with the delicious food he had prepared: the last of the venison steak from his freezer.

"Penny, I cannot make any commitments to you at this time. I am not ready for marriage, but I know I love you very much and want to be with you." He got some soap and wet his hands to slide off the wedding band he had been wearing. He went into the other room to put it away.

"Do you remember when I threw my wedding ring away in Spain, flinging it into a bush? I was pissed off at you and said I no longer wanted to be married to you. Maybe we can go back there and find it," I said with a smile.

"Yes, I remember that," he said.

"I need you to promise me one thing, Rob," I said.

"What's that?" he asked.

"I need you to promise that you will not make love with me until you can give me your heart, whether it takes one week or one year, doesn't matter. I can no longer do 'shallow and casual'. I have realized recently this is who I am; I need a committed relationship before I want to be sexually involved," I said.

"I promise you, Penny; I can do that," Rob said.

So, we slept in separate bedrooms that night, secure in the knowledge that we had been honest with one another and knew more about how each of us operated. It was a wonderful feeling. My love for him grew that night. As I said to him before going to bed, I can now love him better; not necessarily more, just better.

Chapter Twenty Six

"Some individuals are easy to be with, in every sense of the word. They are seldom needy or demanding and are sensitive to the fact that, as important as they are to their partner, they are not the center of the Universe."

Don't Sweat the Small Stuff in Love
by Richard and Kristine Carlson

Penny:

Thursday morning Rob had a meeting related to his volunteer work in the community. A group of retired scientists and school teachers give their time to the schools, putting on workshops and river/nature walks for students as young as fifth grade. Nancy had invited me to go with her to an area between Farmington and Rumford where a group of investors was putting together a condominium deal, renovating some of the old factories now for sale. Rob and I agreed to meet at his house for dinner; this time he was cooking leg of lamb, having slaughtered a sheep the previous fall. I was looking forward to this, as I was raised on lamb. My father raised chickens and sheep for many years.

It was a beautiful sunny day, perfect for a drive. The condo deal looked promising and would have tempted me had I been interested in living in town. Nancy and I got along very well, talking the whole way over and back. It was the same when I was there a few weeks before, looking for land. Nancy had introduced me to her friends when we went to clubs, doing line-dancing. She knew Rob and his ex-wife, but said little about them except that the wife was the one doing most of the talking when they met at the Eagles Club or the supermarket. Rob was very quiet, almost withdrawn. Neither one of us was interested in doing a bunch of gossiping, so we left it at that. She did say the guy Sandy left Rob for was a widower who was looking for a replacement not long after his wife died. That made me shudder, as I knew the feeling of being used when I realized David didn't care who he married as long as he got what he needed. I told her Rob used to be quiet with me but now is so expressive and open it surprises me. We agreed people do grow up, some of them quite nicely.

"Karma, hello, what a surprise," I said, when I answered my cell phone. "Hey, we may get dropped, as I don't see many cell towers around here. I'll call later if that happens, okay?" I asked.

"Penny, I am wondering how things are going with you and Rob; I haven't heard from you," she inquired.

"Rob told me he loves me; I've been meaning to call and tell you that," I said. I was certain she could see my smile through the phone.

"That's good news. I don't have to ask how you feel, but I will," she continued.

I told her some of what had happened the past few days. I then asked her about his path. "Karma, do you remember telling me you had a vision of him, back in Mexico many months ago, and he was not on the same path as I am?"

"I do remember saying that, but I don't see that now. Why don't you ask him?" she said.

"I will, and another thing that I am concerned about is how much do I compromise? In the past, I have bent over so far that I couldn't stand up straight — women tend to do that — and I cannot allow that to happen again."

"You are a very aware woman; I have confidence you won't go too far," she said, before we hung up, promising to talk again soon.

Dinner that night was superb. He wouldn't let me do the dishes so we just talked in the kitchen about anything and everything. I then told him about Sandy's former roommate who came up to me after Economics class and told me about Rob and Sandy meeting when she was hitchhiking and him telling her he was married and not planning to get divorced. And about the abortion, which he paid for, even though he said the child wasn't his. Was all that true, I asked? Yes, pretty much, was his reply. When did you meet Sandy? In January after we separated? Around then, he said.

"Are you going to be available for her when she is ready to face her anger, a lot of it toward you? Wasn't she really young when you got together? Maybe nineteen?" I asked.

"No, she was eighteen," he replied.

"That's about the age you were emotionally at the time. If it hadn't been her it would have been some other young girl. Maybe you needed someone you could be the grown-up with, don't you think?"

"It's possible," was all he said.

This was the night he also asked me to move in with him, leaving my home in Tennessee, as he couldn't leave Maine.

"Don't worry; I've known all along you are a package deal. Maybe I can move here and sell the house in Tennessee sooner rather than later. But you first must see my home there, as it will help you understand just how important it is for me to have creative living space — I have fourteen colors in my 1500 square-foot home. I have a lot of art on the walls, oak floors, ceramic tiles, and other wonderful touches. This house is cluttered, which I need to take a good look at if I'm to live here. Can we renovate or fix up anything?" I asked.

"Sure, we can talk about that. I do have to tell you I want to spend time alone here in the winter, ice-fishing, cross-country skiing, just enjoying winter," Rob said.

"That's fine with me; if you are here in the winter, you will be alone, for sure," I said, laughing.

The plan was for me to stay Thursday and Friday nights and leave Saturday morning for New Hampshire to visit friends before my Sunday flight back to Nashville. Rob said he could drive down to Tennessee in a few weeks to spend time with me before making plans for my move up there. He also needed time to make room for my things.

The next morning Rob woke up early, banging pans around, grinding coffee beans in the kitchen, which woke me up. It was 5:30 a.m. He had trouble sleeping. "I need to talk to you; I can't sleep, Penny," he said, looking so nervous I asked if I would be needing tissues for my nose. Was this going to make me cry? He indicated that he hoped it wouldn't.

"Penny, I met Sandy in September, four months before you and I separated. We began the affair soon after," he began.

I was sitting there, stunned. I had no idea! Tears weren't quite coming to my eyes; the shock was so great that I couldn't even speak, let alone cry.

"I know you didn't know about it. That's not all of it. I had brief affairs with two other women during the same time-frame, but I decided on going with Sandy. I considered it over between us, as you and I had talked of separating," he continued, nervous, as I wasn't saying much. He didn't know if I was going to scream, cry, walk out and never see him again, or forgive him. I just kept saying I had no idea, shaking my head.

"You mean you were sleeping with three females, then coming home and having sex with me? You were such a shithead." My tone became more sympathetic as I told him it must have been really hard for him to be involved with Sandy and come home to me. Of course, I did burst into tears after that. He apologized, saying he never meant to hurt me, was just so confused and immature at that time he didn't know what to do with his life.

It took me awhile, maybe a few months, asking more details when I could handle it, but I did forgive him, just as he had forgiven me. I forgave the promiscuity that day; after all, who was I to be a hypocrite, and hadn't we set it up to have other lovers? I just never meant for him to fall in love with someone else. Sex is one thing, falling in love is another thing. Of course, it could have happened to me, falling in love with someone else, if I hadn't been so much in love with my husband, even at the end.

The thing that floored me was the deception. Then it hit me. Oh, now I get it! That's why his mother said he left his wife for another woman and then she left him for another man! I was that wife who was left and everyone knew it. Everyone knew about it. Except me. Then I remembered a couple hang-up phone calls that fall, before we had separated. Must have been her, the girlfriend.

We all have "deal-breakers" and mine is when someone lies to me. I'm done with them if they don't see the folly of being deceptive. I'm especially finished if they're not committed to changing. Of course, this was in the past, but how quickly could I get myself back into the present and see who he is today? It goes back to the question: Do I trust who this man is today? The answer is "mostly, yet not totally." Only time will tell if he deserves that trust. I have to trust him 100% if we're going to have a future.

Here's where my natural ability to keep a "wait-and-see" attitude comes in handy.

Chapter Twenty Seven

"A gourmet who thinks of calories is like a tart who looks at her watch."

James Beard, famous chef

Penny:

I had told Rob in a letter that only goodness can come from forgiveness. I certainly meant that. After my return to Tennessee we spent the next few weeks talking on the phone every morning for an hour or more, and during the day for awhile, but especially at night before going to bed, often two to three hours. Our phone cards were being used up quickly. Neither of us had good cell coverage at our isolated country homes.

"Penny, I know of a lovely place in Pennsylvania, near Pittsburgh, where we can camp out for a few days and get to know each other. I want to make love to you for the first time in a natural place. I am excited about being with you; it's been over thirty-four years since we made love," Rob said.

"I would love that; I, too, am eager, yet surprisingly not at all nervous, about making love with you again," I said.

"Honey, we make love every time we speak or look at each other; have you noticed that? We have incredible magic," he said.

I quietly said, "Rob, thank you so much for being who you are now, for doing this courting. Yes, there is phenomenal magic between us."

I flew to Pittsburgh and Rob picked me up. We went to "Target" and I bought a tent, while Rob looked for ice. We met near the door, ready to leave for our adventure. He had brought his queen-sized air mattress and pump, and I had sneaked into my luggage two down pillows and aqua-color Egyptian cotton sheets, that have a subtle pattern of pale green vines. Very romantic. Rob brought the rest of the camping equipment in his truck. Our plan was to camp out all the way to Tennessee, which is actually only a couple days from Pittsburgh, but we could spread out the trip.

I had been reading a book about Tantric sex when I was in Maine and Rob had asked to read it, so I left it for him. This is something we both had an interest in when we were married; the yogis and hippies had been spreading the word. Yet, our sexuality was so youthful and explosively-awesome that we never really investigated the more subtle approach that Tantric brings to a couple. Of course, Tantric sex requires a couple to be intimate, forgiving, and honest with each other, qualities we lacked forty years before.

Another thing I have come to understand about my sexuality is that our bodies change as we age and the "old way" of doing sexual intercourse, goal-oriented, always heading toward having orgasms as we know them, may be partly responsible for the sexual problems people have as they age. Viagra was invented for a reason, as was the operation that gives a man a "penis-pump," inflating him on demand. Tantric sex is a practice that helps us understand that orgasmic waves are just as phenomenal as the old way of being youthful and explosive. Actually, it is better as we age. Yet, in this Puritan country of ours, even though obsessed with sex, is a lack of true understanding of our bodies and sexuality.

Our first night together in the tent was a revelation to both of us, as we began to realize just how close a couple can become when there are no barriers between them. I had told Rob one of the things I love about him is he doesn't put me in a box; I can push my hands out into the energy field around me and it is all open. He totally accepts me for who I am, eager to know more about me. As a couple madly in love with one another we began an approach to spirituality through sexuality.

Of course, we did giggle a lot that night, doing very little sleeping but not for the reasons one might think. You see, I had accidentally bought a Junior-sized tent, one for kids with tiny sleeping bags. All we had to sleep on was a big, queen-sized air mattress that had to be forced into the tent before we could zip it up. And then we had big problems getting the tent opened when we needed to go outside to pee in the middle of the night. The length of a kids' tent is about five feet and we are over five-

and-a-half-feet tall, so there was mostly sitting up for us all night. A position like that works well for Tantric sex, of course.

Sex just keeps getting better all the time, with more intimacy than we ever thought possible. The level of satisfaction is higher and higher each time we make love (which we do a lot), surpassing any satisfaction we felt from the "old way" of practicing sex together.

Rob was very thoughtful when he saw my Tennessee home. He actually apologized for forcing me to have only white walls in the home we had built in Somersworth, the one we still lived in when we divorced, more than thirty-three years earlier. I had asked for colors but he insisted on an all-white house. In Tennessee he became aware of my creative side for the first time since meeting me as a young waitress helping my friend paint her apartment.

As I watched how Rob operates I saw clearly that the same attention to detail I had no respect for many years earlier is a beautiful strength in this man I love. One of his greatest strengths, actually. I pointed this out to him, saying how much I respect it, and that I also see how the Shadow side of being detailed can bog one down so he is unable to function. I feel that is partly where his cluttered home comes from: he has to read everything before disposing of it, even though he hasn't looked at the stuff for twenty years and probably won't ever use it. Put those constraints on a task and it won't get done. My wanting him to clear out things, to make room for me, to move over emotionally, can also be seen as his being obliterated. I could just take over his life, changing much of what he finds secure in his home. Don't forget, he had a basis for this fear of being over-run, this inability to let go of "things," as I used to be a pushy bitch, lacking respect for who he was and what he needed.

This fear of being pushed aside, in fact, was what caused our first disagreement. We rented a U-Haul truck in Tennessee, which Rob drove (pulling his truck behind) after spending the day filling it with the help of four hired men. I followed him, driving my Honda, and we camped out along the way, getting the honeymoon we didn't have when we got married. By now I had bought a bigger tent, but we still found a lot to giggle about in bed with one another. We arrived at his home, now mine, on Friday night.

When I wanted to talk about where to put my things and changes I might want to make Rob resisted, saying "Let's not talk about this now." Of course, I burst into tears, wondering if I'd made a mistake emptying out my house, even though I knew it was the only way to sell it. I felt vulnerable; did I already begin to bend too much?

We weren't really cozy with each other that night, neither of us sleeping as well as we had until now. Usually we just curled up together, intertwining our legs and bodies, peacefully sleeping, waking in the night to make mad passionate love. In the mornings we'd awaken to a smile from the other. None of this happened that night, and we both missed it.

Saturday morning Roger, Rob's best friend, came over early to help clear out the garage to make room for my tote boxes and other items not going into the house. I worked in the house, not daring to take down any pictures of his, yet feeling comfortable moving around his furniture, adding bits and pieces of my art work here and there. When Rob came in for lunch he was amazed at the transformation of a corner in the dining room/living area. "Wow! That looks really good, Penny," he exclaimed.

I quietly replied that this was all I had in mind; I was not trying to wipe him out. He relaxed and agreed I could do what I wanted, as he trusted me now.

Peace and harmony, something Rob and I had always craved, were now inside each of us so strongly that they just took over and resolved the issue. The ease with which we resolved our misunderstandings also showed us that peace and harmony will always be with us, taking care of things automatically. Maybe the pain we had given to each other before made us suffer enough; now we could reap the rewards of having gone through all that negative stuff together.

I realized, over the next months, that one of the greatest gifts Rob is able to give me is knowledge and understanding of nature. I thought I was a real "nature girl" growing up but am now, at age sixty-four, having fun learning even more: For instance, why many people hate the taste of venison — the hunter goes for the antlers (a buck old enough to have a large rack seldom tastes very good), rather than killing an eighteen-month-old doe that is tender and not gamey-tasting. I also learned how to identify tracks of certain animals. Even though we couldn't see moose and bears we sometimes saw their tracks going to our watering hole. Rob showed me embankments where snapping turtles lay their eggs, but explained that the coyotes, skunks, raccoons, and foxes are also watching and few of these turtles would survive much beyond being eggs.

Our favorite dates soon became drives to find deer, even though they were all over our land. Each time we'd see one was as exciting as the first, especially during the summer starting in June when the fawns — usually twins, two to three weeks old — came bouncing along behind their mamas like little puppies.

"What's going on? Where are the twins? The mother's going ahead!" I exclaimed one June day after losing sight of the fawns off in the woods. Rob, ever so patient, said the babies quickly learn to hide, crouching down in a nearby bush, while the mother goes ahead to get us off-track. The fawns have no scent of their own the first few weeks, which protects them from coyotes — for awhile, at least. By the time they become "scented" they are fast enough, and aware enough, to evade their predators.

The lessons about animals, nature, and gardening are daily, often subtle ones, ones I feel privileged to learn. We've settled into a wonderful life together, very thankful to find each other. The magic of it all makes us glow. And Mother Nature's treasures just add a sacred touch to our life.

Chapter Twenty Eight

"When the enchanted woman has come into her power, then and only then has she the inner strength to turn her face toward someone else."

Marianne Williamson

Penny:

While Rob was driving my Honda CR-V on our trip to Mexico in October I was in a mood to discuss relationships, especially ours. Our summer had been very productive. We cherished every moment together. We gave dinner parties so I could meet his friends, all of whom quickly became my friends. After all, if you see a friend who is in love with a woman who adores him you are usually able to like her, aren't you? We not only knew each other better all the time; we also realized just how compatible we really are. And how lucky. We hadn't said much about either of our second marriages; we were busy building our own memories. But now I was curious to hear what he learned from his marriage to Sandy, of how it related to us.

"Rob, you told me about Sandy's cheating on you early in the marriage, and that you told her you didn't want to know what she was doing. Wasn't that your way of shutting her out, just as you did me?" I asked, with my usual "gentle impertinence."

He thought for a minute and said he realized only a couple months into the marriage that he was doing the same thing to her, refusing to communicate, that he had done to me. He realized that he should have lived on his own after our divorce before getting involved with someone else. They'd had a fight — he called her the "Queen of arguments" — and he clammed up. Couldn't talk to her.

So, I'm asking which comes first: The angry woman who wants her man to talk with her because if he doesn't talk she doesn't feel loved? Or the man who just clams up because no one wants to talk with an angry woman?

"Penny, she and I never learned to talk to one another. I felt early on that she wasn't interested in anything I did. We weren't compatible. I learned to open up only after she and I were divorced. I had to live on my own for a few years, reading every self-help, psychology, spiritual book I could find. I probably wasn't ready for you even six months before we got together," Rob said during one long stretch of a Texas highway.

"David and I weren't at all compatible; he was always trying to make himself look better than me," I said. "Such power plays. It was tedious dealing with him. Sounds like Sandy and David could be twins. I closed him out of my life a few years after Benjamin was born. That's one reason I am having such a good time with us; it's even more of a joy when compared to my experiences in marriage," I continued. "I also read every book I could find that would help me understand what his game was and how I could deal with it, which I did by knowing myself better. Understanding myself gave me power."

"Penny, do you remember the letter you wrote to me last spring, telling me who you are now?" Rob asked.

"I remember nearly every word I wrote to you, but you didn't understand me, did you?" I asked.

"No, I didn't understand much of what you said in the letter but, after meeting with you I could see how much you've changed. I also knew I wasn't on the same path as you were when I received it. As I re-read your words, some of them many times over the next few months, I found myself feeling totally in-sync with you. Somehow, we got to the same place. Now we are walking together. I'd call that a miracle, wouldn't you?" the love of my life asked. He was a man I had loved even before time began.

"Yes, baby, I call it a miracle," I replied, feeling deeply loved by him.

"Wow! Rob, it just hit me, I figured it out! Remember I told you we all have deal-breakers, and that mine is when a person lies to me, but doesn't apologize or change, just continues lying?" "I remember, Penny," Rob quietly answered.

"After visiting with your parents a few weeks ago I realized your father's behavior is much like mine used to be — fits of rage, need to control, self-absorbed, shuts out those close to him — and I see how this affects his wife and sons, especially you. You were set up by your father's behavior and unconsciously you had in your mind what your 'deal-breaker' is, even though you couldn't articulate it. After all, his birthday is the day before mine and he appears to have many of the Shadow-side traits of our astrological sign, Cancer. Add this to the fact that your mother is repressed; she rarely speaks above a whisper. She cowers near her husband. You thought all women were supposed to be as sweet and kind as your mother." I asked him if any of this made sense to him. He quietly said he'd think about it.

"You know, Rob, we didn't stand a chance. Recently you told me that a few years after our marriage you said to my father that nothing you did was right in my eyes — the same way I was raised, by the way, with constant criticizing — and he said to work it out with me. He could have helped you had he known how, but he was just passing on the legacy from his father's wrath, and had no clue how to handle it, anymore than you or I did. I criticized you, just what your father did to you and what my father did to me, and that makes whatever I say to you seem even more negative. Like the little boy being reprimanded. I understand it all now," I said.

"You're right, darling, we didn't stand a chance," Rob said, with a hint of sadness.

The second challenge in our relationship came after Rob proposed to me, but couldn't tell his daughters about our engagement. After three months of his "trying to find the right moment" I took off the amethyst/gold ring and told him we are no longer engaged. If he decides he can honor our agreement, he needs to ask me again. Yet do it before telling them we are engaged, because only then will I decide if he has anything to offer me. After all, if a man can't treat the "love of his life" with respect I must ask this question: What do I have? A man who can't keep his word? A man who cares more about what his "grown kids" think than how I feel? I'd rather be alone. At least I'd be keeping company with someone who has a deep respect for me, one who doesn't lie, with enough courage to never allow others to get away with power plays.

Of course, I spent a few days crying, wondering where I'd go — don't forget, I'd sold my home in Tennessee by now. After all, I am only human. I cry like everyone else.

Finally, I decided to go to my home in Mexico to think for a few months. What else could I do? Stay here and get myself sick, worrying about what to do next?

"Please stay here; help me work it out," Rob said to me after a few days of this "rough patch" between us. I knew he was sincere. I also knew guilt is an unproductive emotion. If he's feeling sad about leaving his family — Heather and me — to start another, he needs to understand that it couldn't have happened between us any other way. It truly did work out for the best, for many reasons. After all, I didn't like who he was then and I felt the new wife got the "booby prize" when she got him.

"Barbara, Rob can't tell his girls about our engagement," I said one day during a phone call. "And he's probably right; they won't like it. But what does this have to do with us? They're grownups with kids of their own. I put away the engagement ring." I had called Barbara, a good friend since grade school, who was in New England for the summer. Her advice always cuts to the chase.

"Penny, when Harry and I got engaged seven months after meeting through the Internet one of his daughters made a nasty comment about us and he looked at her, saying very firmly that she has her life, he has his and for her to butt out of his! His tone left no room for argument. In the two years since then she's tried a couple times to interfere and I have stood up to her. She's afraid she won't get 'her inheritance,' but I've got news for her: Harry and I will probably never get married simply because I don't want to," Barbara said, laughing.

After we hung up I told Rob (who could hear parts of the conversation as he walked in and out of the dining room doing his own work) what Harry had said to his daughter. The look on Rob's face was as though a light bulb had been turned on.

This talk with Barbara reminded me of the phenomenon some of us noticed a few years before when so-called "grown kids" were telling their retired parents how to live their lives. I'd had a run-in with my own daughter about it, but stood my ground. None of my friends would have even considered telling our parents how to live! These "kids" must be worrying about their inheritance. Or they can't let go of their childhoods.

Well, to make a long story short, the energy in our home lightened up and Rob talked to me about coming to an understanding of where he'd been wrong in his idea of what family is. We're not supposed to give these kids power; they're grownups, let them go to live their own lives. And NEVER allow them to interfere in ours.

A few days later I (no longer thinking of going to Mexico) realized that — once again — my man came through for us. When he got down on one knee to propose (I had to help the old man get up) I said yes. And we began to plan a three-day wedding bash with live music, boating, food, and friends for the following summer. We also decided to go to Brazil to meet with my friend, Marilia (who's Brazilian, with a love story as wonderful as Rob's and mine) and her husband, Bill, an American who is a gems dealer. They live near one of the largest emerald mines in the world. We could pick out our own stone, get it cut into a square gem, and have a jeweler make our own design. All for less money than buying a boring diamond, which is usually mined by slaves.

As for his girls: they did react the way he suspected they would — by being indifferent or physically turning their faces away from us. Or both. But, we chalked it up to lack of maturity. After all, look at the stupidity Rob and I displayed when we were in our early thirties. We're not born all grownup; we have to go through Earth School to get educated.

If one is able to shift perspective about the tale of Rob and me and how we loved and hurt each other, then learned how to turn the love-that-turned-to-hate back to love again, one would be able to see how it all had to happen the way it did. How each turn became an opportunity to grow.

As I told Rob's mother on my first visit in thirty-four years with his parents, where they welcomed me back to the family with open arms and hearts, Rob and I don't know if we have one year together, or thirty years. We just live each moment to its fullest. After all, isn't this all we have? The past is gone, the future isn't here, but the present moment is where awareness is. This is all we need. And each time my man becomes aware of a problem or situation, thereby "coming through for us," the trust continues to grow stronger.

I wrote on the inside cover of a book of poetry I bought for Rob the first month we got back together: "Rob, you and I shared the beginnings. Now, we are together for the endings. During the middle you were tucked inside my heart. I love you. Penny."

Epilogue

"What goes around, comes around."

The Law of Karma

Betsy:

My brother, Kevin, welcomed me into his life with so much love, with total acceptance, that it made me do some hard thinking on the drive home, and over the next few weeks.

I have not always been nice to others. I don't know why, maybe I just wanted to reject them first before they had the chance to reject me.

Larry convinced me that I should send my Cousin Penny a thank-you note. After all, if it weren't for her interference I'd never have met my real mother. I wouldn't know Kevin, along with all the other family members who came to a reunion the following summer. I did send her that thank-you, as I was raised to do.

But, I still don't like her.

Penny:

I chuckled when I got my cousin's card. It was obvious she really didn't want to thank me. Some people are so stubborn. The good thing is I don't have a need to change her.

Other good news is this: I held out for getting everything on my list — spiritual growth, money intelligence and independence, generous with everything, including sex. I also put in the margins "a carpenter would be nice, and so would a gourmet cook." I can't remember what else was on the list but one day I found it in an old notebook and realized I got ALL that I asked for. Just goes to show we should hold out for what we want. No settling for second best. Rob and I got the best in each other.

Now we continue to grow and thrive. Every single day is a lovely surprise for each other with random and deliberate acts of kindness and love. We are careful to love each other fully, remembering how careless we were in the past with the gifts we were given. We appreciate being given this second chance.

And one more thing: Do you remember all those dreams Rob and I had of living a simple life in the country filled with love, peace and harmony? We realized recently that we did get them after all. We're living them now. Together.

About the Author

Pamela Dow was born with a suitcase in her hand, which is used when she travels and goes on Vision Quests. She began writing poems and short stories by age eight; her father saved much of her work, which she found after his recent death.

She reads at least two books at a time, both fiction and non-fiction; when not reading or writing she's in the garden at her 75-acre haven in Northern Michigan, with elk and deer for neighbors. Or she's at her home in Mexico. Or traveling the world, recently returning from Machu Picchu and Lake Titicaca. Turkey and Greece are next.

Both Ways Are Best, a semi-autobiographical story, is her first novel, but not her last.

To contact the author, please go to website: www.PamelaDow.com